STRATEGIC ALIGNMENT

Managing Integrated Health Systems

A Book of Cases

STRATEGIC ALIGNMENT

Managing Integrated Health Systems

Editors
Douglas A. Conrad
Geoffrey A. Hoare

AUPHA Press/Health Administration Press
Ann Arbor, Michigan   1994

97 96 95 94 93   5 4 3 2 1

Library of Congress Cataloging-in-Publication Data

Strategic alignment : managing integrated health systems : a book of cases / Douglas A. Conrad, Geoffrey A. Hoare, editors.
    p.   cm.
  Includes bibliographical references and index.
  ISBN 1-56793-003-4 (softbound : acid-free paper)
  1. Health services administration—United States—Case studies. 2. Health planning—United States—Case studies. I. Conrad, Douglas A.   II. Hoare, Geoff.
  RA395.A3S85   1994   362.1'0973—dc20   93-34353 CIP

The paper used in this publication meets the minimum requirements of American National Standard for Information Sciences—Permanence of Paper for Printed Library Materials, ANSI Z39.48-1984. ∞™

Health Administration Press
A division of the Foundation
  of the American College of
  Healthcare Executives
1021 East Huron Street
Ann Arbor, Michigan 48104-9990
(313) 764-1380

Association of University Programs
  in Health Administration
1911 North Fort Myer Drive, Suite 503
Arlington, VA 22209
(703) 524-5500

Contents

Acknowledgments

This casebook is the product of a wealth of collaborators, both individuals and organizations. The editors wish to recognize in particular the diligence and patience of the case writers, who have produced multiple drafts of their case materials and teaching notes and who generously shared their time and intellectual capital with us. The book is truly our joint product. Catherine Robinson and Pat Mitchell of the Western Network for Education in Health Services Administration played a major role in organizing, promoting, and staffing two major symposia on strategic alignment, at which many of the case materials and ideas reflected in this book were tested in an executive education format. Sherril Gelmon of the Accrediting Commission on Education for Health Services Administration and the Association of University Programs in Health Administration (AUPHA) gave very graciously and thoughtfully of her time in organizing double-blind peer review of initial drafts of these cases, and also organized an AUPHA symposium at which our concepts regarding managed care and selected cases were presented to an audience of health care executives and faculty. Bob DeVries and Kaaren Johnson of the W. K. Kellogg Foundation served ably and insightfully as the program officers for the grant that supported the coeditors and several of our collaborators in developing the cases that this book comprises. We wish to express our gratitude to the W. K. Kellogg Foundation for its financial support of the larger project on vertical integration and managed care of which this book is a major component. We owe a special thank you to Ed Kobrinski, who has been unstinting in his encouragement and creative in his substantive ideas for this text. Finally, we bless our families for putting up with the long hours this book has required of us. Mary, Jenny, and Betsy Conrad were always there for Doug, as were Lea, Nora, and Gabe for Geoffrey.

Introduction

Theoretical Framework and Structure of the Cases

Douglas A. Conrad and Geoffrey A. Hoare

This casebook reflects the transformation of the U.S. health care system that has been underway over the past ten years. Beginning in the early 1980s, particularly with the introduction of Medicare prospective payment by diagnosis-related groups (DRGs) for hospital inpatient services, market forces have increasingly pushed hospitals, physicians, other providers, and health services financing organizations toward vertical integration. Closer coordination between the suppliers of inputs to health services (e.g., physical capital, materials, capital-embodied technology, physicians) with those who deliver and distribute the system's outputs (e.g., physician visits, hospital discharges, and health promotion and disease prevention services) has become the essence of the successful health care organization of the 1990s.

The emphasis on vertical integration in the 1990s has supplanted the focus on horizontal integration that was so evident in the 1970s and early 1980s. Indeed, the pressures of certificate of need and rate review regulation, coupled with the continuing predominance of usual, customary, and reasonable charges reimbursement for physicians and retrospective cost-based reimbursement for hospitals, acted as catalysts for hospitals and physicians to seek economies of scale through hospital mergers and consolidations and the restructuring of the form of

1

physician practices—particularly the rise of single-specialty groups. The twin towers of Medicare DRGs and the resource-based relative value scale (RBRVS) introduced in the early 1990s for physician payment under Medicare have cast a long shadow over the health care market. Together, they are stimulating vertical integration in health care of an intensity equal to the horizontal changes of the earlier era. Growth and employer and consumer sensitivity to the cost of health care, matched by increasing awareness of providers that better integration of the health services components is required to achieve cost-effective care delivery, have fueled the drive toward more closely aligned health services organizations.

These market dynamics are not fully understood, but we hope that the cases in this book will considerably add to the breadth and depth of knowledge and understanding concerning strategic alignment in health care. We have chosen the cases so that they collectively capture the range of strategic choices health care organizations must make in adapting to environmental and internal change. The cases highlight aspects of vertical integration—for example, formal changes between hospitals and physician group practices or hospitals and long-term care or rehabilitation facilities and contracting relationships between a closed-panel health maintenance organization (HMO) and external (outside the panel) providers of specialty services—but examples of horizontal integration (e.g., hospital mergers) and diversification into new service lines (e.g., a hospital venturing into wellness services for the community) are also incorporated to enrich the book's characterization of strategic alignment.

Our philosophy in developing this book was (1) to provide a conceptual framework on which instructors could rely in their choice and ordering of cases and (2) to represent the complexity and diversity of strategic alliances being formed in health care in the 1990s. Our paradigm draws on strategic management theory, particularly a strategic adaptation framework articulated by Geoffrey A. Hoare.

The steps in the process of strategic adaptation are (1) environmental assessment, (2) strategy making, (3) building and balancing systems and structures, and (4) implementation and reassessment. Duncan, Ginter, and Swayne (1992) present an extremely useful paradigm for strategic management that fits our view of strategic adaptation quite well: *situational analysis* of the organization's internal and external environments leads into *strategy formulation*, which requires *strategic implementation* at the level of programs, budgets, and organizational structures. Strategic control ties together the adaptive process by reviewing goals, measuring performance relative to goals, assessing the strategy, and taking corrective action when indicated. The seminal work of Michael Porter (1980) provides a state-of-the-art model for analyzing environments and formulating strategy in conformance with market conditions. Porter's analysis pinpoints the forces driving industry competition as crucial to strategy development: (1) the bargaining power of buyers and suppliers, (2) the threat of substitute products or services, and (3) the threat of new entry. These forces collectively shape the nature and extent of rivalry among existing firms and the degrees of freedom for any given organization in crafting its strategy.

Figure 1 displays the process of strategic adaptation as we see it. The organization first analyzes its internal and external environments and then develops strategies that may or may not involve new internal and external alliances. In the system-building phase, the organization assesses and potentially redesigns its basic organizational structure so that the structure fits the strategy. As Paul Allaire, the chief executive officer (CEO) of Xerox, describes it (Howard 1992), this process amounts to "organizational architecture." The last stage in the strategic adaptation process is implementation and reassessment. In this phase of organizational change, new structures—with their concomitant task allocations, internal hierarchies, decision-making and management information systems, human resources mix, and patterns of reward and recognition—are united with refinements to strategy as the organization actually implements its initial strategic and structural choices. This phase is not the end, for the process of strategic adaptation is inherently continuous, but the system implementation and reassessment phase is a critical step in the feedback loop of environmental assessment–strategic choice–structural change–reassessment and the redesign of strategy and structure.

In our own work (cf. Conrad et al. 1988; Conrad and Dowling 1990; Hoare 1987), we have attempted to develop a theoretical synthesis of one of the leading strategic adaptations under way in the health care market in recent times—vertical integration and managed care systems. This case book represents an attempt to extend that work and integrate its themes within a broader array of strategic and structural changes underway in the environment for health services. The strategic alliances we refer to in this casebook spring from a number of underlying rationales, but foremost, economies of sharing and synergies between related steps in the value chain of producing health services are the fundamental drivers behind vertical integration and managed care. Thus, economies of complementarity are the principal explanation for vertical integration, as we have come to understand that concept in health services. In contrast, economies of scale and the spreading of fixed costs across larger volumes explain the drive in the early 1970s for horizontal integration in the health care system.

As Chandler (1990) has described so eloquently in his master work regarding the emergence of managerial capitalism in U.S. industry, the strategic alliances in health care represent staged responses to market

Figure 1 The Strategic Adaption Process

I. Environmental assessment and strategy-making

The organization's internal and external environments and its strengths, weaknesses, opportunities, and challenges in that context are assessed.

Strategy is formulated to match the environmental conditions facing the organization.

II. Building and balancing systems and structures

The strategy demands the creation of organizational structures, human resources and information systems, and governance relationships, which must be built and balanced relative to each other.

III. Strategy implementation and reassessment

As strategy is implemented, the underlying structures and systems are continually reevaluated and adjusted.

pressures for increased efficiency. The essential trajectory in health care has been, first, to tap the economies of scale in horizontally integrated multihospital systems and shared service alliances of independent hospitals. This early stage, which established larger volumes of acute care throughput in the acute care hospital, laid the groundwork for future movement to a more vertically integrated system in which the complementarities between related services and the symbiosis between related stages of service in the production of health care were tapped by organizations working together, as well as individual organizations enhancing their own internal structures to create stronger alliances between subsidiary units. In parallel with this movement in general industry, from horizontal to vertical integration, has been systems' experimentation with corporate diversification. Economically, these efforts at diversification into services that are unrelated or only partially related to the core business of health care can be explained by the search for economies of scope—that is, reduced costs from sharing of inputs across unrelated services. The cases in this book illustrate these themes and provide an indirect test of the theoretical paradigm for these different sources of economies as explanations of different forms of strategic alignment.

This book examines the elements of vertical integration and managed care as forms of strategic alignment for health services organizations. As developed in some of our earlier writing, the determinants of vertical integration fall into five basic categories (cf. Conrad and Dowling 1990):

1. A series of environmental changes, such as heightened cost sensitivity among large organized purchasers and a shift to prospective payment arrangements that have redefined the health services product as a more all-inclusive unit and that have forced providers to bear pricing and utilization risks

2. The search for savings in production cost through the sharing of fixed inputs and the tailoring of hand-in-glove complementarities and synergies between related stages in the production of health services

3. Savings in transaction costs, which are the resources devoted to informing oneself on the terms of a given exchange or transaction between parties in the market place, and the cost of writing and enforcing those contracts and exchange relationships

4. Overcoming marketing imperfections due to regulatory constraints or monopoly power of either buyers or sellers (or both)

5. The endogenous development of new managerial and intraorganizational forms to facilitate tighter linkages between internal

organization units and to manage interorganizational exchanges among alliance partners

The cases in this book illustrate these themes in different forms, explaining the adoption of vertical alignments in response to changing environmental conditions and competitive demands for reduced production and transaction costs. The cases highlight organizational forms and cultures devoted to strengthening the alliances formed in particular circumstances.

A central theme that emerges from a comparison and a contrast of the cases illustrated in this text is that of *core competencies,* as elucidated by Prahalad and Hamel (1990). The cases offer an object example of the reality that the internal competencies of the organization, coupled with its ability to construct linkages to other organizations and to tap their competencies through a commitment to organizational learning, represent the roots of organizational competitiveness. Several of the cases in this book demonstrate how organizations have agreed sometimes to collaborate with one another to enhance their individual competencies and competitive position, while in other situations going back to competition. The vertical alliances discussed in this book exemplify what Zuckerman and Kaluzny (1991) refer to as "opportunistic" and "stakeholder" alliances. Opportunistic alliances tap the complementary needs and resources of different organizations for their immediate competitive advantage. Stakeholder alliances build on those same complementarities to exploit interdependencies between customers, suppliers, and employees of a focal organization. These alliances have also been characterized by Johnston and Laurence (1988) as "value-adding partnerships," in which otherwise independent organizations band together to manage the flow of inputs and outputs for a given set of goods and services.

Several of the individual cases probe the internal requirements of vertical integration, which have received insufficient attention in the empirical literature in health services. The first requirement for both vertical and horizontal alliances to be successful is to create and maintain a sense of functional unity between previously disparate units. This unity requires a series of mechanisms for administrative coordination and integration, as well as structures for coordinating patient care. As we trace the history of successes and failures of the integrative alliances presented in this book, we return to the theme that, for such vertical alliances to work, they need to have a strong local market focus, as well as a series of both administrative and patient care coordinating mechanisms that enhance the continuity and efficiency of care.

The table of contents for the casebook shows how the cases fit into the cycle of strategic adaptation in health services organizations discussed above, which are represented as Parts I, II, and III. Part IV presents a case that illustrates all the stages. Case 1, "Competition, Integration and Diversification: Seven Hospitals of Growthville, U.S.A." by David B. Starkweather, examines the evolution of local markets for hospital services. The case reveals how pricing policy, competition, and the scope of services are affected as the market structure evolves through the stages of, first, horizontal integration, then, hospital diversification into new services, and ultimately, more vertically integrated hospital systems. In a sense, this case provides a health services example of the historical stages of industrial markets described by Alfred Chandler (1990).

The next two cases focus on strategy development while also illustrating the transition from strategy to building and balancing the structural and process components of a more integrated health care system. Cases 2 and 3, "Western Health Care Systems: A Health Care Delivery Continuum," by Robert C. Myrtle, and "Strategic Choices in Building an Integrated Health Care Network: The Buena Vista Clinic Acquisition Proposal," by Carol K. Jacobson, deal with the integration of hospitals and physician practices. Both reveal the issues in developing alliances between previously separate groups, the establishment of incentives to coordinate behavior, and the need to manage relationships of strategic collaboration over time. In particular, the case by Myrtle forces the analyst to review the administrative and clinical integrative mechanisms against the functional and structural alternatives for achieving that integration. Jacobson's case, on the other hand, emphasizes the specific human and organizational capital tied up by the partners in developing an integrated hospital-physician arrangement. Thus, her study provides a strong health care application of the transaction cost framework developed by Williamson (1975). Williamson emphasizes that customized goods and relationships ("transaction-specific capital") and small numbers of contracting parties tend to raise the costs of contracting between parties, thus favoring vertical integration.

Case 4, written by Nancy J. Packard, takes place in the context of the 20-year history of a hospital's development of linkages between acute hospital inpatient care and long-term care. The case background shows those difficulties in a dynamic external environment. By tracing the effect of the early Medicare extended care policy through the revisions of the early 1970s and the more recent enactment of Medicare Prospective Payment System for inpatient hospital services, Case 4, "Linkages between Acute and Long-Term Care Services," demonstrates how an organization can cycle back and forth between alternative ownership and administrative relationships in the acute/long-term care portion of the continuum of health services. Issues with respect to staffing, quality of care, and the volume of patient flow between related facilities offer the analyst a unique opportunity to explore the internal requirements of vertical alliances and the crafting of strategy in light of intraorganizational realities.

"Corporate Restructuring: Phase II" by James D. Hart and Mary Ann Goeppele, which is based on the same organization as Case 4, looks at a different stage in the organizational process—that is, the organization's governance mechanism. We use this example to introduce the section on building and balancing systems and structures. This case describes the second phase of the corporation's move toward a management board model for governance. Case 5 opens a window that offers a view of the subtle and complex relationship between management and governance in the vertically aligned organization. An added complexity is the organization's desire to maintain a diversified base of health services activities; so in this case, one must wrestle with the differing demands of diversification and vertical restructuring.

Case 6, "Centralization and Decentralization in a Vertically Integrated System: The XYZ Hospital Corporation" by Arnold Kaluzny, presents another important application of the principles of system building and structural balancing. This case deals with a multi-institutional system with 18 owned or operated health care institutions in four coastal states. The multi-institutional system is seeking a new corporate structure to respond to five design problems:

- The inability of the current structure to recognize and deal with corporate problems in a timely fashion
- The leadership of the corporation being overly involved and often consumed by specific institutional issues
- The consequent opportunity losses associated with strategic issues not getting the attention they deserve
- Role conflicts between institutional administrators and corporate-level personnel
- The inability of current policy to effectively reconcile conflicting statutes and guidelines affecting member institutions operating in different states and market and legal environments

Through a variety of exercises, the analyst is required to weigh and balance the organization's need to differentiate administrative functions and yet to coordinate them over time. The flow of the case emphasizes how the appropriate structure for the corporation is contingent on the characteristics of its environment and the nature of the organization's own goals. These goals work through the internal demands, tasks, technology, and information bases of the corporation and its constituent member institutions. The thrust of the case study is to force a decision among the structural options, based on how those different structures would most appropriately meet the contingent demands of the environment.

Continuing with the attempt to build a kind of "strategic architecture" for vertical integration and related forms of organizational alignment, Cases 7 and 8 focus on one form of vertically integrated organization—the HMO. Case 7, "Organizational Control Issues for a Health Maintenance Organization Subsidiary" by Jenifer Ehreth, delineates these issues for an HMO subsidiary of a parent diversified insurance corporation. The case traces how one of the early physician gatekeeper, independent practice association (IPA)-model HMOs designed four kinds of controls: financial, managerial, claims, and provider. The case captures some of the early tensions in developing integrative relationships between primary care physicians and related subsystems of specialists, hospitals, and other ambulatory care providers. The transfer pricing mechanism used between the parent and its HMO subsidiary draws special attention in this case and allows one to examine the agency relationship between the insurance company principal and HMO subsidiary agent in this application.

Case 8, "Make versus Buy Decisions in a Closed-Panel Health Maintenance Organization" by Douglas A. Conrad, is set in the middle to late 1980s. The focus of the analysis is on internal information systems, incentive and accountability structures, and budget mechanisms for managing the purchase of outside patient services. While not a central theme of the case, the organization's growth strategy in the marketplace also shapes the movement toward the purchase of external services by this staff model HMO. Thus, the case provides the reader a glimpse of the internal issues and external contracting challenges posed by this strategic positioning and market evolution of the closed-panel HMO.

Introducing the section on strategy implementation and reassessment, Case 9 examines the competitive marketing strategy adopted by a community hospital. "Marketing in a Buy-Right Environment" by R. Scott MacStravic highlights a series of environmental and market factors that have forced the hospital into examining approaches to marketing its services to organized purchasers. The case narrative reviews three implementation processes that translate the marketing plan into practice: (1) efforts at marketing intelligence; (2) product and market development; and (3) marketing communications, with emphasis on creating a signal of the commitment to service for the institution and the development of a true working partnership with purchasers. The key challenges that the organization faces are how to implement the three elements of the marketing strategy and to create a plan that is successful in differentiating the product of the hospital, while providing an appropriate balance of attention to cost containment.

Case 10, "Geriatric Assessment Center," also by MacStravic, deals with the creation of a geriatric assessment center by a community hospital in a major metropolitan area. This study exposes the case analyst to issues of strategy development and the steps in the implementation of a comprehensive marketing plan. The case contrasts a marketing strategy emphasizing the multiplicity of customers for a geriatric assessment center (market management) with an earlier, more limited, boutique approach. Thus, the case targets the design of a strategy that looks at the three *p*s of marketing—product, promotion, and price—while also defining a broad market for focusing the marketing strategy. The implementation portion of the case considers how market segments are developed and the specific sales and cross-sales arrangements that might be developed to implement the plan.

Case 11, "Capitated Medicaid and St. Joseph's Hospital" by Bradford Kirman-Liff, provides a penetrating look at a major medical center's Medicaid managed care contracting process. The case reviews the hospital's implementation of its contracting strategy and offers the case analyst an opportunity to reassess St. Joseph's strategy decisions.

Case 12, "Analyzing the Financial Performance of Hospital-Based Managed Care Programs: The Case of Humana" by Joseph S. Coyne, traces the evolution of Humana's hospital-based managed care product. The case narrative and accompanying financial data allow the analyst to probe the implementation problems associated with Humana's strategy—particularly the conflict between hospitals' short-run incentive to fill beds and the long-run corporate goal to function as a managed care company.

Case 13, "The Institute for Preventive Medicine Health Plan" by Gordon Brown, Keith Boles, and L. Jerome Ashford, concludes the book and serves as a capstone integrative case. The case elucidates the development of this HMO from its origins as a clinical research corporation. The case documents the history of strategy development for the Institute for Preventive Medicine (IPM), as it moved from a research corporation to a prepaid health plan with enrollment limited to primary beneficiaries who were union employees of Southern Pacific Railroad, to its evolution as a partner with a medical group, which resulted in the formation of an HMO. The consistent pattern for the organization is to adopt strategies that are opportunistic, high risk, and focused on rapid growth. The early emphasis is on locating a niche in a marketplace otherwise dominated by the Kaiser Health Plan, with a potential market focused on very small local businesses and some individual enrollees.

As the case continues, the organization undertakes a major restructuring that involves changes in corporate culture and management style. The case moves through this combination of strategy reformulation, system building and balancing, and an in-depth financial analysis of IPM and the role of finances in strategy development.

Strategy shifts again at the beginning of part three of the case, when IPM adopts a preemptive strategy of moving into a new geographic market, seeking to change its competitive positioning in the marketplace while at the same time changing its benefit package. In the last part of the case, it becomes clear that IPM cannot survive as a freestanding entity, and it begins to look for a partner in purchase or merger. The case ends as IPM becomes investor-owned. Thus, the cycle of strategic adaptation, from strategy formulation to system and structure building and balancing, to implementation and reassessment is systematically illustrated in this case history.

Case Applications

The cases in this book are intended to serve a variety of purposes. Fundamentally, the logic of the case studies and their interrelationships suggest their utility for a course in strategy and strategic management. However, individual cases will be useful in structuring units for courses in organizational behavior and organizational design and development, marketing and marketing strategy, microeconomics and finance, and health politics and policy. This casebook could serve as a very effective fundamental text for a course in managed care, as well as providing background materials for course work in risk and insurance.

The philosophy of the cases and their complementarities also make them useful for a capstone, integrative seminar in health services management. By presenting the strategic adaptation process in its several constituent parts and providing a series of different micro and macro case examples, this book is meant to enrich management curricula and to provide some diversified educational products that go beyond the traditional hospital setting. The cases have been developed with an eye toward long-term shelf life, and we hope that they continue to serve their purpose well into the twenty-first century.

The choice to tie the order of the cases to the flow of the strategic adaptation process reflects our conceptual framework for this book. We hope that the faculty and students of programs in health services administration will use this casebook as one of their programs' core texts. In analyzing these cases and confronting the problems they pose, the student will draw from a wide range of disciplines and managerial perspectives.

Table 1 presents a matrix of the disciplinary and curriculum areas addressed by the cases in this book. The case materials are inherently interdisciplinary, which should facilitate broad use of the book as a

Table 1 Disciplines, Curriculum, and Areas by Case

Case	Disciplines, Curriculum, Areas Addressed
1. Competition, Integration, and Diversification: Seven Hospital of Growthville, U.S.A.	Microeconomics, strategic management, organization theory
2. Western Health Care Systems: A Health Care Delivery Continuum	Strategic management, organization theory, behavior
3. Strategic Choices in Building an Integrated Hospital-Physician Network: The Bueno Vista Clinic Acquisition Proposal	Microeconomics, strategic management, organization theory, managed care
4. Linkages between Acute and Long-Term Care Services	Organization theory, strategic management
5. Corporate Restructuring: Phase II	General management, organization theory, governance
6. Centralization and Decentralization in a Vertically Integrated System: The XYZ Hospital Corporation	Multi-institutional systems, organization theory and development, strategic, general management
7. Organizational Control Issues for a Health Maintenance Organization Subsidiary	Management accounting and control, organization theory and behavior, managed care
8. Make versus Buy Decisions in a Closed-Panel Health Maintenance Organization	Strategic management, general management, managed care, microeconomics, managerial control
9. Marketing in a Buy-Right Environment	Marketing, strategic management and planning
10. Geriatric Assessment Center	General management, marketing, strategic planning
11. Capitated Medicaid and St. Joseph's Hospital	Microeconomics and finance, strategic management, general management, organization theory, managed care
12. Analyzing the Financial Performance of Hospital-Based Managed Care Programs: The Case of Humana	Financial accounting and management, strategic management, managed care
13. The Institute for Preventive Medicine Health Plan	Organization theory and development, financial accounting and managerial finance, risk and insurance, strategic management, general management, managed care

core text in integrative seminars within residential and executive management education programs and as a source of extensive supplementary materials for discipline-based and applications courses throughout the curriculum.

References

Chandler, A. D., Jr. 1990. *Scale and Scope: The Dynamics of Industrial Capitalism.* Harvard: Belknap Press.

Conrad, D. A., and W. L. Dowling. 1990. "Vertical Integration in Health Care: Theory and Managerial Implications." *Health Care Management Review* 15 (Fall): 9–22.

Conrad, D. A., S. S. Mick, C. W. Madden, and G. Hoare. 1988. "Vertical Structures and Control in Health Care Markets: A Conceptual Framework and Empirical Review." *Medical Care Review* 45 (Spring): 49–100.

Duncan, W. J., P. M. Ginter, and L. E. Swayne. 1992. *Strategic Management of Health Care Organizations.* Boston: P. W. S. Kent Publishing Company.

Hoare, G. 1987. "New Managerial Roles in Multiorganizational Systems: Implications for Health Administration Education." *Journal of Health Administration Education* 5 (Summer): 423–39.

Howard, P. 1992. "The CEO as Organizational Architect: An Interview with Xerox's Paul Allaire." *Harvard Business Review* 70 (September–October): 106–21.

Johnston, R., and P. R. Laurence. 1988. "Beyond Vertical Integration: The Rise of Value-Adding Partnerships." *Harvard Business Review* 66 (July–August): 94–101.

Porter, M. E. 1980. *Competitive Strategy: Techniques for Analyzing Industries and Competitors.* New York: The Free Press.

Prahalad, C. K., and G. Hamel. 1990. "The Core Competence of the Corporation." *Harvard Business Review* 68 (May–June): 79–91.

Williamson, O. E. 1975. *Markets and Hierarchies: Analysis and Antitrust Implications.* New York: The Free Press.

Zuckerman, H. S., and A. D. Kaluzny. 1991. "Strategic Alliances as an Emerging Health Care Organizational Form." *Frontiers of Health Services Management* 7 (Spring): 3–23.

Part **I**

Environmental Assessment
and Strategy Making

Competition, Integration, and Diversification: Seven Hospitals of Growthville, U.S.A.

David B. Starkweather

Part I: Introduction

If environments grow increasingly uncertain and turbulent, organizations form interorganizational links. This is a concept drawn from the theories of organizational exchange and interdependence. Such is the case for U.S. hospitals: environmental change and uncertainty have increased in the past decade, heightened by deregulation and the introduction of market forces. This has yielded three responses on the part of hospitals that are relevant to this theory: (1) the number of hospitals entering multi-hospital systems has increased [1]; (2) the form of interhospital linking has shifted from looser forms providing for individual hospital discretion and autonomy to tighter forms leaving little or no discretion [2]; and (3) the structure of relationships has shifted from more distant links (i.e., between hospitals in widely dispersed areas) to more proximal affiliations (i.e., between hospitals in the same geographic areas) [3].

This case study is about the process by which such restructuring occurs. Fundamental to this process is a change in the nature of relationships between organizations. Typically, there are four stages of change:

This article has been reprinted from *Journal of Health Administration Education* Vol. 8, no. 4 (Fall 1990), with permission of the Association of University Programs in Health Administration.

competition, exchange, symbiosis, and dominance. As described by Blau and Scott:

> One can see that the outcome of competition at one stage changes the object of competition at the next. In the earlier stages all units compete against all others. Differential success in this competition for relative standing has the result that the least successful are no longer able to compete with the most successful, and this change leads to the establishment of symbiotic relations that aid both parties in their continued competition. But now the two groups have different objects to their competition: the more successful units compete with one another for dominance, while the less successful units compete for survival. . . . Relations between units have also changed, since some former competitors have now become partners in exchange. Differential success in further competitive processes enables a few large organizations to dominate a given market [4].

This case study provides an illustration of this process.

A striking feature of the evolution seen in this case is the role of concentration as both a response to increased competition and a vector of change in restructuring hospital markets. A related phenomenon is the relationship of vertical and horizontal integrations to each other: initial corporate reorganizations provide the vehicle for subsequent horizontal integrations; then horizontal integrations achieve a new critical mass and market dominance, yielding more vertical developments. The resulting increase in the market power of health care providers stimulates concentrations among the purchasers of care, thus rebalancing the power equation and moving health care toward a system driven by negotiated prices.

Organizationally, this process is called *strategic alignment.* The case reveals how the numerous hospital managers of Growthville use strategy to create their realigned enterprises.

Part II: Overview of the Community

Growthville is a metropolitan area comprising more than ten incorporated cities and unincorporated areas. It lies less than fifty miles from another densely populated city of almost one million people. Growthville is an economic leader in its state, widely known for its concentration of high-technology industries. It is the fourth most populous city in the state.

Population of Growthville tripled from 200,000 to 600,000 in the twenty-year period between 1960 and 1980. By 1985 it had grown another 300,000, to 900,000, and by 1988 it had topped one million. Estimates for 1990 project a continuing population increase for Growthville, although not at the same extreme rate.

Caucasians represent 73 percent of Growthville's population. Sixteen percent are of Spanish origin, 8 percent are Asians and Pacific Islanders, and 3 percent of the population is black. The median age is 28.4; 30 percent of Growthville's population is between 18 and 44—a significant factor in competition in health care delivery. Over 26 percent of the population has four or more years of university-level education.

In 1985 the median household income was $38,200, making this community the seventh most affluent market in the United States. Eighteen percent of the households have an income between $12,500 and $23,500, compared with 23 percent of the households statewide. By contrast, 15 percent of Growthville's households have incomes of over $62,000, compared with 11 percent for the state as a whole.

Employment in Growthville is high and is distributed in the following areas:

Agriculture	1 percent
Manufacturing	36 percent
Government	18 percent
Services	22 percent
Other	23 percent

Thus, approximately one out of every three workers is employed in manufacturing, primarily in high technology, with several corporations employing over 20,000 persons each.

In short, Growthville contains those ingredients that make a strong and healthy economy: an attractive place to live; a geography with room for growth; a youthful and high-income population that is increasing rapidly; production characterized by clean, light manufacturing; and a well-qualified work force.

These factors have contributed to the early and strong competitive behavior among hospitals.

Hospitals

There are fourteen hospitals in Growthville, of which seven figure prominently in this case.

Miseracordia Hospital. Miseracordia Hospital is owned and operated by a Roman Catholic order. Its services are typical for a community hospital of this size and type, including an organized outpatient department and a home care program. Its prime service area is a lower-economic section of Growthville to the west, with many persons of Spanish origin.

The basis of Miseracordia's strategic response to competition is its location: it believes that it has a superior location because it is the only hospital in the western part of Growthville; it has developed outpatient activities to serve this population; and it has a strong local reputation for its market share of labor and delivery services and its services to the elderly.

Miseracordia boasts the largest charity allowance among Growthville's nongovernmental hospitals, but its percentage of Medicaid patients is declining. Miseracordia's CEO does not see the hospital remaining a free-standing institution. He distinguishes between an "affiliation" and a "merger"; given Miseracordia's assessment of its locational advantage, the CEO sees an affiliation yielding an "agreement between hospitals to stay out of each other's territories."

Queen of Angels Hospital. Queen of Angels Hospital, also owned and operated by a Catholic order, is the oldest hospital in Growthville, having been established in 1889 when the community was a small town serving an agricultural area. Its strategy has been one of diversification. It was one of the first hospitals to reorganize corporately, by creating a parent corporation that is also the eastern regional corporation of the order's national multihospital system. Queen of Angels believes in diversification outside of the health field; in 1984 it made more than a quarter of a million dollars on its activities outside of the health sector.

In the early 1980s the management of Queen of Angels assessed the "new market" as one in which "consumers are changing their shopping habits; they wish to and will seek care in different environments." This meant to Queen of Angels that there should be strong vertical developments coupled with a separation of services that treat the sick from those that are oriented to the well—primarily young and affluent persons. Its strategy focused on planning a surgi-center across the street from the hospital, a second surgi-center in the rapidly growing North County area, an off-site magnetic resonating imaging center, and an off-site personal fitness center.

Queen of Angels sees its prime competitors as other fee-for-service hospitals or groups of hospitals. There have been serious affiliation talks with Miseracordia Hospital. Queen of Angels has established a relationship with an out-of-state HMO and seeks to draw other local hospitals into its "network" in order to serve a patient population dispersed over a wider geographic area.

Good Shepherd Hospital. Good Shepherd, the largest hospital in the community, is also the newest. It was built in the early 1960s in a fast-growing suburb of Growthville and has grown with its population sector.

Its general hospital services are augmented by numerous specialty and subspecialty programs.

In 1986 Good Shepherd joined with Valley Community Hospital to form Health Value, a multihospital system also including Beeler Hospital, a 56-bed community hospital serving a small agricultural community to the north of Growthville. Beeler Hospital had joined with Good Shepherd in 1985 in an affiliation that would make possible—with Good Shepherd's financial backing—the replacement of Beeler's obsolete physical plant on a new site.

Valley Community Hospital. Valley Community Hospital, established in 1923, is another of Growthville's older hospitals. It is located in the center of Growthville, in what can be called its inner-city district. As such, the hospital has served large proportions of indigent patients for most of its history. Unlike other fee-for-service hospitals in Growthville, Valley Community has an established group practice of 55 physicians. Located adjacent to the hospital, it has afforded opportunities in recent years for numerous joint doctor/hospital projects.

By 1987 the three-hospital combine of community hospitals making up Health Value faced the possibility of competing with another hospital system comprised of two religious hospitals. Further, Health Value and the Catholic hospitals saw considerable overlap in their geographic markets.

Large HMO Hospital. Large HMO Hospital is a part of a prepaid health plan and a closed-panel medical group. All three components operate as an integrated system. The prepaid health plan provides all of the patients for Large HMO Hospital.

The strategy of Large HMO Hospital is based on the view that "the hospital and its physicians must be seen as one." This refers to the entwining of Large HMO Hospital with its parallel closed-panel medical groups in order to (1) serve a prepaid population of enrolled members, (2) operate the hospital, and (3) staff numerous outpatient clinics operated on and off site.

The CEO of Large HMO Hospital believes that future competitors will be other emerging HMOs and that the competition will be based on both price and service. The hospital now enjoys approximately 30 percent of the health care market in Growthville.

Large HMO's competitive threat thus far has come from the south, where Large Employer (20,000 employees) and St. Royale Hospital have collaborated to establish a preferred provider organization plan that has drawn members away from Large HMO. It believes that another employer (25,000 employees) may do the same.

County Medical Center. County Medical Center is a government hospital, owned and operated by the Growthville County. It is a tertiary hospital offering many services, in part because of its close affiliation with a medical school to the south that provides its medical staff and uses the hospital as an acute care teaching unit.

Survival has not previously been a problem for this hospital, given its subvention from county government and its close relationship with a nearby medical school. But County Medical Center would now view the future as bleak were it not for recent major changes that have the potential for success. First, the Center is promoting services used by privately insured patients. This includes the hospital's burn care unit, neonatal unit, spinal cord injury unit, cardiac care unit, and specialized disease services. These services are being marketed across to a wide geographic region, because County Medical Center has joint ventured with its affiliated medical school in a helicopter service that brings patients to the hospital.

The hospital's second thrust relates to the prepaid market. A preferred provider organization (PPO) type of health plan has been initiated, aimed at the 11,000 employees of the Growthville county government. Its major competitor in this endeavor is Large HMO, and its strategy is to obtain "Large HMO disgruntleds."

St. Royale Hospital. St. Royal Hospital is a large hospital immediately to the south of metropolitan Growthville. It is relatively new, having opened in 1962 to serve the population of a suburban and industrial community that was rapidly expanding due to the buildup of electronics and aerospace companies. St. Royale is owned by a hospital district, formed pursuant to state legislation that permits local special-purpose public entities to provide a tax base for the construction of hospital facilities. While St. Royale is thus a government hospital, it, unlike County Medical Center, has no obligation to serve the indigent. Indeed, the state-enabling legislation stipulates that district hospitals like St. Royale must operate on a self-sufficient financial basis.

Table 1.1 summarizes the key characteristics of the above seven hospitals, including their strategic and competitive features.

Medical staffs

Table 1.2 summarizes and compares the active medical staffs of six of these hospitals. At Valley Community there is a much larger proportion of primary care physicians and a smaller proportion of medical specialists. At Good Shepherd there is a larger proportion of specialists, particularly in the medical specialities.

Table 1.1 Summary Characteristics of Seven Growthville Hospitals, 1987

Hospital	No. Beds	Ownership	Occupancy	Special Strengths	Strategic Strengths	Competitor(s)	Relationships
Misericordia	204	church	75%	obstetrics pediatrics rehabilitation emergency	sole hospital in West Growthville	Valley, County Medical Center	possible affiliation with Queen of Angels
Queen of Angels	329	church	75%	cardiac surg. radiation hemodialysis obstetrics	diversified, wellness, ambulatory care	Valley, Good Shepherd	possible affiliation with Misericordia
Good Shepherd	403	community	58%	cardiac surg. premature nursery psychiatry chemical dependency	size, reputation, specialized services	Queen of Angels	joined with Valley Community and Beeler in Health Value
Valley Community	352	community	59%	cardiac surg. radiation hemodialysis psychiatry chemical dependency emergency	inner-city location, service to indigents, medical group	Misericordia, County Medial Center, Queen of Angels	joined with Good Shepherd and Beeler in Health Value

Continued

Table 1.1 Continued

Hospital	No. Beds	Ownership	Occupancy	Special Strengths	Strategic Strengths	Competitor(s)	Relationships
Large HMO Hospital	546	HMO	71%	obstetrics pediatrics chemical dependency surgery emergency	dominates HMO market, low cost	emerging HMOs, St. Royale	Large HMO, Medical group
County Medical Center	305	county	79%	burn center neonatal spinal cord emergency	teaching, tertiary services	Valley Misericordia, Queen of Angels	nearby medical school
St. Royale	396	district	69%	obstetrics pediatrics radiation emergency	location, district support, little uncompensated care	University Hospital, Large HMO	Large Employer's PPO

There is substantial overlap in medical staff memberships among the fee-for-service hospitals of Growthville, notably among the first four listed in Table 1.2.

Prepaid health plans

In addition to Large HMO, with a 30 percent market share in health insurance, there are six other smaller health plans and PPOs that have been contracting with community providers since 1983. Combined with Large HMO, they represent in excess of 270,000 enrollees, or 40 percent of the total health insurance market. The hospital patient volume associated with each of these health plans has created an aggressive and competitive contracting situation, which is further stimulated by the multiple-choice health benefit environment among local employers. Sixty percent of all local employers offer two or more health plan alternatives to their employees, 55 percent of all local employees are fully or partially self-insured, and 70 percent of these employers use brokers to search and negotiate price contracts. This has stimulated the multihospital linkages that are so important to provider access and availability for prepaid plan members. The degree of over-beddedness in the community, in addition to the current power of these plans to force large discounts for hospital services, has encouraged several of the providers to consider and/or initiate health plans of their own.

Table 1.2 Composition of Medical Staffs

	Misera-cordia (N-169)	Good Shepherd (N-475)	Queen of Angels (N-167)	Valley Community (N-487)	County Medical Center (N-315)	St. Royale (N-555)
Primary	43%	42%	23%	54%	33%	25%
Psychiatry	0	6	0	4	4	8
General surgery	8	10	14	7	3	4
Surgical specialties	23	15	26	18	13	11
Medical specialties	17	20	23	10	35	50
Hospital-based practices*	8	8	14	7	13	2
Total	100%	100%	100%	100%	100%	100%

*Includes hospital-based specialists of radiology, pathology, anesthesiology, etc. but excludes all other physician types in county medical center who are physically located within the hospital. All figures exclude interns and residents in training.

Financial performance

Table 1.3 summarizes the overall financial performance of six of the seven case study hospitals in Growthville from 1981 to 1988. Note the drop in occupancy percentages of all hospitals, with the exception of County Medical Center. This resulted in substantial excess capacity in the fee-for-service hospitals by 1985–86. In turn, this excess influenced the strategies of several of these hospitals. We note also a general leveling in the operating margins of the fee-for-service hospitals, with only St. Royale improving its position.

While operating margins were flat, there were increases in non-operating margins at most of the hospitals, with the one exception of Valley Community, which experienced a slight drop. Clearly, nonoperating income became more important, and in three of the hospitals the nonoperating margins were greater than the operating margins in 1985–86. This reflects the diversification strategies pursued by these hospitals.

There was a remarkable increase in the assumption of long-term debt in three of the four fee-for-service hospitals. The notable exceptions are Good Shepherd and St. Royale, which reduced their proportion of long-term debt relative to unrestricted assets. Most of these commitments in long-term debt were made in 1982–83 and first appeared in the financial statistics for the following year. This corresponds with the time that these hospitals "awakened" to the fact that they faced an era of high competition.

Good Shepherd and St. Royale experienced improvement in operating margins in the period 1985–88. Valley Community experienced a substantial drop in occupancy over time. Likewise, there was a dramatic drop in operating income, but as a downscaled hospital its operating margin recovered in 1987 and 1988. This hospital also increased its debt, but at a period of time later than its competitor hospitals. The case will describe how Valley Community shelved its capital investment plans of the earlier 1980s because they were too expensive, and later developed an alternative strategy that was eventually funded.

Uncompensated care

Table 1.4 shows the distribution of charity and government patients among the six hospitals. The changes shown on this table stem primarily from a decision of the state legislature in 1984 to shift its method of reimbursement to hospitals for the care of indigent and low-income patients from one based on costs to one based on negotiated prices. Hospitals throughout the state could choose whether or not to bid for

Table 1.3   Financial Statistics of Growthville's Hospitals

	Misera-cordia	Good Shepherd	Queen of Angels	Valley Community	County Medical Center	St. Royale*
1981–82						
Occupancy (%)	84	69	78	73	67	
Gross revenue (thousands of dollars)	36,676	49,813	49,487	50,582	60,336	
Net operating income (thousands of dollars)	2,156	4,405	4,749	2,346	−17,588	
Operating margin (%)	8	10	11	5	−38	
Nonoperating margin (%)	2	2	1	.4	23	
Long-term debt/unrestricted assets	.04	.28	.91	.83	n.a.	
Acct. receivable/total current assets	.73	.82	.91	.83	n.a.	
1983–84						
Occupancy (%)	64	58	86	61	77	68
Gross revenue (thousands of dollars)	40,043	60,769	59,455	61,564	94,004	74,569
Net operating income (thousands of dollars)	−754	2,498	0	701	−19,086	3,422
Operating margin (%)	−2	4	0	1	−22	5
Nonoperating margin (%)	n.a.	n.a.	n.a.	n.a.	n.a.	n.a.
Long-term debt/unrestricted assets	.52	.21	.45	.20	0	.08
Acct. receivable/total current assets	.77	.79	.82	.88	.74	.92

Continued

Table 1.3 Continued

	Misericordia	Good Shepherd	Queen of Angels	Valley Community	County Medical Center	St. Royale*
1985–86						
Occupancy (%)	75	58	75	57	79	61
Gross revenue (thousands of dollars)	58,606	79,088	96,902	74,259	130,007	82,097
Net operating income (thousands of dollars)	450	7,636	5,011	4,298	−23,226	5,631
Operating margin (%)	1	11	7	2	−27	8
Nonoperating margin (%)	4	3	2	3	16	n.a.
Long-term debt/unrestricted assets	.50	.15	.48	.49	0	.07
Acct. receivable/total current assets	.77	.88	.90	.69	.89	.94
1987–88						
Occupancy (%)		65	78	38	81	92
Gross revenue (thousands of dollars)		86,597	93,088	47,336	148,552	84,445
Net operating income (thousands of dollars)		7,171	4,400	2,650	−30,366	8,733
Operating margin (%)		9	6	7	−34	11
Nonoperating margin (%)		n.a.	n.a.	n.a.	n.a.	n.a.
Long-term debt/unrestricted assets		.12	.47	.46	.10	.06
Acct. receivable/total current assets		.90	.86	.66	.57	.91

*Data for 1981–82 not reported to the state agency.

the state business. The state needed sufficient contracts in each area to provide accessible care for the indigent populations it supported.

The four major fee-for-service hospitals in Growthville had remarkably different strategies. At both Miseracordia and Queen of Angels, institutional commitments born of religious mission inspired the hospitals to continue serving Medicaid patients; thus, both hospitals submitted bids and obtained contracts. Queen of Angels expected to lose money on its contracts. This was true even though the proportion of Medicaid patients subsequently dropped from the prior percentage of 12 to about 8. At Miseracordia, by contrast, the effect of the Medicaid contract was judged to be positive, at least in the immediate postcontract period. The differences in financial effect on the two hospitals may be due to differences in the price of Miseracordia's contract relative to its marginal costs, as compared with that of Queen of Angels. It may also be due to differences in volume, since Miseracordia's proportion of Medicaid patients—30 percent—is substantially larger. Good Shepherd did not seek or obtain a contract with the state inasmuch as its mix of Medicaid patients was relatively low and it had decided not to continue serving these patients. This was part of a strategy on the part of Good Shepherd to go after the private insured market. It calculated that its main and only obligation to Medicaid patients would be in its new north county facility, where the hospital would be the sole provider.

At Valley Community there was a split in the hospital and medical staff over whether the hospital should contract with Medicaid. The appraisal of the hospital management was that the hospital had to eliminate its Medicaid patient population if it was to rid itself of its image of a "county type" facility and acquire a new image as the quality provider for the central and eastern part of the city. Understanding that reductions in volume would ensue, Valley Community decided not to submit a Medicaid contract proposal. The management believed that the financial effect of this decision would be positive for the long run.

At St. Royale Hospital the decision was made in early 1985 to forgo a Medicaid contract. The hospital felt it was already providing care at a low and reasonable cost and there was no justification to cut rates even further by the bidding process. St. Royale was under no community service or religious obligation to solicit and obtain a contract for Medicaid patients.

The results of these strategies are seen in Table 1.4. Most of the Medicaid patients perviously served by Valley Community sought hospital care at Miseracordia, Queen of Angels, or County Medical Center. Even so, the table shows Valley Community continuing with a 6 percent payer mix of Medicaid patients. This is due to an agreement it struck with Growthville County to the effect that in exchange for designation

Table 1.4 Care of Charity and Government Patients

	Misericordia*	Good Shepherd	Queen of Angels	Valley Community	County Medical Center	St. Royalet†
1981–82						
Bad debts and charity deductions/charges	.05	.02	.03	.03	.10	
Total deductions and allowances/charges	.24	.09	.15	.14	.20	
Percent gross revenue from Medicare	28	26	39	36	21	
Percent gross revenue from Medicaid	32	2	9	22	31	
1983–84						
Bad debts and charity deductions/charges	.04	.03	.03	.03	.07	.02
Total deductions and allowances/charges	.23	.10	.11	.17	.20	.11
Percent gross revenue from Medicare	31	28	43	34	21	32
Percent gross revenue from Medicaid	30	6	7	22	42	7
1985–86						
Bad debts and charity deductions/charges	.04	.03	.02	.06	.17	.02
Total deductions and allowances/charges	.29	.10	.18	.21	.36	.11
Percent gross revenue from Medicare	34	28	48	40	14	36
Percent gross revenue from Medicaid	29	2	8	6	36	1
1987–88						
Bad debts and charity deductions/charges		.03	.02	.04	.26	.02
Total deductions and allowances/charges		.09	.15	.18	.40	.05
Percent gross revenue from Medicare		29	45	34	14	33
Percent gross revenue from Medicaid		2	10	6	38	0

*Data for 1987–88 not reported to the state agency.

†Data for 1981–82 not reported to the state agency.

as a countywide trauma center Valley Community would agree not to transfer any Medicaid patients to County Medical Center. This meant that Valley Community was obligated to treat Medicaid and other indigent patients in its emergency room and also provide follow-up inpatient care if needed.

In summary, the hospital market in Growthville was competitive even after the merger that created Health Value. Table 1.5 shows that Large HMO, Health Value, St. Royale, Queen of Angels, and County Medical Center all had market shares between 10 and 20 percent. University Hospital and Miseracordia had market shares between 5 and 10 percent. The Herfendahl-Hirschman Index of concentration was approximately 1400, a level that would indicate that some additional mergers could take place without endangering workable competition.[1]

Part II: Discussion Questions

1. The hospitals described in the Introduction are of relatively similar size; none are clearly different. What is the effect of this on hospital competitiveness?

2. "There is substantial overlap in medical staff members among the

Table 1.5   Growthville Market Shares and Concentration Index, 1987

Hospital	*No. Admissions*	*Market Share (%)*	*Square*
Large HMO	31,801	20.34	413.72
Good Shepherd	19,235	12.30	
Valley Community	11,194	7.16	
Beeler Hospital	3,516	2.25	
		(21.71)	471.32
St. Royale	19,515	12.48	155.78
Queen of Angels	15,724	10.06	101.13
County Medical Center	15,643	10.00	100.09
University	13,952	8.92	79.62
Children	661	.42	.18
Misericordia	10,651	6.81	46.40
Gates Community	6,983	4.47	19.95
North Oaks Hospital	1,794	1.15	1.32
Others	5,688	3.64	13.23
Total	156,357	100.00	1402.74 (HHI)

fee-for-service hospitals of Growthville." Does this have the effect of increasing or decreasing the competition among these hospitals?

3. Table 1.4 shows the distribution of charity and government patients among the six hospitals. There is considerable variation in the burden of uncompensated care, both among hospitals and from year to year. How does this variation affect the hospitals' strategies vis-à-vis horizontal and vertical linkages?

4. Concerning the decisions of Miseracordia and Queen of Angels to contract with the state for Medicaid patients, given their different Medicaid case mixes, what different price calculations and negotiating tactics might the two hospitals have adopted?

5. How did Valley Community reach its conclusion that dropping its Medicaid business would be financially beneficial in the long run?

Part III: The Beginnings of Horizontal/Vertical Concentration and Diversification

Good Shepherd

In 1984 Good Shepherd altered its strategy dramatically, from one suited to the prior situation of less competition to one better suited to the new competitive forces. This change is well reflected in the statement of its chief executive officer of twenty years: "I have become a convert to the idea that health care delivery is consumer driven."

Good Shepherd's former strategy was a traditional one, aimed primarily at physicians and seeking to provide quality services through them. The hospital sought to obtain the commitment of physicians to the "greater good" of the hospital while at the same time avoiding their financial involvement; hospital officials believed that the efforts of doctors relative to the hospital should be devoted solely to providing quality service. The hospital sought and obtained a good deal of participation from physicians in its planning for new services.

Good Shepherd Hospital realized that it had benefited from the patient flows of a high-growth geographic area for its first twenty years but that such would not continue in the future. For this reason it looked to the north county area, which was slated for dramatic population expansion in the late 1980s and 1990s. An opportunity was presented by Beeler Hospital, a smaller and older hospital near this population growth corridor; in 1985 Good Shepherd affiliated with Beeler under terms that stipulated that Good Shepherd would help Beeler capitalize a new hospital in the area. Good Shepherd saw its investment in north county yielding a 400-bed medical center in approximately thirty years.

Good Shepherd's relationship to other hospitals brought about two corporate reorganizations. The first, in 1985, created a new holding company of which the prior existing hospital became the principal subsidiary. This component of the hospital's affiliation with Beeler was needed in order to construct the latter's replacement facility in north county and thus also strengthen Good Shepherd's service delivery capacity. A second reason for reorganization was to change the mechanism by which physicians were involved in decision making; corporate reorganization would allow their involvement in a "timely fashion." This was viewed as a prerequisite for proceeding with an urgent care center. With the traditional hospital medical staff structure, decision making would have been too slow and the center would not have been built. By contrast, corporate reorganization permitted the decision on such projects to be made at the level of the holding company, thus bypassing the hospital medical staff.

The second corporate reorganization occurred in 1986 in order to accommodate Valley Community. This was a minor restructuring relative to the first one; the main change was to increase seats on the parent board for officials of Valley Community.

In the words of the CEO of the new Health Value Corporation, formerly the administrator of Good Shepherd: "Providing the base for an HMO was one reason for this merger, but it was also undertaken for future survival. Only those hospitals who have achieved horizontal integration will weather the squall."

By 1987 Good Shepherd's competitor analysis had concluded that its major threat was Large HMO—not the other fee-for-service hospitals. Its strategy was to use Health Value to form the basis of a counter HMO. It also saw groups of doctors as major competitors, as evidenced by the physician-owned breast center and ambulatory surgery facilities opened in the immediate proximities of Health Value's hospitals.

In 1989 Good Shepherd started construction of a 100-bed facility in the north county area, pursuant to its earlier affiliation with Beeler Hospital.

Valley Community

As with Good Shepherd, Valley Community also dramatically altered its strategy in the mid-1980s. This change was fashioned around two major events: (1) having to choose whether to contract with the state for Medicaid patients and (2) its affiliation with Good Shepherd.

In 1982 Valley Community found itself a "classic inner-city hospital": older physical plant, large indigent population, flight of the affluent patients to the suburbs, and an aging medical staff. Valley Community had one of the largest Medicaid populations in the state for a community hospital: 26 percent.

Starting in 1983 Valley Community was among the first to undertake sophisticated market and product line analyses. This led the hospital to a decision to emphasize six specialized and focused programs: obstetrics, oncology, trauma, orthopedics, rehabilitation, and outpatient surgery. These analyses by the hospital also indicated that Good Shepherd had the highest rating in the Growthville market with respect to quality, although not price, and that Valley Community ranked highest with respect to access to medical care.

In 1984 Valley Community's CEO led his organization through a corporate reorganization that was intended to "get out of the inpatient business and into health care delivery." Further, he realized by this time that the 1983 product line strategy was too expensive; it would cost $80 million in capital investment, and the plan was "overly fixed" on inpatient care. So in late 1984 the strategy was abandoned in favor of one that would change the physical image of the hospital from its "older, downtown county-like" presence to one that would differentiate the facility from other hospitals and present Valley Community as the "quality private hospital for central and western city." A $20 million investment was planned and initiated. It included a new ambulatory surgery facility, remodeling of inpatient surgeries, improvements of amenities in patients' rooms and public areas, and a $2 million "landmark development" of the hospital's entrance and lobby area.

Valley Community's plan for future services was to continue its six "focal services" on a reduced-investment basis. With an eye toward the population growth and demographics of the western area of Growthville, an area served primarily by competitors Miseracordia and Queen of Angels, Valley Community planned to expand its acute pediatric services and to start an adolescent psychiatric unit.

Linked to this change was a decision in 1984 to get out of the Medicaid business, based upon the management's realization that "the other hospitals will do better if we do worse." This referred primarily to Miseracordia and Queen of Angels.

The opportunity to make this change arose in 1984 as a result of the state legislature's decision to change the method of reimbursement to hospitals for Medicaid patients, from one based on historically defined costs to one based on negotiated per diem prices; this was developed from bids submitted by any hospitals interested in the state's "Medicaid business." Valley Community decided not to submit a bid, despite its long-standing history of service to a substantial number of Medicaid recipients.

Its failure to secure a Medicaid contract led to an immediate drop in hospital census from 340 to 200. Numerous beds were taken out of service. Twenty-five percent of the work force was dismissed. These moves made the hospital "leaner and stronger."

This move had a substantial effect on the medical staff of the hospital. Numerous older physicians whose practices emphasized admission of Medicaid patients were now unable to admit their patients, and many other physicians whose practices included some Medicaid patients altered their admitting patterns to use other hospitals. This change fit with a long-term intent of Valley Community to integrate more closely with a smaller number of doctors who were of central importance to the hospital. In particular, there was a 55-doctor medical group that owned facilities adjacent to the hospital and practiced exclusively in Valley Community. The construction of a facility for the medical practice on the hospital campus further enhanced this change. All of this led to a "smaller, more clearly linked, more homogenous medical staff" and to the opportunity for new hospital/doctor relationships based on joint corporate ventures.

Valley Community initiated merger talks with Good Shepherd. It did so following a complicated series of relationships with Beeler Hospital in which Valley Community saw "the chance to change Good Shepherd from a competitor into an ally." Specifically, in the early 1980s the management of Valley Community had been used by Beeler on a consulting basis to develop its plans and strategies for the future. One feature of the plan was for Beeler to seek an affiliation with another hospital in Growthville in order to support its construction of a new facility in the population corridor of the north county. There was every expectation that Beeler would seek an affiliation with Valley Community, given the consulting relationship and given the additional advantage of Valley Community's ownership of a twenty-acre plot in north county that the hospital had purchased in earlier years; it would be ideal for Beeler's relocated facility. But instead, Beeler issued a request for proposals (RFP) to several hospitals. Both Valley Community and Good Shepherd responded, along with others. Good Shepherd was chosen for the affiliation. It was through this process that Valley Community came to view Good Shepherd as a possible merger partner.

The merger: Health Value

In 1985 Good Shepherd viewed itself as a "healthy institution" and saw Valley Community as "hungrier" for an affiliation due to its inner-city location, its older plant, its aging physicians, and its high proportion of government-sponsored patients. To Good Shepherd's CEO, there were four short-term advantages of a merger: (1) to provide for improved contracting capacity through the networking of three facilities and the physicians relating thereto, (2) to obtain economies of scale in administrative areas and efficiencies through elimination of duplicate patient services, (3) to improve borrowing capacity, and (4) to help Beeler in north county with its new construction. In the long run Good Shepherd's CEO saw the merger as essential to its survival because of the necessity to create a critical mass and an asset base sufficient to generate revenue and obtain capital.

Officials of Valley Community saw the same short-term and long-term advantages. Valley Community's management stressed the competitive advantage of a market presence in a broad enough geographic area to support contracting with employer and insurance groups, as well as the operation of its own HMO. In 1985 it had analyzed twelve submarkets within Growthville and calculated that a market share of at least 20 percent in each of the twelve would be necessary in order to hold a competitive position in the future. It calculated that the combination of Valley Community, Good Shepherd, and Beeler would obtain this 20 percent share in nine of the twelve areas. Further, the combined efforts of the three could develop stronger positions in all twelve submarkets than any of Growthville's hospitals, with the exception of Large HMO, would be able to obtain separately. In the view of officials from Valley Community this combination of market spread and depth, coupled with the insurance arm of an HMO, would place it and the other two hospitals in a strong position in the future prepaid and capitated health care environment. The market shares of the key competitors in Growthville are shown in Table 1.5.

In 1986 Good Shepherd and Valley Community merged. Both hospitals continued as relatively autonomous entities even though they were owned by a new parent corporation. The new umbrella corporation, Health Value, was established with minimum holding company powers, namely, the four statutory powers that are required of a parent corporation by state law: (1) appointment and removal of board members of subsidiary corporations, (2) approval of sale or other disposition of assets of subsidiary corporations, (3) approval of any mergers, consolidations, or dissolution of subsidiaries, and (4) approval of any changes of the bylaws or articles of incorporation of the subsidiaries.

The hospitals increased the powers of the parent corporation later on, but for its initial two years Health Value consisted of a centralized management operating three hospitals that maintained separate boards, financial objectives, and balance sheets. During this time Health Value was prohibited from making a profit; the entire revenue of Health Value came from management contracts with the three hospitals. Further, it was initially stipulated that there would be neither buildup of reserves for future development nor any master indenture for common borrowing.

In 1987 Health Value created two new subsidiary corporations, both "diversification companies." One is not for profit and deals with activities that are themselves nonprofit, such as a visiting nurse association and health promotion activities. The other is a for-profit company and deals exclusively with taxable entities and joint ventures with physicians, such as a lithotripter center and an outpatient cardiac catheterization laboratory.

Because of the limited corporate powers of Health Value at the time, the new subsidiary corporations had to be capitalized separately by the participating hospitals, as they were in early 1988 to the amount of $9 million.

Health Value's strategy

The overall competitive strategy for Health Value, as described by its CEO, was a mix of (1) broad geographic coverage throughout Growthville, (2) comprehensive services, developed through both vertical and horizontal integrations and developments, (3) quality, and (4) market responsiveness. He also defined Health Value as being a lower (but not lowest) cost producer: below the 50th percentile of rates in the community. Thus, Health Value's strategy was primarily one of comprehensive service provider with some inclusion of a lower cost tactic.

Health Value's management identified eight "critical success factors" for its short-term future. They were:

— efficient array of patient services
— diversification
— patient acquisition through contracting
— adequate reimbursement
— capital access/acquisition
— linkages—local, regional, national
— M.D. partnerships
— strategic cohesiveness

Health Value officials speculated that failure to be the lowest cost producer (i.e., to match or underprice Large HMO) might lose market share in the future, but they disagreed as to whether Health Value would have to cut quality in order to achieve lower costs or to maintain market share. The CEO believed that there is "plenty of quality left," but other officials were less sanguine. The management recognized that the provision of a full range of services was costly and that this range might have to be cut in the future in favor of lower costs.

Health Value's management emphasized the "positive image" of the organization in the community, based primarily on Good Shepherds reputation for quality and efficiency. It believed that Health Value could exploit this advantage in the future.

Health Value officials saw Queen of Angels Hospital, in collaboration with others, as becoming very price competitive. They saw price reductions cutting profits of all hospitals and hospital systems in Growthville, to the point that some hospitals would be sold or closed. Because of this, Health Value executives carefully watched the competitive moves of Queen of Angels, with particular regard to its potential affiliation moves with other Growthville hospitals. They were dubious that Queen of Angels' affiliation moves with Miseracordia Hospital and with nearby Gates Community Hospital would come to pass, or if they did that they would strengthen the hospitals competitively. This assessment was summarized by one Health Value executive:

> Each of the three hospitals in the Queen of Angels' affiliation has recently become more centralized. Queen of Angels has become more centralized to the national system of the owning order, in a reorganization that led to the departure of Queen of Angels' CEO. Miseracordia's order has strongly centralized its decision making in Boston, leaving Miseracordia's CEO as some sort of vice president for public relations. And Gates Community Hospital is owned by a for-profit hospital corporation that was centralized to start with and has become more so due to downsizing.
>
> Further, physicians are departing from Miseracordia Hospital to practice at Valley Community or Queen of Angels, leaving Miseracordia as a hospital to be salvaged. The salvager might be Large HMO or some for-profit outfit; but I doubt it will be Queen of Angels.

Doctors as collaborators or competitors

The new competitive environment in Growthville made the hospital-doctor relationship even more crucial—indeed, the most important element of vertical integration.

Since physicians were, in varying degrees, a part of the hospitals' strategic decision-making process, they had to be brought along quickly and with confidentiality as competition for patient revenues quickened. Further, as the hospitals sought to move away from inpatient activity toward ambulatory care, they were invading the traditional domains of doctors as fee-for-service practitioners.

Thus, Health Value was faced with the dilemma of whether the physicians on its three medical staffs were partners and participants in market development, or competitors. The strategy and the results were quite different at Good Shepherd and Valley Community.

At Good Shepherd there had been a general practice of involving physicians in strategic planning. This was described by the CEO as "the two-edged sword" of involving members of the medical staff in strategy when these persons were not accustomed to business decision making or to entrepreneurial discretion. "Pretty soon the whole world knows what we are doing."

Specifically, Good Shepherd had the problem of including physicians in a hospital strategy concerning the development of new ambulatory services when the same physicians were themselves developers of these services. Additionally, Good Shepherd saw the prior existing medical staff structure as inappropriate for new, market-oriented developments. The hospital medical staff had formed itself into a physician corporation of 400 for the purpose of creating a vehicle for contract negotiations with PPO insurance carriers. While this provided an opportunity and potential for all physicians to become involved in business development, the hospital management found the medical group too large and too cumbersome for specific projects such as a magnetic resonating image center. This and other projects needed to be joint ventured with smaller groups of physicians.

The solution to these problems was to abandon the Good Shepherd Hospital and medical staff structures as the mechanisms for making and implementing strategic decisions and instead to pursue these vertically integrated projects through the parent corporation, Health Value. The creation of Health Value's two subsidiary corporations, one for nonprofit and the other for profit-making developments, made this organizational tactic entirely possible.

At Valley Community the commitment had been made earlier on to involve physicians in the hospital's strategic planning. Major efforts were made to "help the doctors prepare for the changing environment" through a well-developed lecture and seminar series and a series of retreats for all physicians. One result was a readiness on the part of the hospital's physicians for joint venturing with the hospital on a number of projects.

Valley Community set a goal of eight ambulatory care clinics "ringing the new market." Seven were developed under various arrangements with doctors, notably the 55-physician Growthville Medical Group. Three of these were primary care centers (urgent and continuing care) in three smaller Growthville subcommunities to the north and west. Three additional clinics, without urgent care, were located to the south and east.

All six were owned and operated by the Growthville Medical Group, with hospital financial backing. A seventh, to the north, was owned by the hospital and contracted to the same group for the provision of medical care. The stated purpose of these clinics was (1) to wed the Growthville Medical Group to Health Value, thus avoiding a splinter that had developed under similar circumstances in other communities, (2) to be well positioned geographically in the numerous submarkets, and (3) to create referrals to Valley Community and thus to Health Value.

These developments were possible largely because of the Growthville Medical Group, which had its offices adjacent to Valley Community. The group's facilities were older and in need of refurbishing. In 1987 Valley Community made a "general commitment" to help the group refurbish its site and building. This commitment was made in part to provide the Growthville Medical Group the "parity" relative to another group of physicians that would become tenants of a new medical office building being built on the hospital campus—and to which Valley Community was loaning money to assist in construction.

In short, within the same corporation, Health Value, two remarkably different pathways of hospital-physician integration and coventuring were pursued. This was because of the different prior histories and cultures of medical staff involvement in hospital planning, the different medical staff substructures of the two hospitals, and the relative novelty of the new parent corporation as a development tool.

The new contracting

Changes in hospital reimbursement provided further stimulus for horizontal and vertical restructuring. The 1984 changes in state law that permitted the state to contract for Medicaid patients were accompanied by parallel legislation permitting insurance carriers to contract in a like manner. PPO arrangements quickly formed and found early ascendancy in Growthville. All of the fee-for-service hospitals in the community struck numerous PPO contracts, based either on discounts from hospital-set prices or all-inclusive per diem rates. Most hospitals felt they were forced to make these price reductions: each hospital sought agreements with numerous carriers in a strategy of "cover all bases and future possibilities" at a time when it was impossible to determine which PPO carriers might become dominant. Queen of Angels moved the fastest: by 1986 it had over thirty contracts in place, based on the calculation that in the near future this "wholesale business" would constitute 75 percent of its activity. Valley Community had 25 contracts in place, representing approximately 15 percent of its business. Good Shepherd had 25 contracts in place, representing 7 percent of its business.

During the first two years of the new negotiated price era, Good Shepherd and Valley Community Hospitals were still operating as autonomous financial entities, albeit under Health Value's corporate umbrella. Accordingly, they (1) took specific strategic decisions relating to contracting with the state government for Medicaid patients, (2) adopted a "cover-all-bases" strategy in relationship to private insurance carriers contracting for PPO business, and (3) made minor and selective adjustments in hospital-set rates where they felt that price sensitivity was a factor in either losing volume for failure to reduce prices or gaining volume in the presence of such reductions. All of these changes were made through a certain amount of trial and error, but experience with the new price environment was gained along the way. Furthermore, these changes were made in the absence of any centralized, coordinated, or developed policies or process for setting competitive prices.

Part III: Discussion Questions

1. Health Value CEO said, "Only those hospitals who have achieved horizontal integration will weather the squall." In what way was his statement true?
2. Why did small Beeler Hospital open up its "be taken over by" talks to numerous organizations other than Valley Community?
3. Health Value's first success factor was creating an "efficient array of patient services." How would the merger have affected this efficient array of services?
4. Health Value's sixth success factor was the creation of "linkages local, regional, and national." Given the local nature of medical care delivery, what advantages would there be to regional or national linkages, if any?
5. During 1986, what was the disadvantage of numerous contracts each with substantial discounts?

Part IV: Concentration of Power and the Countervailing Response

By 1987 the competitive forces had become even more obvious and powerful, and for the first time the hospitals fashioned pricing policies and practices with some systematic market rationale. The three main features of the new rationale were (1) centralization of contract negotiating for all three hospitals of Health Value, (2) response to the entry into the market, on the purchasing side, of a trade association of seven large employers representing approximately half a million employees and their dependents, and (3) ownership of health plans.

Centralized price contracting

The problems associated with negotiated contracts received a great deal of attention in 1986 and 1987, and the number of signed contracts was high. In 1987, 20 percent of Good Shepherd's nongovernment revenue was from business sold at discounts from full price. However, at Valley Community the percentage of contract patients was higher: one-half of nongovernment patients.

Granting these differences, the management of Health Value foresaw that the percentage of contract patients would increase dramatically in the near future. Its forecast was that by 1990 the HMO percentage of the total insured health care market would increase from the 1986 level of 40 percent (of which 30 percent belonged to Large HMO) to 60 percent. The management believed that the multihospital properties of Health Value, with its service capacity in a broad geographic area in Growthville, would be increasingly advantageous in negotiating with insurance carriers and employers. This would be so because, though insurance is arranged by the work place, employees and their dependents live throughout the Growthville area and want access to nearby health care; it followed that the provider that could offer this had a clear market and negotiating advantage.

These were the reasons, then, for the decision in early 1987 to centralize contract negotiations across all three hospitals and to negotiate contracts that included all three hospitals wherever possible. The Health Value management used six criteria in its price contracting strategy, as follows:

1. Health Value would sign agreements on behalf of its three hospitals with all hospitals at the same price level.
2. Exclusivity would be sought when possible, or a maximum of one competitor.
3. Long-term relationship would be sought: three to five years.
4. Contracts would be based on knowledge of the number of lives covered by the employer or carrier.
5. There would be a combined physician and hospital package, including a joint agreement on signing or not signing together, with both parties willing to walk away from a contract if either was unsatisfied.
6. There would be physician control of utilization review.

While no relative weights were assigned to these six criteria, the Health Value management stressed those factors that were impacted strongly by competition and discounts.

Health Value's management acknowledged that there would be difficulties in applying these criteria due to lack of data on marginal costs in the three hospitals and in the system and to lack of data on the number of employees and dependents who were covered by proposed contracts.

Enter the Employers' Association

The importance of this centralized contracting decision was further reinforced by the sudden creation of an association representing seven of the very large employers in Growthville who were all self-insured. These seven employers represented approximately half a million employees and their dependents, constituting an extremely powerful purchasing force. With the trend toward self-insurance, it was widely expected that by 1988 the number of employers in the association would expand to upwards of 60 or 70.

The seven large employers formed Valley Employers' Association in late 1986 for the specific purpose of dealing and negotiating with hospitals and doctors, and doing so directly rather than through insurance companies or other intermediaries.

Valley Employers' Association published the following as goals and purposes of the organization:

— To assist member companies in containing health care costs
— To work cooperatively with the community's health care providers that are committed to delivering cost-effective medical care
— To support an alternative delivery system that is effective and satisfies members' needs for such a system
— To provide individual company members with flexibility regarding participation in alternative delivery arrangements in the area
— To make available area wide alternative delivery system management information

In particular, Valley Employers' established a preferred provider program "to enhance the efforts of its member companies . . . in arrangements that control health care expenditures and maintain quality health care services."

In early 1987 the Association issued a request for proposal, to which Health Value and others responded. The RFP called for submissions of price and other contract features. The Association did not then negotiate for its member companies based on these responses. Rather, it first turned the responses over to its consultant for analysis, and then to the seven individual companies, which negotiated directly with providers. Health Value then negotiated with seven companies.

Health Value and its competitors faced an element of uncertainty as to whether the seven companies would negotiate exclusive contracts with just one provider system, or whether they would contract with all providers in the area. Health Value's management assumed the former and submitted lower prices based on the assumption that increased volume would be obtained if a contract was signed. But as it turned out most of the seven companies were unwilling to "cut out" any of Health Value's competitors; in other words, they signed contracts with other hospitals regardless of their bid prices (which Health Value surmised were higher). The companies explained that they were under pressure from their employees and unions to do this in order not to reduce their access to care and also to allow them to continue traditional physician and hospital relationships.

A more serious problem was that some of the big employers wanted to "buy a piece of Health Value but not all of it." In other words, Health Value was contracting centrally for all three hospitals and assumed that any contracted employee or dependent would then be able to go to any of its three hospitals. But some employers wanted to contract with one or two of its hospitals but not all three.

There were two reasons for this. First, some purchasers were under pressure from Health Value's competitors to exclude one of Health Value's hospitals in order to protect their market. Officials at Health Value learned that the source of this pressure was Queen of Angels, its aggressive competitor, because the request for "cut out" was aimed at Valley Community Hospital.

Queen of Angels prevailed in this because it had convinced some purchasers that it was the sole provider in the western area and thus they had to contract with it. The purchasers did not realize that Valley Community enjoyed a substantial share of the same market and could thus also serve its patients. Such was the nature, at the time, of hospital market competition for price-negotiated contracts.

The second reason insurers and employers sometimes wanted contracts that excluded Valley Community was costs. Valley Employers' Association had obtained comparative cost data on the many hospitals in Growthville from a state commission to which all hospitals were required to report. The Association knew that the costs in hospitals varied, including those for the three hospitals that made up Health Value. Some employers calculated that if a high-cost hospital were eliminated from the contract Health Value could thereby reduce the overall contract price.

These circumstances caused some dissent within Health Value. Health Value's CEO believed that it was necessary to "alter some prices by individual hospitals" in order to maintain or obtain contracts in the future. He also believed that Health Value must on occasion negotiate contracts that exclude a Health Value hospital. The CEO of Valley Community believed quite strongly to the contrary, that the three hospitals "must hang together; and if one hospital were eliminated Health Value should walk away from the contract." "We need to sell Health Value; now is the best opportunity and we ought to leverage that chance."

As an expression of this general goal, Valley Community's CEO assigned the following priorities to negotiating strategies: "First, all three hospitals are in; second, sign exclusive contracts; and third, walk away from a couple of contracts to make the point."

As a result of the first round of negotiations with the employers of Valley Employers' Association, Health Value signed one exclusive contract with a company self-insuring for 6,000 persons, involving services by Good Shepherd and Beeler but not Valley Community. Another exclusive contract was signed with a company self-insuring for 3,000 persons, calling for service by all three Health Value hospitals. The third contract was nonexclusive, with a company self-insuring for 50,000 persons, also including all three hospitals.

And by late 1987, after eight months of centralized contract negotiations with numerous parties, Health Value's management had signed 23 new PPO contracts and 3 HMO contracts, 2 of which were exclusives. This brought the total number of contracts to 63. Of these, 55 were with PPOs, and 8 were with HMOs. These represented about 68,000 patient days of care, or 38 percent of Health Value's total business.

Health plan ownership

The Health Value management calculated that an alternative strategy to contract price negotiating at arm's length with PPOs and HMOs was to "own our own." Thus Health Value became involved in three new ownerships, in a dynamic example of vertical integration. The first was Southern State, an HMO operating primarily outside of Growthville but in the nearby metropolis sixty miles away. Health Value acquired ownership of 13 percent of this HMO through an investment of $5.7 million. Southern State had an enrolled membership of 65,000. The co-owners were all other hospitals in the region, but not in Growthville. Since Southern State was not at the time operating in Growthville, Health Value became its exclusive avenue for doing such. Health Value's CEO estimated that Southern State could contribute 10 percent of Health Value's patient volume by 1990. The advantages of Southern State were its regional proximity, its successful history of performance elsewhere, its hospital ownership and control, and its marketing strength with small businesses.

Health Value's second investment was in Death Guard, a nonprofit HMO formed in 1986 by four hospitals in Growthville, each of which contributed $100,000. The four hospitals were Good Shepherd, Valley Community, St. Royale, and Gates Community. The county medical society was also an owner. Death Guard had 100,000 enrollees. In 1988 Health Value decided to walk away from this investment, for two reasons: (1) Health Value's investment with Death Guard conflicted with its new investment in Southern State, and (2) Health Value did not control Death Guard, and the HMO was channeling its patients to competing providers. Death Guard represented 4 percent of Health Value's total business, but the percentage was declining.

Health Value's third venture was as the majority stockholder in Professional Claims Managers. At the time Professional Claims Managers was a "third party" claims processing organization, but it was soon to become licensed by the state as an HMO. The strategy was to "get inside the doors of the large employers" with the claims processing organization, then exploit the opportunity to tie the employers into an HMO. This organization was started by St. Royale Hospital, a hospital to the south of Growthville with little overlap in patient populations. Health Value was the majority stockholder, however, with an investment of $.5 million. This was because St. Royale, as a district government hospital, was unable to own any portion of the company; instead St. Royale's "investment" was in the form of a loan. Local physicians were also equity holders. The advantages of Professional Claims Managers stemmed from the strength of St. Royale's relationships with certain large employers and its ability to penetrate yet additional firms. Physician ownership was also considered a plus.

This "joint venture" with St. Royale Hospital was part of a larger collaborative arrangement between Health Value and St. Royale. The organizations avoided any corporate restructuring or joint contract negotiating that might invite antitrust concerns. Instead, Health Value committed to "thinking St. Royale when it looks south," and St. Royale would "think Health Value when it looks north." The resulting "mutual advantage society" dealt with cost-saving activities such as common data processing, coordinated program development, and marketing.

Health Value's fourth HMO involvement was with Take Notice, an HMO owned by a large insurance company. Take Notice represented

3 percent of the activity at Valley Community Hospital, where it was associated with the Growthville Medical Group. There was also some minor volume at Good Shepherd. The advantage of Take Notice was its system of putting a single medical group at risk for all claims exposure. But for Health Value this was also a disadvantage since its hospitals were required to bargain with the physician group for payment to the hospitals.

A general problem with Health Value's HMO development was the lack of a physician organization necessary to contract on a capitated basis. At Valley Community Hospital there was the long-standing Growthville Medical Group, which operated as the capitated group for Take Notice, as well as a contracting group with PPO insurance carriers. Additionally, at both Valley Community and Good Shepherd there were large and loose physician groups that were available as contracting vehicles for individual doctors with various PPOs, but in neither of these instances was the group able to bind the physicians on a contract basis.

In connection with Southern State, the HMO offered to form an independent practice associate (IPA) type of medical group, but this was rejected by Health Value and its doctors because Southern State would have insisted that the group operate exclusively with it; Health Value's physicians wanted the option of contracting with other insurers. Instead, there was under development by Health Value an IPA-type medical group that would be used to serve Southern State. This would include physicians at all three Health Value hospitals as well as St. Royale Hospital. It was anticipated that this IPA would have approximately 400 physicians, each of whom would invest a minimum of a thousand dollars.

Price negotiation effectiveness

In 1988 the CEO of Health Value concluded that its pricing decisions were "amateurish, with little science." He believed the main problem was a lack of a common data base, which was needed so that the impact of centrally determined prices on individual hospitals and on the system could be better known. The CEO also believed that there was a "philosophical question" that had not been settled as to how prices should be set whether based on hospital costs or market driven. The CEO also saw the lack of ability to know what volume would result from a contract as the main problem in contract negotiation. Clearly, Health Value would set its contract prices lower if it felt it was going to get additional new volume. But it did not know whether this volume would materialize, and to date it generally had not. In other words, "We are buying back our current book at lower prices, versus new volume."

There was agreement among management that the basis for determining the effectiveness of Health Value's pricing policies and practices should be overall profitability. This systemwide goal evolved naturally from the fact that contract prices were now negotiated on a centralized basis. A secondary goal was the preservation or enhancement of market share, and it was agreed that this goal would become more important in the future.

On both measures, the management was pleased with the result thus far. The system was "as profitable as it has ever been." And occupancy rates were climbing relative to those at other hospitals in the community. Market share had been maintained, and increased to slightly over 21 percent since the system was created. In short, the management was on the one hand critical of its lack of a clear pricing policy and the lack of information systems necessary to support its price negotiating process, while on the other hand pleased with the results of price negotiations insofar as they had contributed to financial success and market share for Health Value.

Even so, it knew that the Growthville hospital market was moving from one based on service competition to one based on price competition. In this it had some fierce competitors: Large HMO and Queen of Angels.

Part IV: Discussion Questions

1. Health Value officials believed that they might have to reduce the range of services offered in a competitive environment demanding lower production costs. Are there economies of scope that mitigate such a shrinkage, at least for certain service patterns?

2. The case describes a loose collaboration between Health Value and St. Royale. While designed to avoid antitrust concerns relating to market concentration, does the arrangement invoke other antitrust issues such as agreements to divide a market?

3. At both Valley Community and Good Shepherd there were large physician groups formed to become PPO contracting groups for individual groups but unable to contractually bind the physicians as a group. Why is the difference important?

4. Southern State wanted an IPA medical group to operate exclusively with it; that is, the physicians in the group could not contract with other PPOs or HMOs. Given the circumstances at the time, why did Health Value and its doctors reject this? Under what circumstances might they accept exclusive dealings? What are the costs and benefits of such a restriction on vertical development?

Part V: Competitor Response

Queen of Angels Hospital was founded in 1889 as a sanitarium by a local judge known for his charitable works. It was the first private hospital to be built in Growthville. The judge turned the operation of the facility over to a Catholic order, which has owned and operated the hospital for one hundred years. In 1954 a new 257-bed hospital was constructed on a new site, and in 1969 a new wing was added. In 1973 a nearby 80-bed hospital was acquired by Queen of Angels and has since been operated as a pavilion of the main hospital; half of its beds are for extended care. In 1978 Queen of Angels purchased a 32-bed acute hospital in a neighboring community fifteen miles to the southeast. In 1982 a $52 million replacement and remodeling was completed at the main hospital, for a present capacity of 329 beds.

Strategy for the eighties

Queen of Angels' strategy was "derived from an analysis of firms in other industries that are going through deregulation." Its management believed that there were direct analogies between these other industries and the health care field. It made use of these analogies and experiences in its development strategy.

The early 1980s. Diversification was one strategy that derived from this. Starting in the early 1980s, Queen of Angels was one of the first hospitals to reorganize completely. It created a holding company (Charity East) with subsidiary corporations to operate three hospitals (Queen of Angels, the small hospital to the southeast, and a hospital outside the area), an arthritis institute, a medical office building development company, a fund-raising foundation, and a for-profit corporation. Charity East, in turn, is the regional corporation of the order's national multihospital system. The offices of Charity East are fifty miles to the south of Queen of Angels, a distance described by the management as "quite close."

The proprietary corporation owned by Charity East diversified outside the health field. In 1985 it made more than a quarter of a million dollars on its nonhealth activities, which constituted 17 percent of its net income for the year. Queen of Angels started taking market analysis seriously. In both 1983 and 1986 it commissioned in-depth studies of community and public perception, using consultants skilled in public opinion sampling. The 1983 research emphasized the overall institutional image of the several hospitals in Growthville. The 1986 study emphasized the marketing possibilities for several targeted services in specific geographic areas. The hospital used the results in positioning its new services.

Partly as a result of the first of these two studies, hospital officials concluded in 1984 that "consumers are changing their shopping habits; they wish to seek care in different environments." This meant to Queen of Angels that there should be a separation of services that treat the sick from those that are oriented to the well—primarily the young and affluent. Officials at Queen of Angels read their own experience as supportive of this strategy. The hospital had offered an ambulatory surgery service within its inpatient facility but found that patient reaction was "less than desirable" because these "customers" did not want to identify themselves with ill patients.

The hospital's implementation of this "separation" strategy focused on planning a surgi-center across the street from the hospital, a second surgi-center in the rapidly growing northern area, an off-site magnetic resonating imaging center, and an off-site personal fitness center. As at Good Samaritan and Valley Community, physicians—as medical staff representatives on the hospital's strategic planning committees—were actively involved in these strategic developments. The CEO stated that "we will develop these projects through joint ventures with physicians, although the hospital will undertake them anyway if this is not possible."

But instead an independent surgi-center was constructed across the street by some physicians. The hospital management felt that there had been "inside dealing" on the part of some surgeons on the strategic planning committee. The physician-owned ambulatory surgery center performed approximately six cases a day; a volume much lower than expected. The physicians had encountered problems with licensure and code compliance, resulting in a smaller capacity than originally planned. This had hurt the facility financially. The Queen of Angels management believed that the facility was headed for bankruptcy.

Queen of Angels developed a competing ambulatory surgery program located within the hospital. It purposely underpriced the physician's center, calculating that its own "financial pockets are deeper" and thus better able to weather a price war. Many surgeons supported the hospital's offering, based largely on the greater convenience of performing ambulatory and inpatient surgeries close by.

In furtherance of its strategy, Queen of Angels committed $20–40 million in "new service centers" that were calculated to move the hospital away from its emphasis on inpatient care and toward ambulatory care. Accordingly, the expansion of wellness services was a high priority. For example, the hospital considered tie-in sales and package pricing wherein persons receiving cardiac surgery would also receive fitness services (but not vice versa!).

This action was taken in the larger context of the hospital's first organized effort of competitor analysis. The Queen of Angels management saw its prime competitors as other fee-for-service hospitals or groups of hospitals—notably Good Shepherd and Valley Community hospitals. The CEO of Queen of Angels viewed Valley Community Hospital as "problematically weak" prior to its merger with Beeler and Good Shepherd to form Health Value. He had hoped that Valley Community would continue its pre-1983 Medicaid operation because it "took patients who were not good business and who otherwise might come to us."

The CEO believed, further, that the hospital "needs to draw a circle and decide with whom it will compete and with whom it will not compete." In early 1986 the hospital started drawing this line by proposing an affiliation with Miseracordia Hospital. Queen of Angels saw this integration as one between its own "more tertiary" facility and Miseracordia's "more bread and butter" hospital. Queen of Angels would obtain a feeder network and additional volume for its specialized programs. It saw an opportunity through an affiliation to joint venture on several projects, especially a new hospital in the burgeoning county to the north. Queen of Angels also saw Miseracordia as a network partner in an HMO involving numerous hospitals.

For Miseracordia, the possible integration would be based on "mutual needs." These included "external joint ventures," greater financial strength, and the use of Queen of Angels' hospital talent. Miseracordia's CEO also saw in the affiliation the opportunity to create a prepaid health plan that "could be a force in the future bidding with businesses, since they will become more selective and wish to work with fewer hospitals."

In short, during the first half of the 1980s Queen of Angels saw diversification, a shift to ambulatory care and wellness, and coupling with other hospitals as the strategies that would "weather the storm."

The painful reconsideration

By 1987 the competitive environment in Growthville had heated up considerably, and the relations with other hospitals had changed. The years 1985–86 had found Queen of Angels with a solid operating margin of 7 percent but a declining occupancy and heavy debt. Its patients presented real and potential financial problems. Almost half were Medicare, with the hospital now facing full national diagnostic related group (DRG) rates that were calculated to hurt Queen of Angels with its costly labor market. Eight percent were Medicaid, with the proportions likely to rise due to Valley Community's actions. The hospital was heavily in debt, and it had a high volume of accounts receivables not likely to be collected.

The still-new and changing environment induced major changes in Queen of Angels' strategy. The hospital moved away from its prior efforts to be a comprehensive service leader. "We cannot do all things for all people," reported the hospital's new CEO. Instead, it moved toward a strategy of "several market niches." These niches combined specialty services and population groups. They included, in the first category, cardiology, oncology, eye, ear, nose, and throat, neurology, and rehabilitation. In the second category they included a full-blown seniors' program that embraced a home health agency, hospice, and several geriatric-oriented specialty services. In adopting this new thrust, the management realized that it was somewhat constrained in advancing the strategy because of the hospital's commitment to care for indigent patients and its state Medicaid contract: these patients required general hospital service capacity, thus limiting the specialities/niche strategy.

Coupled with this shift was a return to the pre-1980s emphasis on inpatient care. The director of planning and marketing stated: "We have come to realize that our core business is inpatient care. We are still interested in ambulatory care, but we will advance that by working through our doctors." Related to these two strategy changes was the cancellation of investment plans for $20–40 million to be spent on "new service centers."

Merger reconsidered

In late 1987 the management of Queen of Angels reported that there was "no change in thrust" in respect to its merger negotiations with Miseracordia. But Miseracordia had pulled back from the major project that would have stemmed from a merger—the construction of a 60-bed hospital in the population corridor to the north of Growthville. The project was reconfigured as a joint venture between Queen of Angels and Miseracordia, with Queen of Angels providing all the funding. Miseracordia backed away because its analysis of potential referrals showed that very few of the patients coming from the north county area would flow to Miseracordia Hospital; instead they would go to Queen of Angels. This was due both to geographic propinquity and to Queen of Angels' more specialized services.

Further, the Catholic order of which Miseracordia is a part had gone through a substantial reorganization that removed a great deal of local governance and management autonomy. This made it impossible for Miseracordia to negotiate as a principal in further merger talks.

As an alternative, Queen of Angels proposed an "alliance agreement" with Miseracordia and a third hospital, the Gates Community Hospital. This looser affiliation was guided by restraint of trade concerns, since further concentrations among Growthville hospitals could attract antitrust litigation from private parties or the Federal Trade Commission. The document defined "opportunities for cooperation" between hospitals, while the hospitals would otherwise remain autonomous and competitive. The first area of cooperation was collective contract negotiating. The discussions were complicated by the fact that the Gates Community Hospital is owned by a large investor-owned hospital corporation.

Charity care policy

Queen of Angels' overall market strategy was strongly influenced by its mission of community service. Specifically, it operated under a policy that it should earn at least 4 percent net operating income each year and that 25 percent of this net income must go to charitable care. The 25 percent excluded any contractual allowances that stem from Medicare or Medicaid reimbursement or any private contracts. It also excluded bad debts. This 25 percent was represented by a line item in the hospital's annual budget; if the hospital did not achieve this amount of charitable care the "unused" portion of the budgeted amount was sent to the parent corporation, Charity East, for allocation to medical charity in other locations.

Queen of Angel's charity care was administered along clinical program lines through a strong social service department. There was an evaluation of patients' ability to pay in advance of the delivery of service. Some services were rendered free, while others were provided on a sliding scale for partial payment. The maternity service, including prenatal counseling for indigent mothers, was the recipient of substantial charitable aid. Another was ambulatory surgery. A third was open-heart surgery, where the hospital had an arrangement with Growthville's Rotary Club to support a certain number of open-heart surgeries per year. A fourth program was one that waived Medicare coinsurance provisions for patients of households with less than $20,000 annual income.

The Queen of Angels management realized that its commitment to charity care affected the hospital's pricing policies and could seriously hurt the hospital in price competition. The management believed that "this Hospital was chosen on other factors; we need mission and margin, and must be good enough to get both."

A summary of Queen of Angels' reported charity care, compared with that of other hospitals in Growthville, is shown in Table 1.4.

Competitor analysis for the late '80s

In the early 1980s Queen of Angels saw other individual hospitals as its major competitors. But in 1988 it concluded that Large HMO was its major threat. After Large HMO, its chief competitors were Health Value, followed by St. Royale. One effect of this analysis was that Queen of Angels decided not to open a breast screening center because Health Value, in joint venture with two radiologists, had recently established one.

Another key conclusion stemming from this market analysis was that present and future employers and insurance carriers would desire a choice of hospitals or hospital systems for their employees and dependents, not preferred or exclusive arrangements. This perception of the market was different from that of Health Value, which was founded in major part on the assumption that employers and insurance carriers would want broad geographic coverage provided by a single multihospital system with which they could contract exclusively.

It is hard to determine whether Queen of Angels' circumstances dictated this strategy, or the strategy dictated its circumstances. The management did acknowledge the hospital's failure to put together a multihospital system with the potential for geographically spread services offered through centrally negotiated pricing. And further, the hospital did not own an HMO or PPO, or control one in a way that would channel patients to Queen of Angels. Queen of Angels prepared to enter a future that would be "filled with wholesale business of all types," soon to constitute 75 percent of its patient mix.

Queen of Angels quickly became aggressive in both seeking out contract possibilities and in pricing them. By the end of 1987 it had secured 53 contracts.

But the real feature that distinguished Queen of Angels was the depth of its discounting. Its discounts averaged 30 percent, while the mean for the other hospitals was less than 10 percent. (The difference in these percentages was not caused by higher list prices; if anything, Queen of Angels' prices were somewhat below those of its competitors.) In addition, Queen of Angels had a higher percentage of Medicare and Medicaid patients than did the other private hospitals.

In short, Queen of Angels was willing to engage in deep discounting if purchasers were willing to shift patients who otherwise would go elsewhere to Queen of Angels. Whether by conscious decision or not, Queen of Angels appeared to be testing a strategy of being the low-price leader among fee-for-service hospitals.

Health plan development

In 1988 Queen of Angels switched its tactic of the prior two years. Rather than developing a new HMO from scratch, it started working with Southern Health Group to bring that organization's HMO to Growthville. This strategy acknowledged that Queen of Angels had little experience in HMO development or management, whereas Southern Health Group was a long-established prepaid health plan with an enrollment of 350,000 persons in its prime region.

Management expected the HMO to have 5,000 Growthville enrollees in its first year and then double its growth per year thereafter. Development would take the form of a joint venture between the hospital and Southern Health, with both contributing equity. This could not be a single-hospital HMO, so Queen of Angels approached its two alliance hospitals and also sought the involvement of other hospitals. It developed criteria for the selection of these other hospitals: (1) geographic dispersion, (2) strong finances, (3) good reputation, and (4) ownership comparable with Catholic ownership. This development was actually being undertaken by Queen of Angels' parent corporation, Charity East.

The largest barrier to this development was the lack of a physician group to work with the HMO and provide medical care to its enrollees. There existed a "Queen of Angels' Physician's Association" formed for the purposes of channeling contracts between medical staff physicians and PPOs. But this was a "clearinghouse organization" and could not commit its physician-members to contracts. Further, there were no utilization review or quality control functions. There were also two IPAs in existence, each with single contracts with HMOs with which Queen of Angels had no special relationship.

As an alternative the hospital supported the formation of a physician group that would be organized to serve Southern Health. It was called Pro Health, and one of the internists at Queen of Angels' was the driving force in forming it. Approximately 25 physicians were invited and subsequently joined, with an investment of $5,000 each. The physicians were mostly specialists who practiced primary care.

Price negotiations

In 1986 Queen of Angels' payer mix of patients consisted of 46 percent Medicare (DRG reimbursement), 8 percent Medicaid (negotiated price), 35 percent private reimbursement on the hospital's posted charges, and 11 percent price-negotiated contracts. Within two years the percentage of patients whose payment was based on negotiated contracts tripled. The hospital's management anticipated that there would soon be only two types of payment to the hospital: Medicare and price-negotiated contracts (including Medicaid).

Given the hospital's commitment to negotiated prices as a large proportion of its business, Queen of Angels became even more aggressive in both seeking out contract possibilities and pricing them.

The process first involved identifying the possibility of a contract, which came about through the invitation of a purchaser of care or a solicitation by Queen of Angels' contracting officer. The possible contract was then distributed to several departments of the hospital: nursing, marketing, finance, and legal. Responses from these four departments were returned to the contracting officer, who then negotiated with the purchaser. If the contract was satisfactory, it went to the hospital board for approval, and also to Charity East, the parent corporation.

If there was disagreement on price or some other feature of a contract, the problem was referred to another hospital group consisting of the director of marketing, the contracting officer, and the vice president for finance. If these parties agreed to terms that would obtain a contract, it was submitted to the vice president for corporate development and finance for approval. If there remained disagreement, it was submitted to the CEO for resolution. All contracts were then first submitted to the board of Queen of Angels Hospital and thereafter to the parent corporation, Charity East.

Queen of Angels' management acknowledged that its hospital board was deeply interested in the contracts and the prices negotiated, as it "wants to be sure that the management is not giving away the store." Likewise, the parent corporation, Charity East, was concerned. The requirement for approval by these two bodies caused a delay in price setting that made contract negotiations difficult.

Queen of Angels developed a rating system for measuring the importance of a contract to the hospital and thus for determining how far it would go in negotiating price and other features to secure an agreement. The rating scheme had nine factors, with a given number of points assigned to each factor. The nine were as follows: (1) whether Queen of Angels would have an exclusive contract; (2) financial stability of the contracting party, as scored by Best Agent's Guide to Life Insurance Companies; (3) the number of persons insured in Growthville; (4) historic and potential utilization at Queen of Angels; (5) track record of the plan in other areas, in terms of geographic or demographic market penetration and growth; (6) benefits and incentives used by the plan, such as deductibles, copayments, and waivers; (7) ease of administration through provisions such as admitting, billing, utilization review, concurrent review, and discharge planning; (8) coordination of benefits with other insurance coverages; and (9) payment arrangement with regard to timeliness.

On the basis of this process, 57 contracts had been finalized as of late 1988. There was about a 15 percent contract "loss," the reasons for which were either failure to negotiate an acceptable price or the absence of a medical staff group capable of performing on the contracts. The management recognizes that it had a conservative medical staff that was slow to organize and respond to contracting for medical care.

The management at Queen of Angels did not negotiate with insurance companies or employers with Miseracordia or Gates Community as part of the package; instead, these hospitals submitted and negotiated their own prices at their own discretion. Queen of Angels did not know what these prices were, for antitrust reasons. However, Queen of Angels developed a contracting tactic that followed from its proposed affiliation with these hospitals: it offered a "dual choice" to insurers and employers. There was one price if Queen of Angels was the sole contracting hospital and another price, higher, if the contract included other hospitals as well.

Queen of Angels developed these prices by first knowing the number of employees in Growthville for each contracting group. It then calculated two "base prices" for these groups to obtain care at Queen of Angels, one representing a greater discount for the exclusive use of Queen of Angels and the other a higher price "penalty" for greater choice. This strategy was designed to obtain more volume for Queen of Angels.

But this tactic had limited effect, particularly with the group of self-insured employers that had formed the Valley Employers' Association. These employers were constrained in straight price negotiation by pressures from employees and union groups, which wanted to retain the broader access to hospital care that would be lost with exclusive contracts. In short, employers were unwilling or unable to strike exclusive contracts with Queen of Angels based on its best price, which would channel new volumes of patients to Queen of Angels and away from other hospitals. Instead, they maintained contracts with other hospitals, though at higher contract rates.

The Queen of Angels' contracting officer acknowledged that this made price/volume decision making difficult, "because we never know whether we are cannibalizing our own prior volume; it's an information systems game." However, the Queen of Angels' management believed this was a "temporary phenomenon."

Part V: Discussion Questions

1. In 1987 Queen of Angels abandoned its strategy of "all things to all people" in favor of a specialty/niche strategy. How is this strategy limited by (1) the hospital's substantial mix of Medicaid patients, and (2) the hospital's forecast of substantial "wholesale business" of price-negotiated contracts with large employers and insurance carriers?

2. Did the 1987 Queen of Angels/Miseracordia "alliance agreement" offend restraint of trade laws in respect to price fixing?

3. How did the Queen of Angels alliance with Miseracordia relate to its recently established specialty/niche strategy?

4. What assessment did Queen of Angels' competitors, notably Health Value, make of the Queen of Angels/Miseracordia alliance?

5. What conflict could have been expected to arise among the Queen of Angels' medical staff in response to a small number of its physicians joining forces with the hospital in a medical group to support the joint HMO venture with Southern Health?

6. Evaluate Queen of Angels' process of negotiating and approving prices, in particular, with respect to conflict resolution and the decision-making role of the CEO relative to the hospital's board and Charity East.

Part VI: Summary: Three Phases of Strategic Alignment

Phase 1: Individual competitors, monopolistic competition

The first phase in the evolution of corporate changes in Growthville occurred during the early 1980s, until 1984. In this phase each hospital saw itself as an individual competitor and viewed all other hospitals likewise. There was a proliferation of services among facilities to the point of extensive duplication.

Most of the hospitals in our case study went through a corporate reorganization. The motivations for these reorganizations varied, but in the main they had two purposes: to provide a corporate structure outside of the hospital to undertake vertical diversification into ambulatory care, since certificate-of-need laws might block such developments if undertaken directly by the hospitals; and to alter the decision-making process in regard to medical staffs, since these bodies could block moves by the hospitals into lines of business the physicians considered their own.

This first phase of competition in Growthville was further characterized by a market in which there was (1) an absence of well-informed corporate and individual buyers; (2) a preponderance of comprehensive health insurance for consumers; and (3) continuation of cost-based reimbursement to hospitals. These factors in combination yielded a market in which price was not operating. Further, there was (4) a lack of emphasis on productive efficiency within the hospitals (the hospitals did not know or care about their marginal costs, so they could not make the calculations necessary to determine output levels at which prices might be set in relation to these costs) and (5) incomplete and insufficient competitor analysis. For this last reason the fee-for-service hospitals failed to assess properly the effect of prepaid health plans and employer efforts to contain costs. Some hospitals also failed to anticipate the responses of their own physicians to the increasing supply of doctors and the increasing competition. Thus, the market in this early phase could be described as monopolistically competitive. Each hospital was attempting to build market share and market power through differentiation and product development; however, since all were pursuing similar strategies the efforts essentially neutralized one another.

During this period there were no horizontal integrations among hospitals in Growthville. Instead, hospital affiliations consisted of external links with outside multihospital systems: Queen of Angels and Miseracordia hospitals in separate religious systems, and Large HMO owned by a parent corporation. This pattern matched the type of horizontal integration taking place generally at the time among not-for-profit hospitals: cross-regional, holding company–type systems, with regional or national corporations linked to local and autonomous corporations.

By contrast, the local market phenomenon of note in this phase was vertical diversification through corporate reorganization. It appears from what subsequently developed that these reorganizations were useful precursors to the horizontal integrations that subsequently occurred in Growthville.

Phase 2: Consolidation-oligopoly

The second phase of evolving competition started in Growthville in late 1984 and early 1985 and continued into 1987. Hospital executives studying the environment anticipated a period of shake-out. Excess capacity created by cost-based reimbursement coupled with increased marketing expenditures tended to erode the hospitals' net returns. This erosion was hastened by the special circumstances in California, where payment to hospitals for care of Medicaid beneficiaries was shifted from one based on cost to one based on individually negotiated prices. And coincident with this change in Medicaid reimbursement was state legislation that authorized private insurers to negotiate with hospitals for PPO-type price discounts. Employers and insurance companies began organizing new prepaid health plans designed to compete with large HMOs and to reduce hospital utilization. In addition, at the federal level Medicare shifted from cost-based reimbursement to the prospective payment system. In short, hospitals could no longer ignore pricing behavior, even though they were ill equipped for this aspect of competition. And it was clear that demand for hospital services could be expected to flatten if not decline. The days of acute inpatient care as a growth business were over—even in Growthville.

Several hospitals soon realized the futility of the individual-competitor strategies of Phase 1, given the diseconomies of small size and the heavy costs of monopolistic competition. So they shifted strategy from one of independent competition to one of increasing market share and controlling the marketplace through merger. The numerous individual hospital reorganizations of Phase 1 had set the stage for this shift; that is, the new corporate structures made integration easier because holding companies were already in place to act as parent companies to merged subsidiaries. In quick sequence there was a hospital merger among three fee-for-service hospitals (Good Shepherd, Valley Community, and Beeler) and the initiation of merger talks between two additional hospitals (Queen of Angels and Miseracordia), one of which had assumed control of a third hospital several years earlier. Further, County Medical Center established closer programmatic affiliation with a nearby medical school hospital. In short order there was a de facto or projected restructuring of the market from fourteen independent hospitals (seven of which were part of this case study) to four dominating health care systems: two fee-for-service systems embracing seven previously independent hospitals, Large HMO hospital linked with a mutually dedicated prepayment organization and a large physician corporation, and the county-university combination.

During Phase 2 some of the hospitals realized that their competitor analysis needed to include consideration of physicians as market entrants. But there was a dilemma. Since the new competitive environment made close hospital-doctor relationships more crucial, most hospitals had incorporated physicians into the institutions' strategic decision making processes. Yet as the hospitals moved away from inpatient activity and toward ambulatory care, they invaded the traditional domains of their doctors. The hospitals thus faced the question of whether the physicians on their own medical staffs were partners or competitors in market strategy.

The hospitals in our case study treated this problem differently. Since physician competitors came from within the hospitals' organizations rather than from without, the hospitals had to alter their process of competitive strategy development. In the terms of Blau and Scott's formulation presented in the introduction to this case, strategies of hospital-physician relationship involved elements of competition, exchange, and symbiosis, each aimed toward obtaining positions of dominance [5].

Price competition was not an important element of the hospitals' marketing mixes during Phase 2. Hospitals were still trying to set non-contract prices as high as possible to offset contractual allowances on government-sponsored patients, and they grudgingly granted price allowances to the state and a few PPO and HMO plans.

Three fee-for-service hospitals in Growthville took another tack. The 1984 decision of the state to contract with individual hospitals for Medicaid patients provided a specific opportunity for hospitals to decide whether they would continue their social missions of caring for poor patients. Valley Community, St. Royale, and Good Shepherd hospitals decided separately not to negotiate contracts, thus altering each hospital's long-standing mission and abandoning care of persons who could not pay full prices. As a consequence, indigent patients were shifted to Miseracordia, Queen of Angels, and County Medical Center.

In summary, the key dynamic of Phase 2 was rapid concentration along horizontal lines, this time in the local community, where critical mass might be used to stage further vertical developments. Yet the reasons for these combinations were different from what is often proposed. The three related reasons for merger were to restrict competition, expand market share, and obtain market control. The hospitals had experienced the heavy costs of the head-to-head competition in Phase 1 and in some instances had been required to pull back from strategic investments designed to compete on these terms. Limiting competition through merger—and in the process achieving a market dominance not previously envisioned as possible—certainly became a strong desideratum.

Phase 3: Buyer response

The third phase of evolution in Growthville's hospital market started in late 1986 and continued through 1988 and beyond. It consisted of two major phenomena: efforts by the consolidated systems to expand and countervailing organization among purchasers.

As with Phase 1, Phase 3 was brought on by market forces accelerated by continuing deregulation. The circumstances now were (1) continuing decline in hospital use; (2) excess capacity; (3) the quick ascendance of private contracting by insurance companies and large employers; (4) the realization by several hospitals that marginal price contracting with the state for Medicaid patients was a long-term reality; and (5) the dramatic increase in forms of hospital payment (e.g., Medicare's prospective payment systems and HMOs) that shifted risk to hospitals and doctors.

But the major change in strategy for the hospitals of our case study was a new focus on geographic expansion. Now the goal was to expand the geographic base of services needed to capture HMO and PPO contracts with employers whose employees and dependents lived in locations more widespread than the historic markets of the individual hospitals. Now it was necessary to provide services over a broad geographic area—services for HMO patients wherever they might live.

Phase 3 efforts by the hospital systems constituted a new wave of vertical integration and downstream product development based on the critical masses created through the horizontal concentrations of Phase 2. In contrast to the minor vertical developments of Phase 1, Phase 3 activities took place more rapidly and with greater market effect.

Vertical integration and product development took place along two lines. One was the vertical integration of ambulatory medical practice with acute care hospital services, through numerous joint ventures designed to locate primary care or specialty doctors in new markets and to create physician-hospital mechanisms for signing PPO and HMO contracts. As an example, the merger creating Health Value (Valley Community, Good Shepherd, and Beeler hospitals) soon yielded a subsidiary corporation "dedicated solely to the development of innovative health services delivered outside of the hospitals." The first venture was a regional kidney stone center developed in joint venture with numerous local physicians. The next was a network of six geographically dispersed primary care centers developed in a joint venture with a medical group practice that admitted most of its patients to Valley Community Hospital. Plans were also being developed, through another subsidiary corporation, for home care, a range of wellness services for families and corporations, nursing homes, and residential care facilities.

The second line of vertical integration was into health insurance. This move needs to be seen as a response to countervailing power on the buyers' side of the market rather than on the supply side. Health insurance companies were coming to the hospitals and demanding discount contracts. These insurance plans were the gatekeepers to the ultimate consumer market. The competitive struggle thus shifted from one between acute hospitals to one between health plans. But who would control the health plans? Market power would come to whoever controlled access to the ultimate consumer. The hospitals in Growthville calculated that there were several possibilities on the provider side: local hospitals, local hospitals in collaboration with doctors, and coalitions of local hospitals with distant corporations. On the purchaser side there were the indemnity, or prepayment, companies and the large employers.

The hospitals and the physicians in Growthville were thus gearing up for two struggles: over who would serve the new purchasers that were expecting hospital-doctor risk sharing and over who would control the health plans that were usurping the patient gatekeeper role from doctors and becoming the channelers of patients to hospitals.

A second source of countervailing power also emerged, in the form of local employers. In late 1986 there was the quick creation of an association representing seven of the very large employers in Growthville, all of which were self-insured. These seven employers represented approximately half a million employees and their dependents and constituted an extremely powerful and important purchasing force in the entire Growthville health care market. With the trend toward self-insurance, it was widely expected that by 1988 the number of employers in the association would expand to 60 or 70.

The Growthville hospital systems faced a problem in that they did not know whether the seven companies would negotiate exclusive contracts with one provider system or contract with many providers in the area. Most systems assumed the former and submitted lower prices based on the calculation that increased volume would be obtained if a contract was signed. But it turned out that most of the seven employers were unwilling to "cut out" any hospital competitors; in other words, they signed contracts with numerous hospitals even when signing with a single one might have obtained somewhat lower prices.

To summarize Phase 3, the hospital market of Growthville had moved in only a few years from one best described as monopolistic competition to one best seen as a differentiated oligopoly. The horizontal concentrations of Phase 2 formed the necessary basis for the phase 3 set of vertical integrations that emphasized geographic market expansion and new lines of health services delivery. This took place through two developments: (1) restructuring relationships with physicians, since their services were essential to the hospitals' response to the environment of managed-care plans; and (2) corporate extension into the medical prepayment business, since this was the business that would channel patients in the future.

These changes were to be expected since concentration at one level ordinarily leads to vertical integration and restructuring at upstream or downstream levels. Two other subindustries, medicine and insurance, had different market structures and thus their restructuring took different forms. The cottage industry of medicine moved toward its own form of corporatization and concentration for countervailing power through the quick formation of groups necessary for contracting with insurance companies. One existing group structured new and long-term joint venture links with a hospital system.

The subindustry of insurance restructured itself as new parties entered to assume the functions of carrying risk and processing claims: large employers took up the former function and provider-based corporations took up the latter.

These developments in medicine and insurance constituted forms of countervailance to the power developed through hospital mergers; they emerged in different ways and took different forms because of their prior structures.

Summing up across the three phases of this case, the pattern of evolution was (1) emergence of a market orientation by hospitals as the industry moved away from regulation; (2) steady expansion of what the hospitals considered to be their business, to include nonacute hospital and medical services as well as insurance, with vertical integration and concentric diversification serving as the vehicles for accomplishing this expansion; (3) remarkable change with respect to who was competing with whom, stemming from restructuring of hospital relationships away from open competition among many toward domination by a few; (4) a shift in the market from one of consumer choices among physicians and hospitals toward one of competitive choice among health plans; and (5) the emergence of negotiated pricing within the context of the new oligopoly, stemming from the heightened and organized power of corporate purchasers.

Finally, we return to a concept presented in the introduction to this case strategic alignment. The case has described the substantial realignment of our study hospitals to their new and changing environment. And it has highlighted their managers' use of boundary scanning, competitor analysis, and strategy to achieve this realignment.

James Thompson's word for this process is "co-alignment," referring to "the most critical managerial function, and the skill closest to creativity." This case has illustrated this management skill, defined as "the discernment of hitherto unnoticed relationships in the complex environment, calculating their cause-effect relationships, and translating them into appropriate programs of action" [6].

This is both a summary of the performances of our case study managers and a powerful prescription for those who might face similar circumstances and challenges.

Note

1. The underlying economic theory that supports the Herfendahl-Hirschman Index (HHI) holds that monopoly power or near-monopoly power is socially evil because through increased collusion, either tacit or actual, monopoly profits are enhanced. The risk of collusion is believed to increase as the market shares of leading firms increase and as their inequality in market shares increases.

    Theoretically at least, market power can be demonstrated by various behaviors of firms: predatory pricing, excessive profits or price-cost margins, or price discrimination. Or market power can theoretically be determined by various market processes: presence of potential competitors, presence of exogenous barriers to entry, etc. However, there are practical problems of acquiring and preparing proof of these indicators. In most cases, therefore, courts have adopted a market structure method of analysis based on the degree of concentration relative to a defined market.

The measure used is the HHI. This index measures both the number and the size of competitors relative to a market. It calculates the percentage share each firm has of a defined market, squares each percentage, and sums the squares to indicate the degree of concentration. Because it squares market shares, the HHI attaches disproportionate weight to large shares and increases in shares. The HHI's squaring property also magnifies the importance of market share inequality. According to the HHI, a market of three firms with shares of 33 percent each has a lower degree of concentration than a market of three firms with shares of 50 percent, 30 percent, and 20 percent each.

In 1982 the Justice Department issued guidelines indicating, in terms of the HHI, what mergers the government would consider to be illegal under Section 7 of the Clayton Act. (The guidelines were on hospitals.) The Justice Department adapted the HHI after accumulated empirical evidence indicated that market share data and concentration ratios were the best predictors of industry performance, price levels, and profitability. One study concluded that, on the average, a 10 percent increase in market share results in a 2 percent increase in profitability.

The guidelines state that when the postmerger HHI is below 1,000 the market is considered to be unconcentrated, and mergers will not be challenged except in extraordinary circumstances. When the postmerger HHI is between 1,000 and 8,000, concern for monopoly power exists, but the Justice Department is unlikely to challenge a merger that produces an increase in the HHI of less than 100 points. When the postmerger HHI is above 1,800 the market is considered highly concentrated, and the Justice Department will ordinarily challenge a merger unless it produced an increase in the HHI of less than 50 points. Such might be the case, for example, if two marginal competitors merged in order to survive and become a viable competitor to the larger market leaders.

Certain antitrust behaviors such as price fixing and market division are considered so pernicious that they are deemed per se illegal restraints of trade and require no calculation or proof of market power by the HHI method.

References

1. Ermann, D., and J. Gabel. The Changing Face of American Health Care: Multi-Hospital Systems, Emergency Centers, and Surgery Centers. *Multihospital Medical Center* 23 (May): 401–20, 1985.
2. Finkler, S. A., and S. L. Horowitz. Merger and Consolidation: An Overview of Activity in Health Care Organizations. *Healthcare Financial Management* 15 (January): 18–28, 1985.

3. Johnson, R. L. The Myth of Dominance by National Health Care Corporations. *Frontiers of Health Services Management* 3 (May): 3–22, 1987.
4. Blau, P., and W. R. Scott. *Formal Organizations*. San Francisco: Chandler, 1962, at 220.
5. Blau, P., and W. R. Scott. See number 4.
6. Thompson, James D. *Organizations in Action*. New York: McGraw Hill, 1967.

Case 2

Western Health Care Systems: A Health Care Delivery Continuum

Robert C. Myrtle

Introduction

The history of Western Health Care Systems can be characterized as one of progressively responding to current and emerging community health care needs. In the mid-1940s civic and community leaders identified the need for a new community hospital. Under the leadership of Davis Mitac, a prominent businessman, a citizen's committee was formed and plans drawn for building a new community hospital. When Astrid Bennett made a $500,000 contribution for the new hospital in memory of her husband Freemont, these plans were put into motion. A fund-raising campaign was launched, and Western County citizens responded generously, providing hundreds of thousands of dollars for the hospital.

Western Community Hospital opened its doors in April 1952. The first hospital built in Western County in 32 years, the new facility relieved a critical bed shortage by adding 169 medical and surgical beds and 32 maternity beds to the community's health care resources. Through the years, the community leaders who formed Western Community Hospital stayed involved, providing the progressive thinking and direction that enabled the hospital to assume a leadership position in the health care community. This support led to an expansion of beds in 1965 and the addition of a medical office building on hospital property across the street.

While modest renovations have taken place since 1965, the size of the hospital has not changed. Of the hospital's 267 beds, 240 were licensed for medical/surgical patients, 12 were intensive care unit–cardiac care unit beds, and 25 were licensed for maternity services. Last year the hospital maintained a 70.1 percent occupancy level.

Western Health Care Systems

In June 1973, Western's board of directors asked Health Planning Associates to study the health care needs of the community and the changing environmental and economic conditions of Western County and the surrounding metropolitan area. The report noted that the health care environment was rapidly changing. While Western Community Hospital had an excellent reputation and attracted many clients from outside its service area, the consultants noted that the area surrounding the hospital was growing more slowly than other areas in the county. Although many of Western Community Hospital's patients were wealthy or covered by third-party health plans, the report noted that the residents in areas immediately surrounding the hospital were poorer, less well educated, and more likely to be elderly or a member of a minority group. The consultants noted that the areas northwest and south of Western Community Hospital were growing more rapidly, with higher proportions of affluent and better educated residents. While consultants pointed out that there was no critical need for new hospital beds, they noted that a "lack of coordination" in health care delivery and the poor operating performance of several hospitals in the area created a strategic opportunity for Western.

Acting on the recommendations of the consultants, Western Community Hospital made a series of decisions to improve its competitive position in its environment while continuing to pursue its mission of providing quality health care to the residents of Western's service area. In September, 1978, Western signed an agreement to manage Kettering Memorial, a 181-bed, general acute care hospital located in the northeast portion of the county. Six months later Western was asked if it might be interested in purchasing Kettering. The board agreed and formed Western Health Care Systems.

Over the years Western continued to respond to changing economic and environmental changes. In January 1981, Western Health Care Systems acquired William Frances Stair Community Hospital. Located in the southern part of the county, this 250-bed hospital provided Western Health Care with a horizontally integrated delivery system that was geographically and strategically diversified. Over the past few years, Western Health Care Systems acquired the Clearview Rehabilitation Center, a full-service rehabilitation center, and Pleasant Valley Hospital, a 120-bed acute care psychiatric hospital providing a full range of inpatient and outpatient psychiatric services.

Developing a Health Care Delivery Continuum

In 1990, Western Health Care Systems' board asked Hospital Planning Associates to provide a comprehensive review of the health, economic, and service delivery conditions of Western County and the surrounding metropolitan areas. Their report indicated that Western Health Care had been very progressive in its acquisitions. This strategy helped to maintain marketshare in an increasingly competitive environment. The consultants noted that operating margins, while better than most facilities in the area, were declining, primarily because of changes in reimbursement policies and service delivery activities. The consultants stated that "while Western Health Care Systems has extended its presence in key geographic sectors of the area, it must move beyond its present inpatient focus to encompass an expanded service continuum." The consultant report noted four areas that Western Health Care Systems should focus on:

1. Acute care: strengthen its position in this area of patient care by establishing centers of excellence and adopting a product-line management strategy
2. Mental health: expand the role and function of Pleasant Valley Hospital to create a major mental health center providing comprehensive treatment, including prophylactic, therapeutic, and rehabilitative services
3. After care: develop specific services for the care of patients with chronic disease, as well as for those who need outpatient, day, home health, long-term convalescent, intermediate, nursing home, or rehabilitative care
4. Ambulatory care: broaden its focus from facility-based outpatient clinic care to include freestanding ambulatory and urgent care service centers, clinics, and alternative delivery systems and mechanisms

Community Health Network

Shortly after the acceptance of the consultant's report, Western Health Care Systems' board was asked by A. P. Wilinski, President of First Western National Bank, if it might be interested in acquiring an equity position in Community Health Network, one of the region's rapidly growing multispecialty medical groups. Community Health Network was formed in 1929 by George Harrison and his two sons shortly after their graduation from University Medical School. Harrison Clinic, as it was known at that time, experienced steady growth through the 1930s. In 1946 Dr. Harrison retired. With their father's retirement, the Harrison brothers asked a former classmate from University to join their practice on a salaried basis. Over the next five years Harrison Clinic continued to grow and additional physicians were hired. In 1951 the medical group began to experience growing pains. A clinic administrator was recruited, and the five salaried physicians were given full partnership status in the medical group.

The ensuing years saw rapid growth and development in Western County. This growth created an increased demand for medical care, which was met by an increase in the number of physicians affiliated with the medical group. By 1965 the medical staff had grown to 30, housed in two office buildings located in the north-central and western areas of the county.

During the planning for the second clinic, the general partners decided to form a new corporate entity, which they named the Community Health Network. While Harrison Clinic continued to exist as a named unit within the new organization, the Community Health Network soon established its own identity as an important health care provider in the community. At present the Community Health Network operates five clinics in Western County, with a sixth under construction. It has 68 physician partners, employs a support staff that numbers over 270 full-time equivalent (FTE) positions, operates its own clinical laboratory, and has an annual operating budget of $23,318,426. It has contract relations with four of the six HMOs operating in the county. All physicians hold a partnership position in the corporation and are compensated under a base draw, personal productivity formula system. Other employees are compensated on a salary or contractual basis.

While Community Health Network provides a stable and viable practice environment for its physicians, the group has experienced cash flow and organizational difficulties associated with the recent expansion activities and partnership share refunds to retiring members. Although the group is otherwise financially solvent, it has been exploring several organizational and financial options to reverse its current difficulties. It was this search that brought the group's plight to Wilinski's attention.

The Community Health Network Decision

Western Health Care asked Anderson & Anderson, a prominent consulting firm, to study the financial, legal, and organizational implications of this acquisition. Anderson & Anderson reported that the network's physicians were positive about many aspects of their practice. Turnover within the group was quite low, and because of its reputation and location, it experienced little difficulty in recruiting new members. The consultants pointed out that the group's physicians expressed concern about the competitive changes taking place in the health care industry, reporting that some physicians were very unhappy with the continued influx of new doctors to the region and the aggressive moves of several area hospitals to develop satellite clinics and acquire group practices. The report also indicated that several partners felt there was a need for the network to expand into several rapidly growing areas of the county. Funding this expansion, particularly in light of the practice-building activities of different hospitals and the partnership fee refunds to a growing number of retiring associates, did not seem possible under the current capitalization plan.

The consultants noted that the network's senior management was capable, although they focused more on operational instead of strategic issues. Each clinic operated in a quasi-autonomous fashion, with little integration of medical, financial, and administrative systems. Although the network's executive officer had attempted to develop an integrated management and patient care information system, progress was very slow due to the nature of the decision-making processes within the medical group and the concerns of many physicians over how these changes would affect the day-to-day operations of the different clinics. Any attempt to develop organizational structures and management processes that appeared to reduce the autonomy or control in the different clinics was likely to be strongly resisted.

The consultants also pointed out that different members of the medical staffs at Western Community, Kettering, and Stair had strongly stated their concern about the possibility that Western Health Care Systems would also be acquiring group practices to be operated by the different hospitals in the system. One of the most vocal of the physicians was responsible for nearly 20 percent of the admissions to Kettering. Since most of the network's medical staff had privileges at the different hospitals operated by Western Health Care, it appeared that this concern was one that could be managed or diffused.

These issues notwithstanding, the consultants felt that the acquisition offered considerable strategic opportunities for Western Health Care. While the financing of the purchase would create some cash flow difficulties in the short run, the longer-term assessment was positive. And since opportunities such as this one occur infrequently, it is a decision that they suggest Western Health Care undertake.

Questions

You are part of a senior-level planning group that Western Health Care has formed in response to the consultant's report to review the recommendations of both Hospital Planning Associates and Anderson & Anderson. Using the information in Tables 2.1–2.11, and Figure 2.1

1. indicate what strategies and actions Western Health Care should undertake in response to changing conditions and the emerging opportunities that have been identified;
2. prepare an outline describing the risks your strategy entails and the steps that Western should take to overcome these risks;
3. develop an implementation plan and timetable that identifies the level, nature, and means for integrating the strategy you are recommending with the functions and activities of Western's hospitals and other patient care delivery units; and
4. address any other issues critical to the successful implementation of your suggested strategy.

Table 2.1   Western Health Care Systems

	Western Community Hospital	Kettering Memorial Hospital	William Frances Stair Community Hospital	Clearview Rehabilitation Center	Pleasant Valley Hospital
Beds	267	181	250	N.A.	120
Personnel FTE	735	462	691	183	279
Outpatient emergency room visits	93,317	30,577	48,727	106,635	25,419
Gross revenues (thousands)	$75,123	$61,311	$77,985	$9,337	$52,486
Medical staff	376	214	345	37	81
Total patient days	68,316	45,122	65,426	N.A.	40,165

Source: 1992 Annual Report of Western Health Care Systems.

Table 2.2 Community Health Network

	Broadway Clinic Building	Hillside Clinic Building	Tivoli Clinic Building	Harrison Clinic Building	Thirty-Fourth Street Building
Medical staff	18	14	12	10	14
Personnel (FTE)	83	52	38	39	58
Clinic visits	86,112	68,432	53,358	44,986	63,409
Gross revenues (thousands)	$5,652	$4,516	$4,784	$4,104	$4,262

Source: 1992 Annual Report of Western Health Care Systems.

Table 2.3 Western County Population Statistics by Health Facility Planning Areas

Geographic Area	1950 Census	1960 Census	1970 Census	1980 Census	1990 Estimate	2000 Estimate
HFPA 1	58,395	70,075	80,584	97,507	116,444	136,484
Cypress Valley	33,869	41,421	48,677	59,576	71,021	84,585
HFPA 2	50,803	63,768	67,584	86,781	103,964	125,796
Belmont Heights	28,450	36,794	40,903	54,854	62,704	79,069
HFPA 3	76,497	93,199	109,683	134,087	160,650	180,909
Desmond	44,146	53,878	65,492	81,245	95,138	112,358
HFPA 4	123,213	138,817	143,521	150,268	153,424	156,661
Arlington	74,051	81,916	83,257	85,668	88,986	90,096
Western County totals	308,908	365,859	401,372	468,643	534,482	599,850

Source: Western State Department of Health and Human Services, Office of Health Planning and Regulation, 1990.

Table 2.4   Demographic Characteristics of Western County

	1950 Census	*1960 Census*	*1970 Census*	*1980 Census*	*1990 Estimate*	*2000 Estimate*
Age group						
0–14	40.4%	38.7%	35.4%	26.3%	24.9%	22.6%
15–44	43.1	43.3	45.2	49.6	46.4	43.2
45–64	11.7	13.1	14.2	16.3	18.6	22.6
65+	4.8	4.9	5.2	7.8	10.1	11.6
Ethnicity						
Black	9.6	10.4	10.6	10.9	11.3	11.5
Hispanic	N.A.	N.A.	5.9	7.1	7.4	7.9
Other nonwhite	N.A.	N.A.	3.6	4.2	4.5	4.7

Source: Western County Agency for Economic Development, 1988.

Table 2.5   Demographic Characteristics of Western County by Health Facilities Planning Areas

	1950 Census	*1960 Census*	*1970 Census*	*1980 Census*	*1990 Estimate*	*2000 Estimate*
HFPA 1						
Age group						
0–14	41.2%	39.5%	36.2%	31.8%	27.7%	25.1%
15–44	43.5	43.8	45.7	47.9	48.0	48.6
45–64	11.5	12.8	14.0	14.6	16.3	17.1
65+	3.7	3.9	4.1	5.7	7.9	9.1
Ethnicity						
Black	8.5	9.2	9.4	9.7	10.0	10.2
Hispanic	N.A.	N.A.	5.2	6.3	6.6	7.0
Other nonwhite	N.A.	N.A.	3.7	4.2	4.5	4.8
HFPA 2						
Age group						
0–14	41.9	40.2	38.1	35.1	30.3	26.1
15–44	43.2	44.7	45.3	46.7	47.7	48.6
45–64	11.2	11.3	12.1	12.3	14.1	16.1
65+	3.7	3.8	4.4	5.9	7.8	9.3
Ethnicity						
Black	8.3	8.9	9.1	9.3	9.6	9.8
Hispanic	N.A.	N.A.	4.7	5.8	6.1	6.4
Other nonwhite	N.A.	N.A.	3.7	4.3	4.6	4.9

Continued

Table 2.5   Continued

	1950 Census	1960 Census	1970 Census	1980 Census	1990 Estimate	2000 Estimate
HFPA 3						
Age group						
0–14	43.0	42.1	41.2	38.4	34.6	33.3
15–44	42.1	42.1	42.2	43.1	43.8	41.4
45–64	11.3	11.8	12.2	13.7	14.9	16.1
65+	3.6	4.0	4.3	4.8	6.8	9.2
Ethnicity						
Black	8.5	9.2	9.4	9.7	10.0	10.2
Hispanic	N.A.	N.A.	4.7	5.7	6.0	6.4
Other nonwhite	N.A.	N.A.	3.8	4.3	4.9	4.9
HFPA 4						
Age group						
0–14	39.4	38.2	36.0	34.1	32.3	29.6
15–44	43.3	40.6	39.5	37.7	36.5	34.4
45–65	12.2	15.7	17.9	19.5	21.0	23.1
65+	5.2	5.5	6.6	8.7	10.2	12.9
Ethnicity						
Black	10.1	10.8	11.1	11.4	11.8	12.0
Hispanic	N.A.	N.A.	6.0	7.3	7.7	8.2
Other nonwhite	N.A.	N.A.	3.7	4.2	4.5	4.8

Source: Western State Department of Health and Human Services, Office of Health Planning and Regulation, 1990.

Table 2.6   Western County Acute Care Facilities by Health Facility Planning Areas

Facility and Location	Sponsor-ship	Total Beds	Med-ical	ICU/ CCU	OB/ GYN	Pedi-atric	Psychi-atric	Percent Occupancy
HFPA 1								
Oakwood								
Community	Nonprofit	125	99	4	16	6		67.7
Valley District	Public	50	38	2	6	4		83.9
Cypress Valley								
Carson Memorial	Nonprofit	85	60	5	10	10		57.3
St. Lukes	Religious	150	70	10	30	30	10	67.7
Valley Doctors	For-Profit	76	62	4	10			54.3

Continued

Table 2.6   Continued

Facility and Location	Sponsor-ship	Total Beds	Med-ical	ICU/CCU	OB/GYN	Pedi-atric	Psychi-atric	Percent Occupancy
HFPA 2								
University	State	250	145	15	50	30	10	80.1
Belmont Heights								
Western County	County	180	110	15	30	15	10	80.8
HFPA 3								
Overlook								
Community	Nonprofit	80	62	4	10	4		64.7
Ward Howard								
District	Public	50	50					57.4
Desmond								
Cedars-Siani	Religious	133	94	7	20	12		68.6
Kettering								
Memorial	Nonprofit	181	123	8	30	20		68.3
HFPA 4								
IHS Doctors	For-profit	80	76	4				72.3
Wm. Frances								
Stair	Nonprofit	250	190	10	30	20		71.7
Arlington								
St. Bernadines	Religious	153	95	8	30	20		67.3
Western								
Community	Nonprofit	267	195	12	25	25	10	70.1

Source: Western State Department of Health and Human Services, Office of Health Planning and Regulation, 1990.

Table 2.7   Western County Physician Workforce Distribution by Specialty

Specialty	1950 Census	1960 Census	1970 Census	1980 Census	1990 Estimate	2000 Estimate
Primary care	202	223	245	259	365	440
Other medical	24	30	34	48	60	70
Surgical	127	159	178	182	210	235
All other	138	159	172	197	250	290
Total physicians	491	571	629	686	885	1,035

Source: Western State Department of Health and Human Services, Office of Health Planning and Regulation, 1990.

Table 2.8   Western County Physician Workforce Distribution by Specialty and Health Facility Planning Area

Specialty	1950 Census	1960 Census	1970 Census	1980 Census	1990 Estimate	2000 Estimate
HFPA 1						
Primary care	24	32	42	48	90	120
Other medical	3	4	6	11	15	20
Surgical	15	22	31	41	50	65
All other	16	22	30	44	60	80
Total physicians	58	80	109	154	215	285
HFPA 2						
Primary care	23	30	36	50	70	95
Other medical	3	4	5	9	10	15
Surgical	14	21	26	35	40	50
All other	15	21	25	38	50	65
Total physicians	55	76	92	132	170	225
HFPA 3						
Primary care	32	42	57	58	120	160
Other medical	4	6	8	11	20	25
Surgical	19	29	41	41	70	85
All other	21	29	40	44	80	105
Total physicians	76	106	146	154	290	375
HFPA 4						
Primary care	123	119	110	93	85	65
Other medical	14	16	15	17	15	10
Surgical	79	87	80	65	50	35
All other	86	87	77	71	60	40
Total physicians	302	309	282	246	210	150

Source: Western State Department of Health and Human Services, Office of Health Planning and Regulation, 1990.

Table 2.9   Type of Practice

HFPA	Solo	Partnership	Group	Other	Total
1	47	61	59	16	183
2	47	53	39	18	157
3	38	59	84	35	216
4	56	92	46	15	209
Total	188	265	228	84	765

Source: Western State Department of Health and Human Services, Office of Health Planning and Regulation, 1990.

Table 2.10   Community Health Network Statement of Operating
Income and Expense for Fiscal Year Ending July 31, 1992

Patient service revenue		
Private insurance	$13,757,871	
Self-pay	6,062,791	
Medicare	1,632,290	
Medicaid	932,737	
Other	932,737	
Gross Patient Revenue		$23,318,426
Less		
Contractual allowances and adjustments	979,373	
Bad debts	2,565,026	
Total adjustments	(3,544,401)	
Net patient revenue	19,774,025	
Other operating revenue	2,392,657	
Total operating revenue		22,166,682
Operating expenses		
Physician services	6,428,338	
Nursing services	2,881,669	
Other professional services	665,000	
Administrative services	332,500	
General services	443,333	
Office and clerical services	554,167	
Supplies and expenses	1,219,168	
Pension and insurance	3,278,452	
Depreciation	1,108,334	
Interest	2,216,668	
Total operating expenses		(19,127,629)
Nonoperating revenue		
Rental income	30,390	
Investment income	243,124	
Total nonoperating revenue		273,514
Excess of revenue over expenses		3,312,567

Table 2.11   Western Health Care Systems Statement of Operating
Income and Expense for Fiscal Year Ended December 31,
1992

	1992	*1991*
Patient service revenue	$276,240,600	$239,112,600
Less		
Allowances and bad debts	(61,338,640)	(44,479,200)
Net patient service revenue	214,901,960	194,633,400
Plus		
Other operating revenue	10,922,000	7,175,840
Total operating revenue	225,823,960	201,809,240
Operating expenses		
Nursing services	(53,029,570)	(46,116,210)
Other professional services	(95,429,040)	(84,912,700)
General services	(25,858,100)	(25,753,560)
Fiscal services	(14,115,690)	(12,018,930)
Administrative services	(22,054,870)	(13,740,040)
Depreciation	(9,597,084)	(7,626,738)
Total operating expenses	(220,084,354)	(190,168,178)
Excess of revenue over expense	5,739,606	11,641,062
Nonoperating revenues and expenses		
Unrestricted gifts and bequests	421,000	582,000
Income from investments	5,702,400	5,853,650
Gain on sale of investments	2,550,000	613,000
Equity in loss of subsidiary	(1,088,760)	
Net nonoperating revenue	7,584,640	7,048,650
Excess of revenue over expense	13,324,246	18,689,712

Figure 2.1   Western County Health Facility Planning Areas (HFPAs)

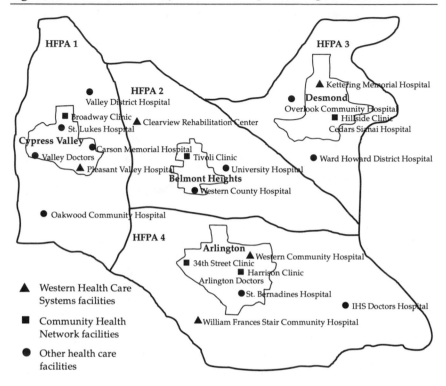

HFPA 1

HFPA 2

Valley District Hospital

■ Broadway Clinic   ▲ Clearview Rehabilitation Center

● St. Lukes Hospital

Cypress Valley

● Carson Memorial Hospital

● Valley Doctors

▲ Pleasant Valley Hospital

HFPA 3

▲ Kettering Memorial Hospital

● **Desmond**

Overlook Community Hospital

■ Hillside Clinic

Cedars Sinai Hospital

■ Tivoli Clinic

● University Hospital   ● Ward Howard District Hospital

Belmont Heights

● Western County Hospital

● Oakwood Community Hospital

HFPA 4

Arlington   ▲ Western Community Hospital

■ 34th Street Clinic

■ Harrison Clinic

Arlington Doctors

● St. Bernadines Hospital

● IHS Doctors Hospital

▲ William Frances Stair Community Hospital

▲ Western Health Care
    Systems facilities

■ Community Health
    Network facilities

● Other health care
    facilities

Case 3

Strategic Choices in Building an Integrated Health Care Network: The Buena Vista Clinic Acquisition Proposal

Carol K. Jacobson

Introduction

In early March 1983, Brian Howard examined the practice acquisition proposal before him. Howard, chief administrator of the Memorial Medical Center (MMC), was preparing for the next day's board of trustees meeting. The proposal to acquire the Buena Vista Clinic was a key topic on the agenda. He knew several board members were opposed to the idea of hospital ownership of medical practices. Howard favored the acquisition, however, and believed the timing was right to evaluate carefully a practice acquisition proposal.

Memorial Medical Center was one of 19 hospitals located in a major metropolitan area. Competition among hospitals in the area was becoming increasingly intense, but MMC had experienced a steady annual growth in admissions and marketshare. The area's rapid growth in HMOs and other managed care plans as well as the efforts of a coalition of business leaders intensified cost-containment pressures. One hospital had closed in 1982, and two other closings were expected in 1983.

The health care industry had changed dramatically since Howard had taken his first administrative position at MMC nearly 30 years ago when MMC was a community hospital. As competition and cost-containment pressures intensified, Howard managed the transformation to a broader health care organization involved in several health care–related ventures. Howard was convinced that the winners in the emerging environment would be health care organizations who were able to deliver quality care at market-sensitive prices, through integrated networks linking physicians, hospitals, and related health care providers with health plans. The question of the moment was, Should MMC acquire the Buena Vista Clinic as one step in building its integrated network?

Howard listed issues that he expected the board members to raise. One of the first issues raised would surely be whether the acquisition would be a sound financial decision. MMC had been a fiscally conservative organization throughout its history and was considered by industry observers to be in the best financial health of all the metropolitan area hospitals. Since the clinic acquisition also involved financing a new medical office building, this was a multimillion-dollar deal. A second issue would be whether a practice acquisition would be a significant departure from the overall direction of MMC and whether it was advisable. Howard was sure that this issue would prompt the physician representative on the board to bring up a third point—the potential resistance of the medical staff. The majority of the medical staff consisted of independent, fee-for-service physicians who would be concerned about hospital interference in the practice of medicine. A fourth concern was likely to be how MMC could control the clinic if it decided to go ahead with the acquisition—that is, could MMC control the cost and quality of medical practice given physician desires for autonomy?

These were all valid issues to consider, but Howard felt the board also needed to evaluate carefully the full impact on the hospital's operations if MMC did not buy the practice and the Buena Vista Clinic were acquired by another party. He was aware that an HMO, Preferred Health Plan, was also negotiating to purchase the clinic. Simultaneously, PHP was promising to admit all of its patients to the metropolitan hospital offering the biggest discounts. If PHP purchased the Buena Vista Clinic and another hospital submitted the lowest bid, MMC would lose a significant share of its admissions to a competitor. What would this loss of marketshare mean to the future of MMC?

History of the Clinic

The Buena Vista Clinic was established by three physicians (two general practitioners and one internist) near the business center of the suburb of Oak Hills in 1950. The founding physicians were joint owners of a new medical office building. As the suburb continued to expand and prosper, so did the clinic. Over the next ten years, the number of physicians in the clinic tripled to nine by adding specialists in internal medicine, pediatrics, obstetrics, and surgery. Each was required to buy into the building. By 1983, the Buena Vista Clinic was a successful multispecialty group of 24 physicians. This number included two physicians who were staffing the urgent care center at the clinic location. (Table 3.1 displays the specialty mix changes.)

Oak Hills embarked on an urban renewal program in the late 1970s. The program was subsidized by federal redevelopment funds. By 1982, the program had progressed to the area that included the Buena Vista Clinic. The building, owned and occupied by the clinic for over 30 years, was scheduled to be torn down.

The scheduled razing of their building prompted a heated debate among the physicians. Many of the physicians no longer wanted to own an office building. A majority were resistant to financing the construction of a new building due to the extremely high interest rates at the time. The physicians quickly dismissed a proposal to buy another building because it would mean moving to a new site. They perceived their current location to be their strongest asset. A small group of physicians wanted to file a lawsuit to stop the dismantling of the building, but the idea was not perceived as feasible.

As an alternative, the Buena Vista Clinic began to give strong consideration to negotiating a contractual arrangement that would link them to a party who would be in a position to finance and build a new facility for them. Because the majority wanted to avoid any type of ownership or financial risk in a medical office building, a joint venture was not a

Table 3.1 Specialty Mix of Physicians at the Buena Vista Clinic

Specialty	1950	1960	1983
General practice	2	2	1
Internal medicine	1	2	6
Pediatrics	0	2	4
Obstetrics/gynecology	0	2	5
Surgery	0	1	2
Family practice	0	0	3
Orthopedics	0	0	1
Urgent care	0	0	2
Total	3	9	24

popular alternative. The physicians began to evaluate the alternative of selling their practice. Several physicians were approaching retirement. Others were just starting to establish practices and were attracted to the idea of a stable income with more predictable hours. With the increasing penetration of managed care plans, the clinic would increasingly depend on capitated contracts to maintain practice volume and would soon need to improve its negotiating skills.

Preferred Health Plan (PHP) expressed interest in acquiring the practice. As talks progressed, the initial enthusiasm of the physicians diminished. The Buena Vista Clinic's practice was predominantly fee-for-service medicine. The physicians perceived that the rules of PHP's capitated plan were designed to limit patient visits and would lower quality of care. In addition, many became uncomfortable with the amount of interference in their practice style that PHP was likely to have. The physicians were told that it might take up to three years to train them in the proper utilization of resources. Most of the physicians strongly disagreed on this point, arguing that physicians are the best judges of how to utilize resources and medical technology to deliver medical care.

In reaction, a small group of clinic physicians discussed looking for other partners. This group decided to approach the MMC, the hospital with which the clinic physicians were most closely affiliated as members of its medical staff. Based on their personal experience and Howard's reputation in dealings with members of the MMC medical staff over his 30-year career, the physicians were confident that the mutual trust that had developed would facilitate productive negotiations.

Memorial Medical Center

Memorial Medical Center was first established as a nonprofit hospital under the name Memorial Community Hospital in 1910. Its mission has been "to be a leader in providing quality health care services to the community that we serve." To fulfill that mission, Memorial Community Hospital merged with a neighboring hospital in the early 1970s and was renamed the Memorial Medical Center.

Memorial Medical Center's marketshare growth during 1982 was the largest of any metropolitan hospital, increasing from 11.8 percent in 1981 to 13.2 percent in 1982. Figure 3.1 shows the five-year record of marketshare growth. To maintain its leadership position in the community, MMC's current goal was to become an integrated health care organization providing a broad line of services. To achieve this goal, MMC planned to establish vertical linkages with other health care-related enterprises and to build outpatient centers for various treatments, including behavioral health, occupational health, and ambulatory surgery.

MMC currently had operating divisions for ambulatory services in home health care, sports medicine, and occupational medicine and for behavioral health services in chemical dependency and mental health. MMC also planned to develop its tertiary care business on the basis of centers of excellence. The first centers would be oncology, neuroscience, and orthopedics.

Memorial Medical Center believed that a key part of its strategy was maintaining and improving physician relationships. In 1983 there were 680 physicians on the medical staff, 325 of whom were considered active members. The majority of its medical staff was fee-for-service physicians in small group practices of less than ten physicians. To survive the expected shakeout in the regional marketplace, MMC needed to ensure that its medical staff was admitting a large portion of patients to the MMC hospital as well as its related enterprises. The marketing and management services of the Clinic Management Division had been helpful in working toward this goal, but there was a growing concern that

Figure 3.1   Memorial Medical Center Annual Marketshare

% Marketshare

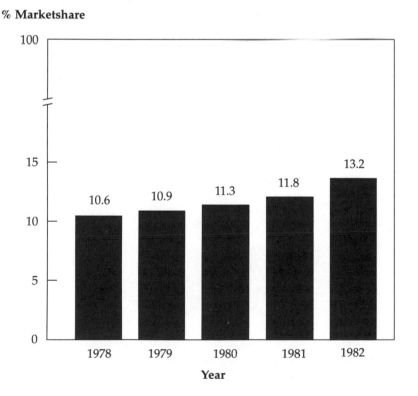

current informal relationships with physicians would need to be formalized under legal structural arrangements. MMC was experimenting with several types of arrangements to determine which was most effective. The arrangements included several joint ventures (some to purchase durable medical equipment, others to set up outpatient treatment facilities), long-term contracts (particularly with hospital-based physicians), and management contracts (to perform marketing services, computerized billing systems, and, in the future, negotiating services to aid physicians in negotiations with managed care plans).

The Acquisition Proposal

In the last week of February, the small group of Buena Vista Clinic physicians extended the proposal in a meeting with Chief Administrator Howard, the director of medical staff relations, and two other top administrators. The physicians conveyed the necessity of a quick decision. Because the clinic had spent several months negotiating with PHP before individual physicians became alarmed with some of the specifics of the proposed acquisition, it was approaching the April 15 deadline that had been given by the city of Oak Hills to make their decision.

Coincidentally, MMC was engaged in contract renegotiations with PHP regarding further fee discounts, perceived by MMC as unacceptably severe. Given PHP's statement that it planned to send all its patients to the hospital with the lowest bid, MMC risked losing PHP's patients to a competitor if it did not agree to the discounts. A nearby hospital was trying to build marketshare by offering aggressive discounts to managed care plans. If MMC gave larger discounts to PHP, however, it faced the prospect of comparable discounting demands from other managed care plans as their contracts came up for renegotiation. Top managers at MMC were increasingly convinced of the importance of taking a stand by refusing to negotiate a discount that would run the risk of pricing below costs.

Partly for this reason, MMC was keenly interested in the Buena Vista representatives' proposal. From the hospital's perspective, the clinic had two key strengths. First, the Buena Vista Clinic was historically either the largest or the second largest admitter of patients to MMC. Clinic obstetricians delivered more babies at MMC than obstetricians from any other clinic, and MMC delivered more babies than any other metropolitan hospital. In 1982 MMC had increased the number of birthing rooms from 9 to 14 and had invested in technological improvements for services to high-risk mothers and newborns. MMC would lose significant volume in obstetrics as well as other departments if the clinic entered into a contractual arrangement with PHP, requiring its admissions to go to another hospital.

Buena Vista's second key strength was its patient mix. Buena Vista Clinic had a large percentage of fee-for-service patients and contracts with multiple HMOs. A clause in its agreement with each HMO limited the number of patients the clinic would accept from that plan, thereby reducing the group's dependence on any one HMO. Other clinics in the area were experiencing serious financial difficulties as a result of overdependence on one HMO. There were frequent threats to refuse to renegotiate with HMOs, but there was a concomitant fear that a physician or clinic could not survive without some proportion of prepaid contracts.

A key MMC strength was its solid financial condition, giving it the capability to finance an office building and practice acquisition. Because top MMC managers wanted it to remain in good financial condition, they were looking for assurances that hospital admissions would be maintained at a stable level without having to offer deep discounts to managed care plans. Howard intended to stress that the acquisition of the Buena Vista Clinic would be one way to protect admission levels without providing deep discounts to prepaid plans.

There were several questions that the board needed to evaluate rather quickly: Did the acquisition of Buena Vista Clinic fit MMC's strategy? If the acquisition did take place, how should the physicians be compensated? How should cost and quality be controlled? How much autonomy should the physicians have in their practice style and admission decisions? What should be the composition of the governing board? How could the acquisition be presented to be palatable to the medical staff? And, just as importantly, if the acquisition did not take place, what were the implications for MMC?

The next section introduces an economic theory to use for evaluating the Buena Vista Clinic acquisition proposal.

Transaction Cost Economics

The strategic question for the board and top managers of MMC is, Given that the choice of an intermediate structure such as a joint venture has been ruled out by the physicians, do contracting conditions warrant the acquisition of the practice? This question is part of the larger strategic question of how vertically integrated MMC should be. Vertical integration can be defined as the incorporation of the stages of production within the boundaries of a single organization. If we identify *acute inpatient care* as the *product* of hospitals, then a vertically integrated hospital might own ancillary services (an input to production), home health or long-term care services (to provide care to the product after discharge), or an insurance subsidiary (the financing mechanism). Each stage of production could feasibly be owned by some party other than the hospital. MMC must determine whether there are cost savings to be gained by bringing a medical practice under common ownership.

With the efficiency pressures on the health care industry, transaction cost economics (TCE), an efficiency-based theory, is a relevant framework for analyzing MMC's acquisition decision. According to TCE, the most efficient structural arrangement for organizing a transaction depends on the attributes of the transaction and the comparative costs of transacting under alternative arrangements. Structural arrangements range from markets (arm's length arrangements) to hierarchies (vertical integration), with intermediate modes (such as joint ventures and long-term contracts) between these extremes.

Structural arrangements between hospital and physicians for organizing the delivery of medical care range from independent hospital and medical staff organizations to vertically integrated health care organizations incorporating acute care hospital facilities, ambulatory care, clinics, and salaried physicians. Intermediate modes include long-term contracts (e.g., with hospital-based physicians), clinic management contracts, and hospital-physician joint ventures.

What determines the relative efficiency of alternative structural arrangements mediating transactions? According to TCE, the key attribute is asset specificity or the "nontrivial investment in transaction-specific assets" (Williamson 1985). Four types of asset specificity can be identified and illustrated.

The first type is *physical asset specificity*, in which unique assets are mobile and highly specialized to a particular transaction, such as diagnostic or therapeutic equipment that is not routinely used by the same type of specialists in other locations. One example is the investment in one-of-a-kind pieces of spinal surgery equipment invented by spinal surgeons for the treatment of spinal injury patients. Physical asset specificity might be increased by an investment in leading edge technology. While the physical assets in this case are not unique, other aspects of the potential acquisition represent a move toward higher asset specificity.

The second is *site specificity*. Here, immobile assets are located in close proximity although there is no technical reason for adjacent locations. The parties choose to locate at the same site to economize on inventory and transportation expenses. In the evaluation of the proposal to acquire the Buena Vista Clinic, site asset specificity emerges as an important factor. As previously reported, the physicians of the Buena Vista Clinic attributed the success of their group practice to its convenient location in the affluent suburb of Oak Hills and believed a substantial portion of the patient clientele would be lost if the clinic moved to a new site. Because 98 percent of the patients drawn from this location are admitted to MMC, the clinic location and patient base are valuable assets for the hospital. However, if PHP acquires the Buena Vista Clinic and negotiates large discounts at a competing hospital, the advantages of the clinic's site and the patient base would be lost to MMC. By agreeing to acquire the clinic, MMC can gain assurances that its physicians would continue to admit their patients to MMC.

The third type, *dedicated asset specificity*, refers to discrete investments in generalized assets, such as expanding capacity, on behalf of a particular buyer with the expectation that the contracting relationship will continue. MMC has made such investments to meet the needs of specialties or product lines identified as centers of excellence as part of its strategy to expand the tertiary care business. To efficiently utilize these dedicated assets and provide a stable flow of patients to the centers, MMC must maintain the volume of admissions. Because of its significant investment in dedicated assets, MMC seeks assurance that the Buena Vista Clinic (as a multispecialty group) will continue admitting its patients to MMC and referring its tertiary care patients to MMC-owned or linked subspecialists and centers of excellence.

The final type is *human asset specificity*, in which skills and experience are specialized to accomplish a specific task. Those physicians who are researchers or innovators in their specialty have the highest degree of human asset specificity. For example, spinal surgeons who are inventing treatment procedures and surgical techniques in the process of treating patients have a higher degree of human asset specificity than the family practice physician who uses routine and established treatment procedures for relatively simple diagnoses.

Human asset specificity may also be acquired by the support staff and is highest among specially trained nurses or technicians whose knowledge and expertise plays a vital role in many medical care transactions. Support team members are often employees of the hospital, so the hospital incurs the expense of additional training and compensation. The supply of replacements for highly specialized staff may be scarce so that the loss of a valued team member would disrupt the team's productivity and result in a costly search for a replacement. Even after a replacement is found, adjustment difficulties may result in a loss of team productivity and effectiveness. MMC has sought to protect its interests by gaining assurances that physicians, whose decisions generate the demand for support staff resources, will admit the volume of patients that will adequately utilize the team and generate revenues to cover employment costs. The benefits of a specialized support staff are enhanced when the relationship between hospital and physician is maintained.

Because of the interdependence resulting from asset specificity, the parties find it difficult to continue to organize transactions through arm's length, market contracts and arrangements to protect specialized investments. Although contingent contracts could be designed, the most obvious structural arrangement for protecting specialized assets is ownership (or vertical integration). For each type of asset specificity, Table 3.2 illustrates the degree of control associated with alternative structural arrangements.

In the absence of specialized assets, the market is the most efficient means of organizing a transaction. For example, a supplier holding out for a higher price than the market can bear risks losing the sale to a competitor because it is relatively easy for a buyer to find an alternative supplier for a general purpose asset. Therefore, the price mechanism offers adequate control, and there is no need to replace the market contract.

When there are investments in specialized assets, however, TCE asserts that exchange in the market encounters problems chiefly because of two behavioral attributes of the parties involved (Williamson 1985). First, although each of the parties intends to act rationally, each is boundedly rational (i.e., has limited cognitive ability to identify, gather, and analyze all of the information required to make a rational decision). Without such information, it is not feasible to design an arm's length contract specifying the responsibilities of each party under all contracting problems that might arise.

Second, each party is potentially opportunistic and cannot be relied on to act fairly or to provide complete information without distortion. Should some unforeseen development arise (say, changing market conditions or government regulation), the terms of the contract might require adjustment. But, because each party tends to bargain for a larger share of the gains (or smaller share of the losses), the process of renegotiation might be protracted and costly—and might ultimately fail. Although the parties are interdependent, each might seek its own self-interests rather than act in the parties' mutual interests.

Table 3.2 Alternative Structural Arrangements

Type of Asset Specificity	Tight Control	Loose Control
Physical	Common ownership	Buyer-owned asset with bidding
Site	Common ownership	Contingent contract
Dedicated	Common ownership	Contingent contract
Human	Employment relation	Autonomous contracting

Recognizing the potential for conflict, the parties may choose to forgo a mutually advantageous transaction—unless they get some assurance that these difficulties can be controlled or eliminated. Choosing a structure that offers such assurances can safeguard the interests of both parties and promote the continuation of a mutually advantageous exchange relationship. Since the clinic physicians have stated in this case that they do not want a joint venture, the most obvious structural choice is common ownership. For a discussion of the advantages and disadvantages of joint venture arrangements between hospitals and physicians, see Jacobson 1989.

The chief advantage of vertical integration is improved coordinating properties: that is, under one owner, the parties can be led to cooperate as a result of the management functions of planning, leading, organizing, and controlling. As contracting conditions change and problems arise, adaptive decisions can be made by management rather than the costly processes of specifying all contingencies in a contract or renegotiating as conflicts occur. The chief disadvantage of internalization, however, is that flexibility for responding to changing market conditions may be restrained. Flexibility is important to hospitals because the development of pharmaceuticals or noninvasive technologies may render current techniques obsolete. For example, if a hospital is locked into an employment relationship with a physician whose specialized technical skill has become obsolete, it would be costly for the hospital to terminate the relationship.

Conclusion

After careful reflection, Howard remained convinced that the Buena Vista Clinic should be acquired and established as a new operating division of MMC. He was confident that the presentation regarding financial issues would convince the board of the project's feasibility. The most controversial issues would be whether a clinic acquisition fit MMC's strategic direction and whether the medical staff would perceive a clinic acquisition as interference in the practice of medicine. Howard personally called the assistant administrator, the director of medical staff relations, and the director of strategic planning to arrange a late afternoon meeting. He wanted a thorough discussion of the issues to anticipate and avoid the development of any cultural or political problems.

Addendum

After considerable discussion, the board approved the acquisition of the Buena Vista Clinic, and its physicians entered into a salaried arrangement with the hospital. The board agreed that MMC's ability to survive in a highly competitive market was connected to its ability to guarantee admissions through closer and more formalized structural arrangements with physicians. Both the hospital administrators and the physicians described the acquisition as a win-win situation. MMC gained the advantage of a stable patient base. The physicians believed that selling the practice to MMC would protect the survival of their group yet not interfere with their style of practice.

The basic terms of the agreement were that MMC would buy the group's building and accounts receivable, finance the construction of a new office building on the current site, provide management and marketing expertise, and create a guaranteed salary pool for three years. MMC and the physicians agreed to share in the governance of the clinic. MMC has majority membership on the governing board, and the physicians dominate the medical review committee that oversees the practice of medicine. Through the medical review committee, physicians will maintain control of how they utilize resources and gain assurance that physician autonomy in practice style will be preserved. Thus, the perception of hospital interference in the practice of medicine and subsequent resistance from the fee-for-service physicians on the medical staff will be minimized. Because MMC is now the owner of the Buena Vista Clinic, it can legally direct the clinic's referrals to its centers of excellence and hospital-owned ambulatory care centers.

One additional matter of concern was the effect of a salaried arrangement on physician productivity. The physician negotiating team strongly believed that productivity is higher among nonsalaried physicians. A fee-for-service physician has an incentive to see more patients and work longer hours because he or she will earn a higher income. Therefore, the negotiating physicians were adamant in their requirement that physicians be in control of the compensation method. MMC guaranteed the salary pool for three years, but physicians will determine how the pool will be distributed. After three years, the size of the salary pool will depend on the clinic's performance.

The success of the Buena Vista Clinic acquisition is signaled by the reaction of other groups. Although MMC still does not have a practice acquisition strategy, several groups have approached the hospital about acquiring their practices as satellites of the Buena Vista Clinic. These practices view MMC as a desirable partner for two reasons. First, other physicians have observed that MMC has not interfered in the Buena Vista Clinic physician's treatment of patients. Second, the physicians want a close association with a hospital that is likely to survive the predicted shakeout in the region. As discussed, this hospital is in relatively good financial health and is expected to be a survivor.

References

Jacobson, C. K. 1989. "A Conceptual Framework for Evaluating Joint Venture Opportunities between Hospitals and Physicians." *Health Services Management Research* 2, no. 3 (November): 204–12.

Williamson, O. E. 1985. *The Economic Institutions of Capitalism*. New York: The Free Press.

Linkages between Acute and Long-Term Care Services

Nancy J. Packard

Introduction

Hospital X, founded in 1960 in a major West Coast city, began as a 115-bed acute care community hospital. Like many hospitals built before the passage of Medicare legislation, the structure and organization of the hospital has, with time, undergone major transitions. Among the most notable changes has been the expansion of the traditional acute care institution to include a range of services along an acute–chronic care continuum.

In contrast to many hospitals that have only recently extended their continuum of care, expansion began early in Hospital X's history. In 1968 the hospital administration made an initial effort to integrate acute and chronic care services through the addition of an inpatient long-term care unit. More recently, a much broader expansion of the organization's service lines has occurred. The original hospital is now a corporation that manages both for-profit and not-for-profit health services subsidiaries. The services provided by the corporation include health promotion and disease prevention, acute hospital-based care, outpatient care, inpatient hospice services, inpatient rehabilitation and skilled nursing care, and home care (see Figure 4.1 for the hospital's service line changes).

The history of Hospital X is one of progressive service expansion. Yet the most recent corporate strategy included not only the addition and

Figure 4.1   Hospital X Service Lines

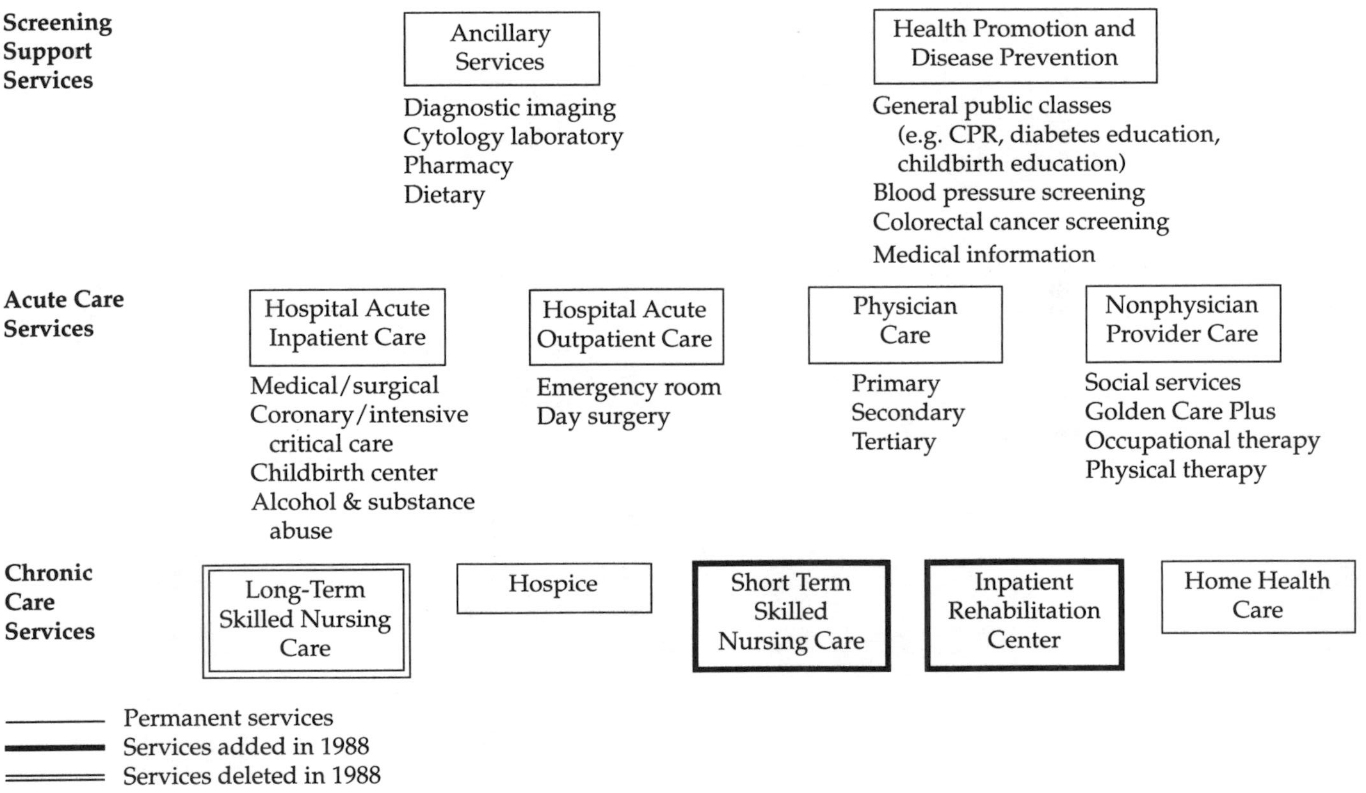

Screening Support Services

Ancillary Services

Diagnostic imaging
Cytology laboratory
Pharmacy
Dietary

Health Promotion and Disease Prevention

General public classes
(e.g. CPR, diabetes education, childbirth education)
Blood pressure screening
Colorectal cancer screening
Medical information

Acute Care Services

Hospital Acute Inpatient Care

Medical/surgical
Coronary/intensive critical care
Childbirth center
Alcohol & substance abuse

Hospital Acute Outpatient Care

Emergency room
Day surgery

Physician Care

Primary
Secondary
Tertiary

Nonphysician Provider Care

Social services
Golden Care Plus
Occupational therapy
Physical therapy

Chronic Care Services

Long-Term Skilled Nursing Care

Hospice

Short Term Skilled Nursing Care

Inpatient Rehabilitation Center

Home Health Care

—— Permanent services
▬▬ Services added in 1988
══ Services deleted in 1988

expansion of service lines but retrenchment as well. The combined strategy reflects a major restructuring of the acute-chronic care continuum. The retrenchment, in particular, involved the elimination of inpatient long-term skilled nursing care, a service that for many years comprised the principal chronic care service provided by the organization. Of the 182 skilled nursing beds owned by the hospital, 140 were eliminated. The remaining were retained for other inpatient chronic care services, including existing hospice care and a newly developed short-term (less than one-month stay) skilled nursing care service. These services were augmented by an expanded inpatient rehabilitation center.

Linkages: Hospital Responses to Regulatory Change

Medicare Extended Care Policy (1968–1972)

The Extended Care Program, mandated in the original Medicare legislation, was instituted nationally in 1967. The program provided reimbursement to nursing homes for the care of Medicare patients who needed skilled nursing care following discharge from an acute care hospital. Through this legislation a rudimentary foundation for the development of an institutional-based chronic care continuum emerged. Specifically, the eligibility criteria for benefit coverage included a minimum three-day hospitalization prior to entry into the nursing home facility. The care provided to the recipients of the extended care program was not long term or custodial. Rather, it was subacute, meaning that it was only temporary or short-term posthospital care.

A major intent of the legislation was to facilitate cost savings for the Medicare program by encouraging the provision of extended care in lower cost facilities. More specifically, it was assumed that Medicare outlays could be reduced if patients' hospital stays could be shortened by their transfer into health care facilities offering less intensive, less costly skilled nursing care. In addition to the perceived cost savings advantages, improvements in the overall quality of care provided to Medicare beneficiaries were anticipated through new access to a broader continuum of care.

Ultimately, the most profound effects of the Extended Care Program were the financial incentives created for hospitals and nursing homes to enter into the extended care business. For nursing home administrators, certification as an extended care facility (ECF) meant a new source of revenue beyond that obtained for the traditional custodial care of long-term, and often permanent, residents. Within less than a year of the program implementation, 4,160 facilities had obtained Medicare certification for the provision of extended care. The majority of these facilities were functioning nursing homes.

Similarly, many hospital administrators perceived new financial incentives for the integration of long-term care services into existing acute care structures. Incentives were now in place for hospitals to consider managing nursing homes for the purpose of providing subacute, extended care to their hospitalized Medicare patients.

Subacute focus and internal management. Administrators at Hospital X, in search of mechanisms to improve the financial health of their hospital, believed that the addition of extended care beds would provide the organization with a new source of revenue. In 1968, in response to the incentives of the Extended Care Program, a nursing home facility was built on the hospital campus.

The nursing home beds were used for persons primarily in need of subacute care. For instance, the majority of beds were used for stroke and hip fracture rehabilitation. The remaining beds were used for a range of inpatient chronic care services including respite care for elderly community residents and short- and long-term care of a limited number of psychiatric and drug-dependent patients.

Administrative synergies, or coordinated management activities between the hospital and the nursing home, evolved almost exclusively in an indirect manner from the fiduciary responsibilities of the hospital board that resulted from the hospital's ownership of the nursing home. The administration of the nursing home was within the purview of the hospital board and was conducted by the hospital administrative staff. Incidental administrative synergies resulted from this relationship and included, for example, paying hospital and nursing home nurses on the same salary schedule and intermittently floating (sharing) nursing staff between the acute and long-term care settings.

Clinical synergies, or integrated clinical activities between the acute and long-term care facilities, also evolved, in a somewhat limited and indirect manner. These synergies resulted not from hospital policy or procedure but indirectly from the federal government mandates that required extended care patients be admitted directly from hospital settings. Communications between hospital and nursing home clinical staff, for example, did occur but were limited to irregular transactions regarding transfers of hospitalized Medicare patients to the nursing home. There were no mandated requirements pertaining to the communication of clinically relevant patient-level information between facilities other than the documentation of the required hospitalization prior to ECF admission. Clinically oriented interactions among acute and long-term care providers at Hospital X were often informal and were enhanced by the geographic proximity of the two facilities as well as the sharing of nursing staff. Neither systematic flow of patient information occurred, nor were there any formal mechanisms in place for enhancing the continuity of care for patients transferred between the facilities.

Outcomes: Unmet expectations. On a national level, the cost-saving outcomes of the Extended Care Program proved disappointing. The original expectation that the availability of extended care would decrease the length of Medicare beneficiaries' hospital stays was not realized. Moreover, the average daily cost of extended care was more than 50 percent higher than had been anticipated (Vladeck 1987). Hospital X, in particular, lost money through the addition of the nursing home rather than realizing a new source of revenue. In the early 1970s, for example, the annual loss of revenue directly attributed to the nursing home operation averaged $150,000. In addition to the unanticipated cost of skilled care, other reasons cited by Hospital X's administrators for the financial losses were poor management, undue influence of selected board members, and poor initial market analysis.

In spite of the unexpected costs of extended care, the quality of care for Medicare beneficiaries may well have been enhanced by the program because of the added services it provided for hospitalized patients. The overwhelming demand for extended care among Medicare beneficiaries is evident in the budget outlays in the early years of the program. Between 1967 and 1969 the number of extended care service claims paid by Medicare rose from less than a third of a million to 1.1 million; the total benefits increased from $100 million to $400 million (Witkin 1971).

Extended care policy revisions (1973–1980)

As early as 1969, federal regulations pertaining to extended care coverage were revised. Out of concern for the vast and rapid expansion of the program, the scope of coverage under the benefit was narrowed. Stroke rehabilitation, for example, was a service no longer covered by the program. For extended care facilities such as the one owned by Hospital X, in which stroke rehabilitation was an important source of revenue, the revisions resulted in major financial losses. The financial losses were compounded as intermediary insurance companies retroactively denied facilities' claims for billings for extended care services no longer covered by the policy.

In 1972 further limitations of the extended care benefits were instituted; facilities were no longer certified as "extended care facilities"; they were now called "skilled nursing facilities" (Vladeck 1987). The incentives for a hospital to be involved in the provision of subacute care of hospitalized Medicare patients in nursing home settings were changed significantly.

Long-term focus and external management. In the mid-1970s, in response to the shifting incentives and financial losses associated with the Extended Care Program, administrators at Hospital X made two important changes in the function and management structure of their nursing home. First, the emphasis of the care was shifted from providing subacute care to Medicare patients to providing long-term care to persons of varying pay sources. Second, the management was turned over through a lease arrangement to an external for-profit nursing home operation.

Outcomes: Continued unmet expectations. Under the new lease arrangement, which lasted for five years, both administrative and clinical interactions between the hospital and nursing home diminished significantly. From an administrative standpoint, all preexisting coordinated activities were discontinued. The for-profit organization assumed complete responsibility for the nursing home administration, including personnel management. No longer were administrative and clinical personnel shared between the two facilities. Moreover, the informal clinical-level cooperation that had existed among care providers in the acute and long-term care facility was also diminished with the discontinuation of sharing nursing staff between the facilities.

Under the lease arrangement, the quality of care provided in the nursing home declined. The majority of residents admitted to the facility required heavy long-term care; 50 percent of the residents were Medicaid-funded. The wear and tear on the facility of the patients requiring heavy care was significant. Presumably due to a profit motive, capital was not reinvested in the facility for upkeep, and as a result, the physical plant reportedly deteriorated. Moreover, family members of nursing home residents often complained to the hospital administrators about the low level of quality provided in the nursing home. Because of a lack of compliance with mandatory care standards, the state Department of Social and Health Services placed the home on probationary status for several years during this period.

Medicare Prospective Payment System (1981–1986)

A prospective payment system (PPS) for the reimbursement of Medicare hospital services was anticipated by Hospital X administrators in the early 1980s. Faced with the necessity of maintaining their competitive position, administrators sought innovative ways to decrease the length of patient hospital stays. To this end, the federal regulatory system, through Medicare PPS, reestablished financial incentives for hospital administrators to reintegrate acute and inpatient long-term care services within one organization.

Under the new reimbursement pressures of PPS, skilled nursing facilities were viewed by Hospital X administrators as a potential solution to the management problems resulting from a reimbursement system such as PPS, in which payments for hospital care were linked to a fixed number of inpatient days according to diagnostic categories. Reducing a Medicare patient's length of hospital stay was generally seen as an effective strategy for maximizing the potential financial gains from a fixed payment system. Within the context of the new PPS, discharging a patient before the maximum number of days reimbursed by Medicare had financial advantages, and discharging a patient no later than the maximum number of days was a financial necessity. A key administrative dilemma was how to minimize the length of inpatient stays without compromising the quality of hospital-based care. To this end, subacute skilled nursing care reemerged as a important strategy for Hospital X's administrators.

Turbulent alliances. In 1981, Hospital X's corporate strategy involved regaining the nursing home lease as a way of obtaining greater control in the nursing home management and increased flexibility in the hospital's use of the facility. The intent was not only to cope with a future PPS. During the years that the nursing home facility had been externally managed, the hospital administration had felt the damaging effects of the nursing home's declining reputation in the community for providing poor quality of care. The initial ownership of the facility by the hospital, as well as the continued close physical proximity of the two facilities, served to perpetuate the community's association of the nursing home with the hospital administration. By regaining the lease, hospital administrators hoped to improve the facility's quality of care and improve its reputation in the community.

Under the hospital's management the administrative liaisons between the hospital and the nursing home were reestablished. Foremost, financial subsidies from hospital revenues were used to support the nursing home operations. Moreover, Hospital X managers were responsible for nursing home administrative matters, including personnel. A new nursing home administrator and a new director of nursing services were hired and were responsible to the hospital administration. At the same time, however, some degree of separation of the administration of both services was formally established. A separate board of trustees was established solely for the nursing home, and the financial accounting was contracted out to an external accounting firm.

In contrast to the strengthened administrative linkages, clinical synergies did not improve and were, as before, more or less incidental to patient transfers from one facility to the other. Assurances for the continuity of care for transferred patients, for example, were nonexistent. Limited clinical information about a transferred patient was shared between care providers in the two settings. Neither formal nor informal communication across the two service lines regularly occurred. Structural barriers to clinical coordination between acute and long-term care services had evolved under the previous external management contract arrangements. Further, major differences in philosophies of patient care had emerged between the hospital and nursing home staff. These different views of appropriate care were perceived as primary deterrents to communication.

Ironically, the informal clinical synergies that had existed under previous management arrangements diminished further with the new reintegration of acute and long-term care services. The decline was related not to prohibitive structural or clinical features of integration but to changing nursing home referral patterns by physicians practicing at Hospital X. The nursing home's reputation under the external management contract for providing poor quality of care had a delayed but very real effect on physician referral patterns; physicians began referring to other nursing homes within the community. Moreover, while the hospital's nursing home had been the major placement source of hospitalized patients needing subacute or long-term care, the social work department instituted a general policy of presenting patients' multiple placement choices within the community.

With the reintegration of service lines, evidence of financial improvements were soon apparent in the nursing home's financial reports. Within one year, however, the accounting system proved to be in error, and the payroll expenses could not be met. In 1983 hospital management fired the nursing home administrator and transferred accounting to hospital-based services. A new nursing home administrator was hired. The primary administrative changes included stabilizing the nursing staff and improving the quality of care. Within six months of the new administrator's arrival, the financial status of the nursing home improved; within 18 months, professionals and community members considered the nursing home to be a well-run nursing home with good quality clinical care. The hospital management promoted the administrator to a higher level of management within the overall organization and early in 1985 hired another nursing home administrator to take his place.

Within a short period of time after improvements were evident, hospital administrators decided again to transfer the nursing home management responsibilities to another external for-profit nursing home operation. Like before, administrative synergies between the two facilities were limited by the separation of management. The hiring of personnel was again transferred to the outside management group, and the directors of nursing services were replaced. Limited formal and informal linkages were retained, however. The external managers retained the nursing home administrator the hospital hired. In addition, an advisory board consisting of selected members of the hospital board was established to guide the nursing home management decisions.

The new management immediately reduced the ratio of nurses per resident from one nurse to eight or nine heavy care residents to one to ten or twelve residents. During this time nursing home staff turnover markedly increased and their level of morale reportedly dropped. Within a few months after the new management took over, the nursing home was closed by the state Department of Social and Health Services due to cited violations in state nursing home standards.

The hospital immediately, and for the last time, resumed management of the facility, and as a result it was reopened by the state agency. Once again, a new administrator and director of nursing services were hired by the hospital management. Administrative synergies were, as before, a by-product of the accountability of the nursing home managers to the hospital administrators. Direct efforts were made to improve the quality of care provided to all residents. Most importantly, a restorative care program and quality assurance program were instituted.

Two important changes had occurred prior to the final reintegration. First, between 1980 and 1985, Hospital X's reliance on inpatient long-term care had increased dramatically. While the hospital patient volume stayed fairly constant during these years, the number of patients transferred annually to nursing homes within the community more than doubled. At the same time, the annual rate of nursing home resident transfers to acute care settings had stayed fairly constant. From 1982 to 1988, the annual percentage of nursing home residents (excluding hospice residents) discharged to a hospital ranged from 26 percent to 33 percent. In addition, the patterns of hospital referral remained consistent; 70 to 75 percent of all hospitalized residents were admitted to Hospital X.

Second, major changes occurred in the payment source of the residents. Prior to 1981 the majority of the residents were Medicaid-funded. However, between 1982 and 1984 only 10 percent were covered by Medicaid; approximately 70 percent of the residents were covered by Medicare, and 20 percent by private insurance. In 1985 a hospice program comprising seven inpatient beds was begun in the nursing home. By 1986 approximately 30 percent of all the nursing home admissions were hospice patients who had an average length of stay (LOS) of one week.

By 1987 the nursing home was generating profits of $250,000 annually. All the profits were reinvested back into the nursing home facility.

The change in the financial status of the nursing home was viewed by administrators as a sign of improvements.

Outcomes: More unmet expectations. Contrary to expectation, the final integration of acute and inpatient long-term care at Hospital X had not proved to be a successful approach for reducing Medicare patients' length of hospital stay. Hospital administrators attributed this result, in part, to the finding that Medicare patients in need of additional care tended to be discharged to their homes with a referral to the hospital-based home care program rather than admitted to the nursing home. In addition, the hospital's costs associated with the placement of hospitalized patients into skilled nursing care facilities had not been minimized through their alliance with the nursing home. The costs associated with hospital personnel arranging the discharge planning for elderly patients, or those costs associated with the delay of nursing home placement, were not minimized.

Increasing competition (1986–present)

The Medicare PPS proved to be initially beneficial to Hospital X's financial position, demonstrated by a 20 percent increase in Medicare payments to the hospital between 1983 and 1986. Late in 1986, however, the profits realized from the PPS program began to decline. The hospital's costs for Medicare patients had increased significantly during the years after the program was instituted. Moreover, the average length of hospital stay for Medicare patients, which had shown some decline in the early PPS years, had begun to rise. Incremental increases in Medicare reimbursement had not been sufficient to cover the increased costs faced by Hospital X administrators for the care of Medicare recipients. In addition, the financial concerns were compounded by a gradually declining hospital census.

Restructuring the continuum of care. In response to the threats of increasing competition in the local hospital industry, the corporation developed a strategic plan to (1) increase the hospital referral base, (2) create a new source of revenue, and (3) decrease inpatient LOS. The specific strategy encompassed, in part, a restructuring of the existing long-term care services provided by the corporation. The restructuring included closing the traditional nursing home services, with the exception of the hospice beds, and converting the remaining licensed skilled nursing beds to short-term (less than one-month stay) skilled nursing care and more inpatient rehabilitation beds. The availability of more inpatient rehabilitation beds was expected to attract more patients who required both hospital care and rehabilitation, thus increasing patient volume. The new short-term skilled nursing service line was expected be a new source of revenue for the corporation and a mechanism for decreasing elderly patient's length of hospital stay.

Changing the organization's mission. For two decades following the construction of the nursing home on their campus, administrators at Hospital X and care providers remained committed to the provision of long-term care services; long-term care was viewed as an integral part of the organization's mission. In the mid-1980s, however, the corporation's administrators began to question the organization's role in the provision of chronic care services. Long-term care services and specifically the nursing home services as they existed were perceived as custodial care and inconsistent with the focus on tertiary care and prevention emerging within the organization. The provision of custodial care began to be seen as inconsistent with the mission of the corporation. In view of the shifting mission, management considered the restructuring of the acute–long-term care continuum to be "getting out of the nursing home business" and making better use of the nursing home facility.

The strategy of restructuring chronic care services reflected not only a shift in the mission of the organization but a basic reconceptualization of the corporation's continuum of care. From the manager's perspective, the restructuring resulted in two changes in the hospital continuum: (1) the elimination of the end point of the care continuum, namely, custodial long-term care, and (2) the building of services that filled the preexisting gaps along the acute–chronic care continuum. Specifically, both rehabilitation and short-term skilled care were viewed as critical intermediary services that lie on the care continuum between acute and custodial chronic care services.

The strategy of filling in the gaps was thought to be consistent with an emerging commitment on the part of the medical staff and management to return hospitalized patients to community living. The rehabilitation and short-term skilled nursing services were anticipated to prevent a patient's need for long-term nursing home placement and thus better serving the needs of the community.

Anticipated outcomes. Beyond the creation of a new financial base, additional benefits are expected from the restructuring strategy. First, the transaction costs associated with the placement of hospitalized patients into settings providing subacute care, which were not minimized under the previous alliances, are anticipated to be reduced substantially under the new arrangements. Having intermediary care services such as the short-term skilled nursing care available to patients who might otherwise be transferred to a long-term skilled care facility is expected to eliminate the time and effort required of hospital staff to secure nursing home placements. Moreover, the quality of care provided to the hospitalized patient who is at risk for nursing home placement is expected to improve: That is, the long-term financial and personal costs of rapid and inappropriate placement in a long-term care facility occurring under the pressures of early hospital discharge might be averted through the availability of a short-term care setting.

Finally, the corporation developed two innovative programs that are expected to improve both the administrative and clinical synergies between the chronic care service lines and the acute care hospital. First, a matrix management board model was instituted in 1987 in which financial, strategic, quality standards, and governance management areas are integrated administratively across service lines within the organization by matrix committees and management structure. For example, the finance committee and the vice-president for finance are responsible for financial management of the hospital, the nursing home, and the for-profit service lines.

Second, the corporation has begun a new case management program in which certain diagnostic groups, such as persons with hip fractures, are monitored by nurse case managers across acute and chronic care service lines according to clinical practice and resource use standards developed for their diagnostic group. A case management structure of this type is expected to formalize provider communication and information flow for given patients across the acute and chronic care settings and to break down traditional philosophical barriers among nurses and other providers working in different care settings.

References

Vladeck, B. C. 1987. "History of Medicare Extended Care." In *Medicare and Extended Care: Issues, Problems, and Prospects*, edited by B. C. Vladeck and G. J. Alfano, 5–13. Owing Mills, MD: National Health Publishing.

Witkin, E. 1971. "The Extended Care Facility." In *Impact of Medicare*, Ch. 11, 92–102. Springfield, IL: C. C. Thomas.

Suggested Reading

Aiken, J. H. "Extended Care: The Hospital's Perspective." In *Medicare and Extended Care: Issues, Problems, and Prospects*, edited by B. C. Vladeck and G. J. Alfano, 15–24. Owing Mills, MD: National Health Publishing, 1987.

Part **II**

Building and Balancing
Systems and Structures

Corporate Restructuring: Phase II

James D. Hart and Mary Ann Goeppele

Organizational Information

This case study describes the corporate reorganization of a 194-bed, nonprofit, acute care, community hospital that has been in operation for the past 27 years. This hospital serves a residential area of a major West Coast city. In the early 1980s the hospital adopted a holding-company corporate structure in response to economic, regulatory, diversification, and taxation issues. The holding company acted as parent for the hospital, a nursing home owned by the hospital, and a newly formed for-profit subsidiary. The nursing home, originally run as a division of the hospital, was separately incorporated when an outside party was retained to run this facility. Activities of the more recently formed for-profit subsidiary include the management of several medical office buildings and the operation of a home health care agency, a sports medicine clinic, and an outpatient pharmacy as well as the management of a joint venture with physicians.

The parent holding company was charged with the responsibility for the coordination and allocation of resources for the three subsidiary corporations. This corporate structure created an overlap of trustee membership on the various boards, a duplication of committees reporting to each subsidiary board, and fragmented communication between the various subsidiaries and the parent board. In 1986, the trustees of all the boards were called together for a retreat to explore ways to improve the functioning of the corporate structure. It was agreed that some modification to the governance system then in place was necessary to address issues of communication and appropriate direction of the activities of the for-profit subsidiary.

Background of the Problem

The 1980s witnessed a proliferation of new corporate structures for hospitals. The proliferation was largely due to increased pressures in the economic arena. The most common model of a hospital corporate restructure includes a parent holding company with several subsidiary corporations. While other models are available, this one appears to be the most prevalent and is the model that this case study will examine.

The impetus for restructuring may have been generated from a variety of sources, but the most obvious source was due to encouragement from consulting and legal firms that sold the concept with great vigor. Generally, the causes most frequently stated for restructuring included the financial impact of Medicare reimbursement and the need to deal with competitive forces. The envisioned culmination of the restructuring efforts was to be additional profit. While there is an element of truth and accuracy in some of the direction given, the implementation of new structures was fraught with difficulty. The creation of multiple corporations often resulted in compounding managerial problems, rather than resolving perceived difficulties for many institutions.

Twenty years ago, community hospitals generally consisted of an acute care facility with limited outpatient services such as physical therapy and emergency. Today these hospitals have expanded their operations to include a broad spectrum of health care services serving a broad array of community needs. Many of these hospitals have diversified vigorously, hoping to find a panacea for many of their financial problems when, in fact, diversification has resulted in the deterioration of their resource base. Managerial efforts have often been stretched beyond effectiveness, and trustees have grown confused and overburdened with information.

To add further complication, the theme of competition has been continually placed before chief executive officers (CEOs). Obviously, tough-minded CEOs must appear to thrive on competition and have often felt compelled to diversify the facilities as an indication of dynamic management style. Meanwhile, in spite of all the talk of competition, the issues of regulation were never removed and in some states have continued to increase. In Washington State, the governmental agencies are fond of the oxymoron *regulated competition*.

Hospital management groups now find themselves not only trying to manage a declining census but also trying to support a wide variety of business entities such as home health services, sports medicine, clinics, freestanding laboratories, skilled nursing facilities, preventive medicine programs for the elderly, and urgent care centers. To complicate matters further, this variety of services has been expanded to include joint ventures with the medical staff.

The most evident danger in restructuring a hospital into a diversified multicorporate entity is the loss of focus on the major purpose of the diversification. Corporate reorganizations were initially enacted to protect the hospital, "the cash cow," and to keep the hospital healthy and viable. Over a period of time, as a variety of diversified activities are started, management tends to become preoccupied with the process of building these allied businesses. This organization experienced what the CEO described as the "deal-of-the-day mentality." The deals became more important and interesting than running the hospital. Interaction with the medical staff took on a new focus with physicians more interested in discussing business ventures rather than quality or service issues. The entrepreneurial mind-set was very easy to slide into and became all-consuming because it is much more interesting and satisfying to manage rapidly growing enterprises than to manage stable or declining businesses.

Identification of the problem areas:
Governing board perspective

Timely and accurate communication proved to be the biggest problem resulting from the 1981 restructure. The restructure established four boards largely composed of outside representatives. In spite of an overlap of membership on the boards, most trustees received fragmented information concerning the activities of other corporations and therefore struggled with identifying their own appropriate role. It simply was not possible to communicate every major issue adequately. While the CEO often repeated the same report at several board meetings, some board members heard the same information two or three times while others never heard it. In an attempt to deal with the communication situation, a proliferation of paper (in the form of minutes, newsletters, and memoranda) to the various boards and their respective members was created in the hope of keeping everyone fully informed. Communication "overkill" and lack of communication were ever-present problems.

Decisions could volley between the four boards for months. For example, the for-profit subsidiary met to agree on the purchase of a parking lot for hospital employees. The hospital board then met to agree on the terms of leasing the property. Finally, the parent corporation met to guarantee the loan transaction for the financing institution only to refer it back to the for-profit subsidiary.

This hospital's problems were further exacerbated because the parent holding company board was charged with the responsibility of coordinating and allocating resources for all the corporations. The members of the hospital board believed that the hospital was viewed by all other subsidiaries of the institution as the cash cow. Resistance from the hospital board grew as they saw monies being drained away from the hospital to establish a series of business entities in the other corporations over which they had no say or control. The hospital board began to perceive itself as a rubber stamp for the parent corporation, and this situation was not acceptable. Lengthy discussions ensued about which board had the major responsibility for the allocation of resources.

The committee structures of the various corporations also overlapped. Quality assurance committees were functioning in the nursing home and hospital, but a committee had not been established for the home health nursing program, causing concern to management and the board. Each entity had a finance committee that made recommendations to its board. Decisions were made at the board level that served the entity but not necessarily the overall corporate good. The same could be said about multiple committees dealing with planning issues.

When reflecting on these poorly defined roles, one must keep in mind that the 1981 organizational structure was blessed by at least two consulting firms and two major, nationally recognized legal firms that purported to have a depth of experience in complex corporate issues. On paper, the organization appeared feasible; nevertheless, practical management of this organization revealed deficiencies. Two obvious questions needed to be asked: How can the various boards be assured that the specific activities they recommend and approve contribute to the best overall use of the organization's resources and management time? and How can the subsidiary boards be assured that the vision and overall plan for the future of the organization is being maintained? It was obvious the boards had become task-oriented and were not fulfilling their mutual responsibilities toward maintaining a unified corporate vision.

Identification of the problem areas:
Management perspective

Management was equally frustrated by the enormous amount of time needed to prepare materials for three to four board meetings each month, not to mention the numerous committee meetings of the several boards. Early in 1986, the CEO wrote a letter to the chairman of the parent board and expressed dissatisfaction with the structure. The CEO did not recommend doing away with the restructured corporate model at that time but recommended a modification of the consultant's model to suit the organization's unique needs. Dialogues with individuals who had several years of participation on the various boards were held to identify the problem areas and to establish guidelines and principles that could be used in realigning the corporations. The CEO also believed that management had committed itself to increased activity under this organizational structure that was not always productive. The organization's focus had been drawn away from serving the hospital to building fiefs and cutting deals. Management time had not been recognized as a resource.

Criteria for Modification

In light of these issues, a board retreat was called. All outside trustees and directors who served on the various boards were invited. Materials presented at the retreat did not suggest solutions but were designed to help the trustees and directors identify structural problems and develop criteria by which to judge an improved corporate structure. At the conclusion of the retreat, the trustees and directors endorsed the development of a structure that would meet the following criteria:

- Adequate communication
- Better cross-corporate coordination of related activities
- Effective overall strategic direction
- Efficient use of board and management time
- Enhanced board recruitment and development programs
- Improved ability for management to carry out its responsibilities
- Safeguarding of the hospital's tax-exempt status

The CEO examined a series of models that would meet these criteria. Initial efforts to explore alternatives began with a review of the health care literature and case studies of other hospital reorganizations. Time was also spent searching for an outside consultant who might provide innovative concepts. Both these efforts failed to yield satisfactory organizational models. Much of what was found suggested even more cumbersome corporate structures than the one already in place.

It became evident that some unique corporate structures had been in place for many years in the industrialized sector of our economy. This organization first studied successful retail companies in its area. These companies did not provide appropriate answers because they did not have the unique problems and complexities of the modern hospital organization. The search then turned to the high-technology industries, where more suitable models were found.

A variety of books further stimulated thinking about the effectiveness of traditional, hierarchical, organizational structures. The writings of Rosabeth Moss Kanter, Ph.D. (1983), a professor at Yale University's School of Management in a book called *The Change Masters*, were particularly influential. The book, based on a study of major U.S. companies, sought to identify corporate management and structural characteristics that contribute to a high level of innovation and success. Kanter's book contends that successful companies are departing from conventional notions of management. Key characteristics of today's highly successful and innovative companies include matrix organizational structures and an emphasis on horizontal corporate communication. These attributes enhance the organization's ability to act quickly as new requirements present themselves, largely because both trustees and managers are able to focus on the broader vision of the overall organization.

As a concept of a new organizational structure began to form, the CEO sought out two members of the governing boards. One individual was the managing partner of a large, national accounting firm. He was asked to describe organizational structures he had encountered, what elements he considered most important to their success, and why. The second board member was a corporate attorney who acts as legal counsel for the largest industrial company in the region. As legal counsel for this high-technology, widely diversified organization, the attorney could identify some usable attributes within its structure. The attorney was asked to describe how a decision flowed through the various entities within this large company and its multiple divisions. From these conversations, it was evident that the successful, diversified organization required empowering management with broader responsibilities and that the governing board must continually focus on overseeing and policy-setting responsibilities. Simplification of the organization appeared to be the answer. Equipped with this information and experience, management began to design options.

Administrative Decision

The presentation of three models

Three organizational models were developed and presented to the board members of the four corporations at a miniretreat held at a local hotel. The format of the session was very specifically focused and enabled the presentation of issues in a minimal amount of time.

While all three models provided that all board members would be asked to serve on the parent board and on the parent board committee structure, they differed by offering progressive levels of consolidation and delegation of operational issues to management.

As illustrated in Figures 5.1, 5.2, and 5.3, all three models provided that five committees would be established at the parent company level and would be matrixed across the operating affiliates to address particular types of issues for all the subsidiaries. All policy issues involving reserve powers of the parent corporation would flow through the appropriate committee for recommendations. The committees include executive, finance, strategic, quality standards, and governance.

The executive committee would be empowered to act on behalf of the parent corporation in emergencies between meetings. The decisions of the executive committee would then be reviewed by the entire board of trustees at its regular meeting. Members of this committee would also determine the compensation of the CEO and establish a conceptual framework for an incentive plan to reward top management for performance. The executive committee would, at a minimum, include officers of the parent corporation and the CEO. (Under the quasi-management board model, chairpersons of each operating corporation—selected among the outside directors of the parent corporation—would also be included as members of the executive committee.)

Each of the remaining board members would select an assignment on one or more of the other matrixed committees, commensurate with his or her interests and expertise. A brief description of the role of each committee follows.

By serving for all the operating affiliates simultaneously, members of the finance committee would be in a better position to audit periodically the financial performance of the operating corporations and to ensure that resources are judiciously allocated throughout the overall corporation. This arrangement would also provide an opportunity to maximize the return on investment and to minimize the cost of borrowed capital.

Members of the strategic committee would focus on periodically updating the strategic and long-range plans for the overall organization. They would also review and recommend management proposals for new products and services throughout the organization, formulate guidelines for an overall marketing plan, and make research and development policy recommendations.

The members of the quality standards committee would define and monitor quality standards to help ensure that patients and physicians receive quality service throughout the continuum of care within the corporate family. Safety and environmental standards and the review of all quality issues would be within the purview of this committee.

Members of the governance committee would take on the tasks of board recruitment, orientation, and development, including education on ethical issues. They would monitor legislative activities at the national, state, and local levels. Members of this committee would also develop the goals and objectives by which the board(s) would perform self-evaluations.

Additional ad hoc committees would be formed, and special subcommittees of the above committees would be appointed as necessary.

The three alternative models provided for progressive levels of management responsibility with the management board model providing the greatest degree of management autonomy. Briefly described, the models included the following.

In addition to asking all outside board members to serve on the parent board, the interlocking board model (Figure 5.1) provided for dual appointments whereby half of the board members would serve on a not-for-profit operating board and half would serve on a for-profit operating board. Under this plan, activities of the nursing home would be merged into the hospital board while the different nature of the for-profit corporation activities would be maintained under a separate operating corporation. Management membership on the operating boards would be limited to the CEO and the chief operating officer (COO) of each organization. The parent board would meet quarterly, and the operating boards would meet during the remaining months.

Under the quasi-management board model (Figure 5.2), in addition to serving on the parent board, selected board members of the parent corporation would be appointed as chairpersons of the three operating corporations while the rest of the operating board members would be selected from the senior management team.

Under the management board model (Figure 5.3), outside board members would serve on a strong, central parent board that would maintain reserve powers over the activities of the affiliated operating corporations. The operating boards would be composed exclusively of members from the senior management team.

Each of these models was designed to help the outside board and management to reflect on the distinct role of the governing board and the distinct role of management. The miniretreat provided an opportunity for thorough discussion of the three options, and at the conclusion of the retreat, the board decided to adopt the management board model on a trial basis. The management board model was chosen for the following reasons: It afforded the greatest opportunity to expedite the flow of communication; it created the least number of meetings involving outside

Figure 5.1 Interlocking Board Model

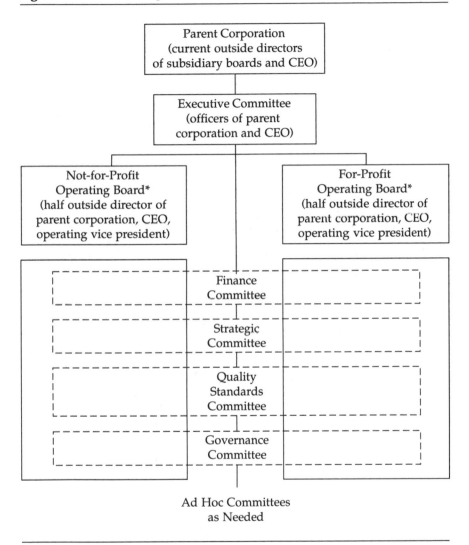

Parent Corporation
(current outside directors
of subsidiary boards and CEO)

Executive Committee
(officers of parent
corporation and CEO)

Not-for-Profit
Operating Board*
(half outside director of
parent corporation, CEO,
operating vice president)

For-Profit
Operating Board*
(half outside director of
parent corporation, CEO,
operating vice president)

Finance
Committee

Strategic
Committee

Quality
Standards
Committee

Governance
Committee

Ad Hoc Committees
as Needed

* No committee structure at operating board level.

trustees; it provided the clearest delineation between governance and management; and it provided the best use of administrative time and talent. In addition, the matrix committee structure to be part of all three models eliminated the need for the structural redundancy present in both the interlocking board model and the quasi-management board model.

Figure 5.2   Quasi-Management Board Model

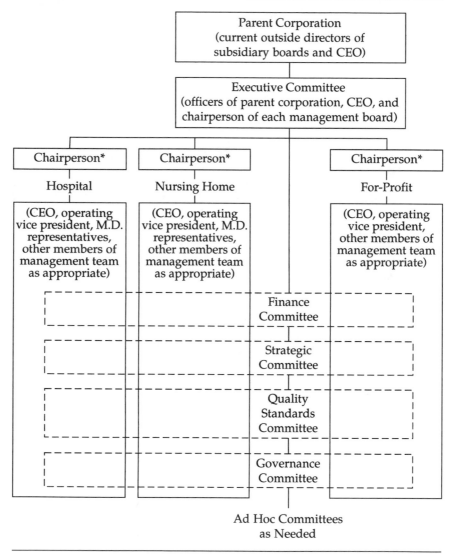

Parent Corporation
(current outside directors of
subsidiary boards and CEO)

Executive Committee
(officers of parent corporation, CEO, and
chairperson of each management board)

Chairperson*   Chairperson*   Chairperson*

Hospital   Nursing Home   For-Profit

(CEO, operating
vice president, M.D.
representatives,
other members of
management team
as appropriate)

(CEO, operating
vice president, M.D.
representatives,
other members of
management team
as appropriate)

(CEO, operating
vice president,
other members of
management team
as appropriate)

Finance
Committee

Strategic
Committee

Quality
Standards
Committee

Governance
Committee

Ad Hoc Committees
as Needed

* Outside director from parent corporation.

If the trustees did not feel comfortable in taking the largest step forward with the adoption of the management board model, the interlocking board model provided the parent board with the greatest degree of board control through its overlapping structure, while the quasi-management

Figure 5.3   Management Board Model

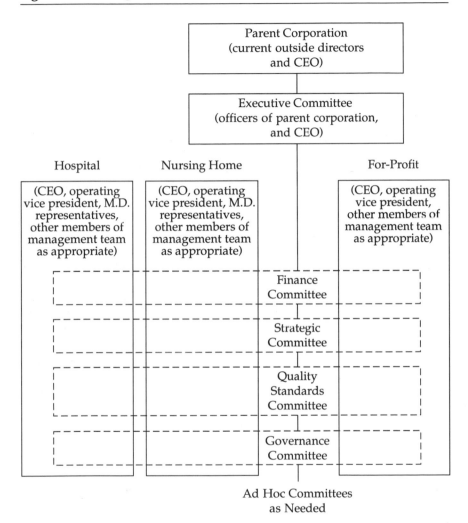

Ad Hoc Committees
as Needed

board afforded a watchdog approach through the appointment of an outside trustee chairperson.

The implementation of the new model

All the outside trustees and directors serving on the various corporate boards were asked to serve on the parent board. The outside trustees were also asked to serve on one or more of the four matrix committees of the parent board to recommend policies for all the operating subsidiaries. The board members demonstrated their willingness to experiment with management's ideas and also demonstrated their commitment to finding the best structure for their organization. Their willingness to risk and to commit to trying the new structure was a clear indication of their confidence in management and in each other.

The decision to implement the management board model occurred in September 1986, and the remainder of that year was spent organizing to implement the new structure. A major part of preparation for the reorganization included the development of functional protocols for the matrix board committees. Issues such as the frequency of committee meetings, record keeping, agenda format, key areas of involvement, reporting functions, and the identification of immediate projects were addressed.

The importance of the matrix committees

It should also be noted that considerable care was taken to limit the number of regular matrix committees to four by focusing on key organizational areas. The key management areas included finance, quality, and strategic issues, while the governance area focused on maintaining a qualified, well-informed parent board. As shown in Figure 5.3, these four committees, each chaired by an outside trustee of the parent board, include the finance, strategic, quality standards, and governance committees. As previously discussed, this simple committee structure allows the trustees to address particular functions for all the operating affiliates, and it is appropriately called a matrix committee structure. The matrix committees are responsible for developing policies, guidelines and recommendations for approval by the parent board on issues presented to them by the subsidiary corporations. Each committee chairperson has an assistant. The assistant is a senior member of the management staff and is responsible for keeping the committee chairperson informed and prepared for committee activities. Each member of the senior management team is charged with the responsibility of proposing the annual goals and objectives of the matrix committee and for seeing that they are properly integrated into management goals and objectives. When completed, both committee and management goals and objectives are shared with the parent board.

Activities of the operating subsidiaries

The subsidiaries, including the hospital, the nursing home, and the for-profit corporation, are governed by boards composed of elected and nonelected (ex officio) board members. Elected operating board members include senior members of the management team. Appointments must be approved by the parent board annually. Nonelected operating board members include the CEO of the overall corporation, the chief of the medical staff, and the president of the auxiliary. Formal management board meetings are held monthly. Agendas, minutes, and other formal records are maintained. The activities of the subsidiaries are reported monthly to the management boards, and management board reports are presented at the monthly parent board meeting. The members of the parent board are welcome to attend any of the subsidiary operating board meetings, should they so desire. The keeping of minutes and the preparation of agendas and background materials is taken as serious business by the management group. The management board meetings are formally run and structured. They are not treated as simple administrative staff meetings, which have a tendency at times to deteriorate into chatting and viewing societies.

Appointing senior members of the management team to the subsidiary boards affords management the opportunity for operational flexibility within the broadly defined policies and budget determinations of the parent board. This arrangement, which vests management with greater power and responsibility, requires great confidence by the trustees of the parent board.

The greatest benefit of the management board model is the improved use of parent board member time. This arrangement allows parent board members to focus on broader policy and strategic issues for the overall organization. On the other hand, there are times when management decisions could benefit from the well-seasoned business advice that parent board members might provide.

The role and composition of the parent board

The major purpose of the parent board is the recommendation and adoption of major policies for overall institution. The control of the overall organization is also maintained by the parent board through reserve powers. Only the parent board may change or repeal bylaws or articles of incorporation of any of the corporations or change resolutions adopted by the subsidiary board. The parent board also maintains the authority to elect and remove trustees of any of the boards and board committees. Other reserve powers include major sale or transfer of corporate property, mergers, consolidations, and acquisitions.

To be effective in its policy-setting role and in the exercising of its reserve powers, the parent board must maintain adequate and balanced representation in a number of key areas. These areas include physician representatives who can monitor clinical aspects of the services offered, individuals who represent community interests, and various business and professional persons (bankers, attorneys, accountants, etc.) whose background and expertise can assist the organization in specific areas.

Results

Key role of the matrix committees

The matrix committee structure has proven highly effective in promoting a number of positive features. Trustees' areas of expertise have been better used. For example, bankers and a partner of a certified public accounting firm participate on the finance committee. Several physicians serve on the quality standards committee. Trustees who do not have a health care or financial background are provided opportunities to develop greater expertise and in-depth understanding of particular aspects of the organization's operation. As the health care industry moves into an increasingly complex environment, it becomes increasingly important to have seasoned and knowledgeable board members who test and challenge the ideas brought before them by senior management. It is also apparent that the reporting mechanisms have been greatly improved and that better policies are being recommended by the matrix board committees. A wider view of all the subsidiaries tends to make the matrix committees more willing to address difficult issues. As an example, this organization is very pleased with the progress made by the quality standards committee in developing a comprehensive quality measurement program that addresses the care offered, not only to the hospital but also in the skilled nursing unit and the home health care agency.

The matrix committees, which generally meet monthly for one-and-one-half-hour breakfast meetings, save valuable board time. The parent board has come to rely on the groundwork done by the various committees in familiarizing themselves with all ramifications of particular issues. The parent board generally acts confidently in adopting matrix committee recommendations with few or no changes. In all likelihood, this stems from the very focused nature of the committees, which engenders board confidence in the information and recommendations that are presented for their review and determination. Confusion has been eliminated regarding the role of the parent board, and the board finds more time to deal with its responsibility to oversee the operations of the various corporations and avoids entanglement in minutiae. We calculate that somewhere in the range of 100 meetings annually involving outside board members have been eliminated from the schedules of board members, medical staff, and management.

The adoption of the new model

After testing the management board model for more than one year, the parent board permanently adopted this innovative management board structure in April, 1988. No consideration was given to alternatives at that time or in the two years that have since elapsed.

Three years later: A retrospection. Both the board of trustees and senior management continue to express satisfaction with the corporate structure, and working relations among the trustees have improved significantly. Management has been able to focus on the development of needed programs and services and on the development of a long-range facility plan for the hospital campus, rather than spending time on problems generated by a cumbersome organizational structure. The key issues identified in 1986 have been efficiently addressed with the adoption of the matrix management board model. Outside consultants indicate that this hospital is fortunate to have found the solution at a time when corporate restructure problems remain an issue in many health care organizations.

Much credit goes to the individuals serving on the parent board. They were willing to test a completely new and unproven approach that provided them the opportunity of setting and monitoring board policies and guidelines while delegating operational responsibilities more fully to management. These accomplishments required a tremendous amount of trust on the part of all involved individuals.

Challenges for the future

This hospital will continue to monitor the current corporate structure, ensuring that it maintains a well-diversified cross-section of outside board members. The organization also recognizes the need to provide its outside board members with sufficient opportunities to explore new assignments and to gain new expertise by varying their committee assignments.

Reference

Kanter, R. M. 1983. *The Change Masters*. New York: Simon and Schuster.

Case 6

Centralization and Decentralization in a Vertically Integrated System: The XYZ Hospital Corporation

Arnold D. Kaluzny

Sitting in a conference room, Jay Smith, the president of XYZ Hospital Corporation, his vice-president for research and planning, Kay Adams, and Bill Jones, a private consultant spending time with the system, were reviewing options for the design of the system. The following are just a few of the recent events confronting Smith and his corporate colleagues.

- At a recent administrative board meeting of the corporation, it was revealed that two system hospitals within the same city were each planning to develop a separate air transport service.
- The medical staff of a large system hospital unanimously passed a no confidence vote in the administration of that hospital.
- An administrator with 17 years of service in a rural system hospital was asked to resign.
- System hospitals and long-term care facilities located in different states are required to conform to individual state statutes and market conditions. Increasingly, the compliance is inconsistent, if not in direct conflict, with overall corporate policy.
- While the corporation historically enjoyed a AAA bond rating by Standard and Poor's, there was some concern that the rating might be downgraded to AA.

The system was obviously facing design problems, and it was becoming painfully clear that

- problems were not being recognized in a timely fashion,
- the president of the corporation and his corporate colleagues were being involved and often consumed with specific institutional issues,
- a variety of strategic issues and opportunities were not getting the attention they deserved,
- there appeared to be a great deal of conflict among administrators and corporate level personnel, and
- corporate policy was unable to reconcile conflicting statutes and guidelines affecting member institutions operating in different states.

The System

The XYZ Hospital Corporation is a religious multi-institutional network in which 24 health care institutions are owned and operated; one is managed, and one is leased. Sixteen of these institutions are hospitals and eight are long-term care facilities. The system has 4,470 licensed acute and long-term care beds and employs 12,931 full time equivalent (FTE) employees. The facilities are located in four coastal states with all facilities near major population centers. Of the sixteen hospitals, three have more than 400 beds, five have fewer than 100 beds, and the remainder average about 230 beds per hospital. Of the eight long-term care facilities, three have more than 150 beds, and the remainder have less than 50 beds.

In addition to operating these facilities, the system in 1985 joined with three other health care systems to create a health maintenance organization (HMO) called the Wellness Health Network. The provider group of the network comprises hospitals owned by the sponsoring health systems as well as several community hospitals. The network has developed managed care programs, or outreach health plans, in two of the regions served by the system. One program currently enrolls more than 25,000 people and has 900 participating physicians providing care, and the other involves more than 600 primary care physicians and dentists with services offered to 98 employer groups, enrolling approximately 20,000 people.

The corporation has a history of providing care to the poor and underserved in the community. While many hospitals have done well financially, other hospitals have reported substantial losses in providing such care, given the economic conditions in many communities. Despite their losses, the corporation has chosen to subsidize the institutions by reallocating profits rather than closing or selling such facilities.

Figure 6.1 presents the current corporate structure and its relationship to the operating institutions. Under this scheme, the executive vice president is the chief operating officer (COO) for the corporation, and theoretically, all institutional administrators are accountable to the corporation through this position. In reality, however, the COO position has never been fully accepted by both corporate and institutional personnel, and many administrators relate to both the president and executive vice-president, depending on the issue. In fact, some of the administrators from the larger institutions relate solely to the president, thus bypassing the executive vice president.

How to Proceed?

Smith had recently proposed a regional structure, and the corporation's board had voted not to implement such an effort at that time. Under this proposal, the four states were defined as regions since each geographic area presented a unique set of problems and opportunities. These problems continue. The group reviewed the options and decided that although the board had already voted against a regional structure, perhaps this was the time to review the options and revisit the decision. It was decided that a special meeting should be called, not to arrive at a decision but to review the options.

Jones set forth the agenda for the day:

- Develop a perspective on organization design. What is it and why is it important?
- Clearly identify problems that result from an inappropriate structure.
- Review structural design options against specific criteria.

A perspective on design

Jones defined organizational design as

> the arrangement and the process of arranging activities, roles, or positions in the organization to coordinate effectively the interdependencies that exist and to improve the effectiveness of the organization.

He indicated that this definition of design stresses both the arrangement (i.e., the particular configuration) of the organization as well as the process of arriving at that configuration. The process is particularly critical since a design is never finished. Rather, it represents the balancing of the organization's differentiation and coordination needs over time.

Figure 6.1 Current Design of XYZ Hospital Corporation

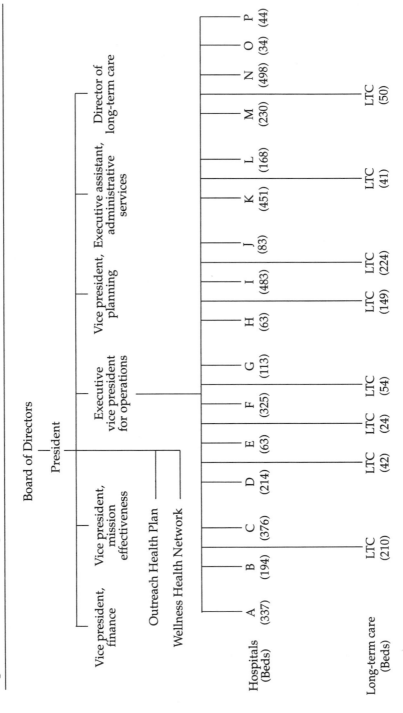

He went on to indicate that these design features are extremely important factors that affect the basic performance of the organization. In fact, in one review of the literature that looked at a number of factors affecting quality, it was concluded that

> Changing the process of care at the individual level is not the only nor necessarily the best means of improving quality of care. To the extent that structural characteristics [design] determine the quality of care, efforts to improve care in the long-term through changing the structure of care [design] may prove to be more cost effective than short-run, quality assurance programs. (Palmer and Reilly 1979)

Secondly, Jones indicated that design is important in that it provides a map reflecting the past power struggles within the organization and perhaps holds the clue to future events within the organization. At the risk of being somewhat presumptuous, one could hypothesize that some of the problems that the system is currently facing could have been predicted given the existing structure of the system.

Finally, he suggested that design is important since it provides the basis for setting realistic limits within which managers function. Structure sets the tone within which basic ongoing processes and culture emerge. Moreover, managers operate on the margin and as the environment changes, structure or restructuring efforts represent the paradigm [or the paradigm shift] within which management operates to adjust to environmental changes. If this structure is inappropriate to the environment, the structure greatly limits the ability of management to be effective, given the challenges that the organization is facing.

While structure is important, Jones stated that the understanding of its role vis-à-vis operations as well as overall performance is embryonic. This understanding is greatly complicated by the fact that there is little agreement on what constitutes effectiveness since different constituent groups within the organization apply different criteria to effectiveness. Moreover, the systematic study of structure vis-à-vis criteria is relatively new, and finally, one cannot overestimate the level of complexity. The notion of design encompasses technical, sociological, political, and psychological factors, and few have the level of sophistication in all these relevant disciplines, thus making this a very slow and difficult area in which to work.

Jones concluded his remarks by suggesting that the appropriate structure is largely contingent on the character of the environment within which the organization functions and the nature of the organization's goals (Duncan 1979). For example, when the nature of goals and environment is simple and fairly static, a more functional type of organization characterized by high levels of centralization is appropriate.

On the contrary, when the environment is complex but in fact can be segmented into more homogeneous components, a more decentralized configuration would be most appropriate. When the design does not fit the environment, organizations tend to experience a number of problems, such as an inability to anticipate problems, an inability to get information to the right people at the right time, or an inability to take corrective action quickly.

Issues and problems associated with the current structure

Given the basic understanding of structure vis-à-vis the environment, the group next discussed various concerns and problems they were currently experiencing within the existing structure. The following issues and subsequent problems were identified.

- There is too much distance between administrators or operating institutions and the governing board: administrators do not have access to the board of directors; response time between the corporate and the hospital levels is too lengthy; those at the corporate level cannot measure the institutional climate and culture or initiate appropriate preventive actions; and the corporate structure does not allow for meaningful input of the board of directors of physicians from the various institutions in administration or of administrators on the governing board.

- There is an ambiguity of roles and difference in perspectives: corporate personnel see the system as highly decentralized while personnel at the institutions see it as highly centralized; there is a lack of common criteria for important policy decisions about resources; there is a lack of consistent criteria for evaluating administrative personnel; the CEO and the board of directors have become too involved with operational activities that do not require their attention. This crowds out other activities and puts their credibility at risk; the CEO and the board of directors have failed to address important policy issues like a strategy for managed care and for long-term care and a cohesive approach to legislative affairs; and the roles of vice presidents involved with planning, operations, mission effectiveness, and public affairs at the corporate level are ambiguous. There is less ambiguity surrounding financial and legal activities.

Structural options

Any decision on structure must be judged against a set of criteria. The board developed the following criteria, which were originally developed as part of the initial discussions on regionalization.

- Strengthen the collective effectiveness and market position of the XYZ System institutions in each area by unifying strategic planning, financial planning, program development, marketing, and the coordination of services.

- Take full advantage of collective resources in seeking out and responding to mission opportunities and market pressures.

- Enhance the effectiveness of the XYZ Corporation institutions by providing greater management oversight and staff support.

- Unify and strengthen the XYZ Corporation voice in state and local public policy affairs and advocacy on behalf of the poor.

- Enhance the effective utilization of management resources.

- Recognize and retain senior executives who are at the top of their organization, thereby providing promotion opportunities for senior associate administrators.

Each of these criteria were discussed and used as a background against which structural options were reviewed.

Discussions, Issues, and Questions

Given the problems facing the XYZ Corporation and the above criteria:

- What structures would be most appropriate?

- What are the advantages and disadvantages of each structure vis-à-vis the criteria?

- Speculate on the advantages and disadvantages of selecting one of the existing administrators within the region and having him or her fulfill the vice-presidential responsibilities along with his or her ongoing administrative functions within an existing institution. Given the obvious disadvantages, how could these difficulties be minimized, and what structural mechanisms (i.e., committees, review processes, etc.) could be developed to resolve problems that you have identified?

References

Duncan, R. 1979. "What Is the Right Structure?" *Organizational Dynamics* (July): 72.

Palmer, R. H., and M. C. Reilly. 1979. "Individual and Institutional Variables Which May Serve as Indicators of Quality of Medical Care." *Medical Care* 17, no. 7 (July): 693–717.

Suggested Readings

Alter, C., and J. Hage. *Organizations Working Together*. Newbury Park, CA: Sage Publications, 1993.

Charns, M. P., and L. J. Smith Tewksbury. *Collaborative Management in Health Care*. San Francisco, Jossey-Bass Publishers, 1993.

Leatt, P., S. M. Shortell, and J. R. Kimberly. "Organizational Design." In *Health Services Management: Organizational Theory and Behavior*, edited by S. M. Shortell and A. D. Kaluzny. Northampton, MA: Delmar Publishers, 1994.

Organizational Control Issues for a Health Maintenance Organization Subsidiary

Jenifer Ehreth

Background

Health care reform initiatives consistently encourage the use of health maintenance organizations (HMOs) as a way of providing cost-effective health services. In the mid-1970s, when the formation of HMOs was first encouraged by the federal government, various organizational forms developed. In one form, the organization contracted with a panel of physicians to provide care. This panel received a reduced rate payment for each service provided by the physician. The patients had financial incentives to use a panel physician as their primary source of health care. This physician acted as a gatekeeper for the use of nonphysician and specialist services and assumed some financial risk for the provision of those services. Many HMOs were formed as joint ventures or subsidiaries of hospitals, physician-owned clinics, or insurance companies. HMO X, a subsidiary of Insurance Company Y, operated from 1974 to 1982 as a prototype of the gatekeeper-model HMO.

HMO X serviced northern California, Washington, and Utah as a subsidiary of Insurance Company Y, which is a nationally recognized insurance company whose product lines are primarily property, casualty, and life insurance. HMO X's product was health insurance coverage in the form of an HMO that included comprehensive benefits such as full coverage for preventive and mental health services with low enrollee cost sharing. Until 1981, HMO X marketed only one benefit package: a standardized, comprehensive plan with no deductible or coinsurance when using panel physicians, a $25 copayment for each general physical exam, and a $2 copayment for each prescription. Pay for participating physicians was put into an account that was divided into two parts. The first part covered the services of the participating physician. Except in a few cases where the physician had more than 200 HMO members, they were reimbursed on a fee-for-service basis at 95 percent of their charges.

The second part of the account was to be used to pay for all services not provided by the participating physician. Hospitalization costs, referral care given by specialists, and procedures, laboratory tests, and x-rays performed outside the participating physician's office were all paid for from this part of the account. The participating physician shared in any deficit or surplus in the account at the end of the year. Premiums were competitive with other comprehensive prepaid group plans. The plan grew to be the largest plan of its type in the nation until, in 1980, enrollment began to decrease and profits fell. The explanation for this turn of events can largely be attributed to the organizational controls used between Insurance Company Y and HMO X.

Control Issues

HMOs have four types of controls—financial, managerial, claims, and providers. Each has unique problems with respect to both information and incentives, requiring separate evaluation of action. Figure 7.1 presents a conceptual framework for control between the parent organization and the HMO. The control system is connected to HMO performance through a process of sharing key information and establishing incentives for HMO managers. This requires a management information system capable of providing the necessary information and a reward system that is perceived as equitable by the HMO management.

Financial control

The managerial decision making at HMO X was independent of Insurance Company Y in keeping with the parent's philosophy of decentralized management. Only summary financial data were submitted to the controller's department for the preparation of the financial reports by Insurance Company Y. Accounting, auditing, and other administrative services as well as marketing, data processing, personnel services, and reinsurance were purchased from Insurance Company Y by HMO X. At

Figure 7.1   Control System Goals

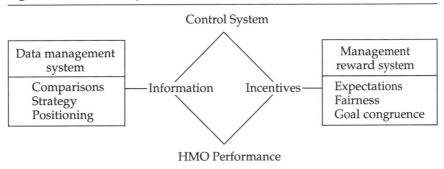

the same time, HMO X had complete control over the funds it received from its sponsor.

For stockholder reporting purposes, HMO X's financial statements were consolidated with Insurance Company Y's statements. Transfer payments between the HMO and the insurance company were eliminated so that the statements reflected only the net financial position. Therefore, transactions between Insurance Company Y and HMO X were known primarily by HMO X management and individual departments of Insurance Company Y. This process reflected the attitude of the management of both organizations that (1) transfer payments were not an issue and (2) the control of funds belonged solely in the hands of the HMO.

As is common in many industries, transfer prices used by Insurance Company Y were approximations of standard full costs arrived at with no actual determination of what the costs might be. HMO X management felt its transfer fees from Insurance Company Y (which ranged from 4.4 to 6.2 percent of HMO X's total expenses) were too high. In response to this perception, the managers constrained the amount of services they received from Insurance Company Y in the areas of accounting, marketing, and data processing. HMO X developed its own marketing function in addition to Y's input. The marketing was not coordinated with the claims processing or the actuarial needs of the firm, so information was not exchanged about the ability to provide the services that were being marketed. Data processing capability was being developed within HMO X in response to management's perception that the quality of Y's data processing of health services claims was inadequate.

Managerial control

HMO X's managers were rewarded on the basis of revenue and sales, or enrollee growth. This system was consistent with the reward system for managers in the parent organization. Casualty, property, and life insurance has characteristics from which reliable actuarial predictions can be made. Once the insurance policy had been sold, so that its premium was set, the firm declared the revenue on its income statement. Since the costs, or claims, were not expected to occur in an imminent reporting period, they were not directly related to revenue on the income statement, and managers did not tie their behavior to maximizing the difference between the premium and the claims of an individual policy. Performance evaluations were more frequent than was the cycle of revenue to expense, and since revenue comes first, it tended to be used to measure performance.

Insurance Company Y did not adjust the HMO X managers' reward system for the fact that the revenue-to-expense cycle for health insurance claims is much shorter than that of casualty, property, and life insurance claims. Health insurance claims tend to be frequent, small claims from many enrollees rather than the rare, large claims that typify the claims of casualty, property, or life insurance policy holders. HMO revenue is closely tied to its expenses. Premiums, coinsurance, deductibles, and provider fees can be adjusted for changes in the level of incurred claims in a rather timely manner.

HMO X's premium prices were consistently low relative to claims. This difference was due to inaccurate claims expense processing and unrealistic actuarial pricing. Both were brought on by an inadequate data processing system. Insurance Company Y was aware of data processing problems and chose to accept the underreporting of claims. Since managerial incentives for both organizations were to maximize revenue, HMO X's management did just that. As Figure 7.2 shows, it continuously increased enrollment, driving up revenue and, by not monitoring its incurred claims expenses resulting from this enrollment, consistently ran in the red. The reason this could continue for seven years without Y applying sanctions to HMO X's management was that the management was increasing revenue as its incentives encouraged it to do. The management was rewarded for the growth in revenue and the growth in sales.

Claims control

HMO X offered a comprehensive benefit package that was designed to be universally competitive with other plans. It was not tailored with knowledge of how a target group could be expected to use the benefits. For example, in designing a mental health benefit, data on the epidemiology of mental illness, utilization rates of mental health services, and existing coverage available to a target population could be gathered. This information could be used to decide how much coverage to offer in an

Figure 7.2   Revenue and Expense for HMO X

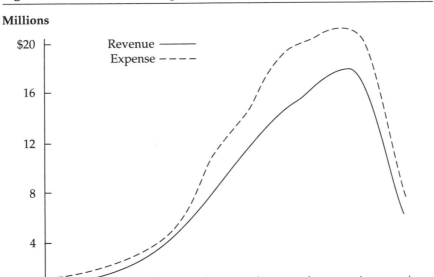

area and to make informed projections of utilization. In contrast, the HMO X benefit package was designed to address expected health care needs generically for any population.

This approach was consistent with the parent company's philosophy of simplifying plans and using its decentralized system of insurance agents, which was successful with property and casualty insurance. Health insurance tends to experience variation across contract groups in the demand for certain services. Therefore, benefit designs can be tailored for claims control to address this variation.

HMO X used the primary care physician as a gatekeeper; it chose to make this physician fully responsible for control over the demand for services. Any services authorized by the primary care physician had no out-of-pocket expenses to the patient except for a $2 copayment for each prescription drug. This practice is common in HMOs and PPOs today. Out-of-pocket expenses are powerful controls on an enrollee's use of services. There is significant variation across types of services with respect to enrollees' discretionary use. For example, an enrollee is more likely to forgo an office visit for a stuffy nose than an emergency room visit to set a broken arm.

Provider control

In addition to claims processing, the information system in an HMO provides feedback to the participating providers on the services that their patients use. This feedback is critical for encouraging providers to make prudent, cost-effective use of health services.

HMO X managers took two steps to encourage physicians' cost-effectiveness. In hopes of educating physicians, they published a newsletter with articles about the organization as well as about health issues. They also made primary care physicians responsible for managing the total care for their patients. Physicians were the financial gatekeepers for their individual patient accounts, which included all costs except those over $5,000 per year per enrollee. The amount in the account was based on average expected costs, adjusted for age and gender. The HMO planned to capitate providers with over 200 enrollees, but few providers reached that number; the average provider had fewer than 50 enrollees.

A dilemma faced by HMO X and other HMOs today is that to encourage enrollees to select the HMO, it needs to allow a wide range of physician choices. At the same time, the more physicians that an HMO contracts with, the less it is able to focus on cost-effective, high-quality providers. In addition, the HMO wants to provide the physicians with as many patients as possible for two reasons. First, that will encourage physicians to contract with the HMO, and second, it will give the HMO more leverage over the physician for claims control purposes. Realistically, this is a difficult situation, in that physicians are in competition for the HMO's enrollees, so that the more physicians who are willing to contract with the HMO, the less likely an individual physician is to increase his or her patient population as a result of contracting with the HMO.

HMO X managers found that primary care physicians did not alter their practice styles and that there needed to be a much larger enrollee population per provider to make enrollee accounts approximate the actuarial predictions on which the accounts were based. It was usually random, expensive events rather than practice style that determined the outcome of enrollee accounts at the end of the year. For example, some physicians with conservative styles of practice carefully monitored each specialist to make sure cost-effective care was given. They took actions such as decreasing the number of unnecessary stays in the hospital, using generic drugs, and substituting clinical judgment for marginally indicated diagnostic procedures. They did everything HMO X intended them to do, only to realize that one or two sick patients requiring costly care determined the deficit or surplus in their account at the end of the year. For those physicians, this realization destroyed the credibility of the individual account management system and the equity of the shared risk incentive for the primary care physicians.

When establishing a loosely structured organization such as HMO X, where the providers are not employed by the HMO and the HMO is a semi-autonomous subsidiary of an insurance company, the management needed to design a control system that provided information for evaluating how well the organization functioned and to provide incentives for individuals to further the goals of the organization. Each component of the control system (e.g., financial, managerial, claims, and provider) has both informational and incentive aspects. For each component, identify what control system aspects were missing at HMO X. How should the control system be changed to provide managers with timely information and properly aligned incentives?

Make versus Buy Decisions in a Closed-Panel Health Maintenance Organization

Douglas A. Conrad

Background

The setting for this case is a large metropolitan area HMO with a closed medical staff as the predominant delivery model. The case focuses on issues regarding purchased patient services in the core urban market area for this HMO, which serves approximately 330,000 persons in an extensive urban corridor. The regions have roughly equal enrolled populations, and they include six districts that basically represent health services primary care market areas. While predominantly a closed, staff-model HMO, this organization has developed several alternative delivery models to respond to dramatic population growth in certain of its target markets.

The HMO views the management of purchased patient services as part of a larger continuum of utilization and quality and cost management. The central idea behind this integrated effort is organization wide continuous quality improvement, developed in three dimensions—the quality of care, the quality of service as viewed by the customer, and the management of utilization. The organization seeks to create a culture and a series of microlevel delivery systems that value, enable, and foster quality. The organization supports this culture through a series of structures:

- The medical services committee, which reviews new technology and provides recommendations to the HMO benefits committee

- The committee on prevention, which develops prevention protocols and provides guidelines for care to the utilization management committee

- Efforts in individual departments and clinical sections that include appropriateness review of existing services, the results of which are provided to the quality of care assessment committee. A parallel committee on practice efficacy has assigned interdisciplinary teams to develop clinical guidelines in specific treatment areas, for example, back pain conditions. All this, of course, is supported by efforts focused on the individual physician, seeking to create a sense of local ownership of the utilization and quality management process. The organization is not looking for standardized treatment algorithms but rather a series of general guidelines that it would obtain throughout the geographical regions served by the HMO.

The organization is a mature-panel HMO. It has the largest penetration of any managed care plan in its local market but has experienced serious competition during the four-year period covered in this case—both from preferred provider organizations (PPOs) and newly emerging IPA-model and network-model HMOs.

The HMO's medical staff has a distinct governance structure and contracts annually with the board. In some sense, the medical staff functions more like a multispecialty group practice. It is completely self-managed with respect to hiring and personnel practices, patient care policies and protocols, and compensation policies. The Medical Director is selected by and reports to the Medical Staff Executive Council. The board–medical staff contract specifies the capitation rate for physician services to HMO enrollees and their respective rights and responsibilities. In addition to capitation, the staff receives non–HMO enrollee revenue for physician services to third parties, the state worker compensation program, and private patients.

The fundamental challenge posed in this case concerns the value judgments and managerial decisions the firm must make in responding to the dramatic growth of its purchased patient services budget. Over a three-year period the budget for purchased patient services has more than doubled, while enrollment during that same period has increased by less than 5 percent. As the organization sorts itself out relative to its competition, it has begun to ask the value question, Is the increasing departure from the pure closed-panel-model HMO appropriate in the light of cost-quality and market considerations, or does the doubling of the outside purchased patient services budget reflect failure to manage these outside costs? This value question gets to the core of how the organization structures itself, the sort of managerial talent it recruits, and the organizational and interpersonal mechanisms it employs to manage the internal and external provision of care.

General Issues for Management of the Cost and Quality of Purchased Patient Services

Managing purchased patient services involves a series of five issues. Those issues are as follows:

- The provision of accurate, complete, and timely data permitting the organization to address the question of whether it is cheaper to buy rather than make in a given market context
- The use of incentives versus controls as mechanisms for managing purchased patient services
- Consistency in control systems across the organization—that is, the consistent application of controls across different locations for similar patient conditions
- The development of key performance indicators and targets for achievement in managing referrals and institutional utilization of outside providers
- The development of clear clinical guidelines and treatment protocols

Case Analysis

The purchased patient services decision is shaped by four broad factors—the budget process, accountability-incentive structures within the HMO, the information system's capacity to track costs and resource utilization over time, and system models for service delivery in primary care market areas.

Budget

The budget is determined through a process by which dollars are allocated for internally and externally purchased services, and in particular, how the transfer of resources is arranged to reflect differential utilization of outside services between different components of the organization (i.e., primary care market). An issue in this area concerns transfer pricing between regional subunits of the organization to reflect the import and export of care across market areas for enrollees of the HMO. This import and export of care can be viewed as an alternative to purchasing services outside the organization.

The organization's budget is apportioned among four areas—medical staff, operations, purchased patient services, and administration. Within the medical staff's budget, which includes both the professional (personal, not institutional providers) services component and closed medical-staff compensation, the import and export patterns of care between primary care market areas are explicitly tracked. Medical staff budget dollars do flow between areas within the HMO to reflect those import and export relationships.

The organization currently uses a top-down approach to its global budgeting, in which the aggregate organizational budget is determined first and then distributed to the department level. The process begins with a projection of enrollment, which is then stratified by the revenues expected for each enrollment type. A margin for capital expenditures is incorporated in the necessary revenue projections as well. Having projected enrollment, the next step is to project expense based on the prior year's budget adjusted by projected changes in enrollment and inflation factors for various line items. A series of special factors such as regulatory requirements, board directives, and other commitments are then factored into those expense projections.

Within the purchased patient services subbudget, the allocation of dollars blends the top-down and bottom-up (decentralized) process. Physician managers, operations managers, and provider relations representatives at the market area level and organization-wide utilization management support staff develop a decentralized budget for purchased patient services, which is then reconciled with the (top-down) aggregate budget for purchased patient services. A key change in the last few years is that the budget for purchased patient services is no longer determined as a residual category after the operations budget (for internally provided services) is set. The budget for purchased patient services is now determined first and reconciled with available internal capacity via explicit trade-offs with the operations and medical staff budgets.

There currently is no explicit budget transfer between the geographic regions within the organization to reflect the importation of services to one region, as it serves the exported enrollees of another region's medical centers. Those budgetary effects are instead implicitly reflected in the historical expense budgets of each of the respective regions. One of the questions for the case is whether that implicit budget transfer for the import and export of services across geographic lines within the organization should be made explicit in the form of transfer pricing between regions. The appropriateness of such an implicit budget reflection of import and export is particularly controversial in a time of changing numbers and composition of enrollees in the HMO. The current data available in the management information system for the HMO do not reflect outside purchased patient services, so the impact of differential outside versus inside delivery by geographic submarket is not captured in the current information system.

Senior staff of the HMO conducted an analysis of the organization's budgetary process to assist the management team in formulating recommendations for improvement in organizational efficiency and effectiveness. All four component budgets of the HMO were examined— medical staff, operations, purchased patient services, and administration. A synopsis of their findings follows:

Medical staff. The aggregate medical staff budget is determined in negotiations with the board. Negotiations usually center on projected salary increases and new FTE requirements. Separate cost budgets are compiled by responsibility area. Until recently the medical staff budget was centrally managed for the HMO, but now it is split into five segments—each of the three regions, mental health, and the medical staff director. The medical staff budget includes non-dues revenue. Physicians do receive additional compensation for extra hours or the provision of services to private patients. A profit-loss system is established regionally, which enables medical staff to accumulate a percentage of revenues less expenses (profit). Table 8.1 outlines the steps in the HMO's evolution toward regional capitation of the medical staff budget. The essence of Phase III, the full regional capitation budget model, is to define a new capitation pool, equal to the expected cost of total physician services to HMO enrollees—irrespective of whether these services are internally provided (within the staff model) or purchased outside. The three model adjusters perform as follows:

- The tenure adjuster seeks to offset the relative advantage (or disadvantage) of having a more (or less) tenured staff composition than other regions.
- The professional purchased patient services (PPPS) adjuster works to offset the disadvantage of one region that historically purchased substantially more specialty care outside the staff model at a higher cost than internally provided specialty care.
- The timing adjuster phases in the full regional adjustment over several years.

Table 8.1   Steps in the Change Process, Phases of Regionalization
Capitation

Phase I. January 1986	Phase II. January 1987	Phase III. January 1988
Introduction of first regional budgets (based on historic patterns)	Regions carry over reserves (net income from 1986)	Historical base eliminated
Budgets capitated at the margin (for 1986 changes in enrollment, from historic base)	All 1986 features continued	Purchased patient services and capitation revenues are pooled and distributed on a capitation basis to create 1988 regional budgets
Creation of interregional transfer pricing mechanism	Medical staff enters into an additional at-risk agreement for the professional fee component of outside professional purchased patient services (PPPS)	Interregional transfer pricing mechanism applied to all enrollment (not just changes to base)
Interregional transfer factors applied only to changes in enrollment from base	Medical staff manages both the staff capitation budget and PPPS budget in parallel	Three adjustments added to smooth phase-in: Tenure adjuster PPPS adjuster 1988 timing adjuster
Nonpremium revenues allocated to the region of origin		
Creation of regional monthly income statements and balance sheets		

Source: An HMO medical director, "Decentralization and Regional Capitation in Prepaid Group Practice," working paper.

Operations. The regional vice presidents work with regional managers to project resource requirements, and the regional operations budgets are submitted to the senior management team (executive vice presidents and the CEO) for consideration at the final organizationwide decision-making stage. Once the HMO-wide allocation is set, the executive vice president for operations then distributes the regional operations budget to the regional vice presidents. There has been a move toward enrollment-based (effectively, capitation for the operations component of the budget) and away from service-based (the analogue to fee-for-service) budgeting, as the process has evolved to more top-down budgetary decision making.

Purchased patient services budget. In earlier years (including year 1 and year 2 of this case study) purchased patient services were budgeted as a residual amount, based on the dollars remaining after the allocations for medical staff, operations, and administration had been determined. Beginning in year 3 expected costs for purchased patient services have been projected by using an actuarial model on a per-enrollee per-month basis with a trend for local health sector–specific inflation. The budget for purchased patient services is allocated to the (subregional) districts or primary medical centers based on the projections, not historical cost patterns. There currently are no direct incentives for control of institutional provider (hospital) costs for purchased patient services. Operations administration is responsible for the institutional component of purchased patient services, while the medical staff bears a portion of the risk for the professional fees, or physician services, associated with purchased patient services.

Administration. The administrative portion of the HMO budget is based on prior year expenses, adjusted for projected increases in enrollment and anticipated changes to administrative workload related to benefit changes or operational needs. Most administrative departments are defined by project, and the budgeting process is relatively straightforward. There are no specific rewards or penalties associated with budget compliance (or unfavorable variances from the budget).

Based on the preceding staff analysis, senior management of the HMO has identified certain themes that reflect barriers to effective budget management and that might influence the efficient choice of internal versus externally purchased patient services:

- The need to own the budget development process at a decentralized level but the lack of strong incentives to do so, particularly in light of the presence of a top-down budget allocation driven by the need to satisfy the capitation constraint of fixed price and the presence of an organizational culture that supports the delivery of patient care over budget management
- Unrealistic base budgeting, reflecting incentives to set conservative targets that managers can meet in the short term

- Insufficient flexibility within the budget to deal with enrollment changes and shifts, differences in patient acuity, and short-term demands on service levels

- Concerns about the quality and availability of relevant information to manage costs—a need for timely and accurate reporting by the appropriate level of detail, including digestible information on new market forces shaping cost and quality decisions (new technology, drugs, changing patterns of illness) as well as clearer communication of budget assumptions and anticipated service levels within the budgeting process

Accountability-incentive structures

These budgetary themes lead into a discussion of accountability—incentive structures within the organization. A key issue concerning accountability and incentives is the structure of the compensation arrangements and risk-reward relationships for the medical staff of the HMO.

The closed medical staff of the HMO are capitated regionally but not as individual physicians, whether primary care physicians or specialists. The medical staff as a whole is technically responsible only for its own staffing costs (the professional component of purchased patient services) and is not given direct financial incentives to manage the facility costs associated with institutional services or the ongoing capital costs of operating clinics. In year 1 of this case study the medical staff as a whole was placed at risk for the first time for the professional component of purchased patient services. The aggregate risk was capped at the level of $100,000 for the professional component only. That organizationwide aggregate cap has risen in year 3 to $500,000 for the medical staff as a whole but is still limited to the professional fee component. The medical staff shares fully in the risk of deficit and the prospect of surplus up to that capped level.

Since decisions about purchased patient services are primarily physician-driven, several risk arrangements have been tested:

- At the total organizational level, if actual PPPS are significantly less than the budgeted amount, the medical staff is given the amount saved as a bonus. Conversely, if the professional component is over budget, medical staff dollars are transferred to the purchased patient services budget.

- Moreover, primary care market areas within the HMO with favorable variances are rewarded by a transfer of funds within the medical staff budget.

- Also, purchased patient services physician managers have been offered salary contracts in which 2 to 3 percent of the individual manager's salary is placed at risk, with the opportunity to gain as much as a 10 percent bonus for favorable area-level variances in the professional component. However, to date, most managers have not opted for this arrangement.

In addition to these accountability and incentive structures, the HMO has implemented utilization management (UM) in varying forms and degrees across different regions and districts. The basic components of UM are referral authorization and preauthorization of admissions, which limit the scope of service, the choice of provider, or care setting before the service is delivered; concurrent review; and retrospective review. Table 8.2 reflects the status of these UM efforts as of year 2 in this case study, based on information collected in the office of the manager with responsibility for the oversight of purchased patient services in the HMO.

Some of the strategic questions faced by the organization in the area of the accountability and risk-reward structure of purchased patient services concern the following:

- Is there a way to change utilization policy to systematically require more people to use inside services, particularly those for institutional care?

- How should enrollment changes, both in numbers and composition by market segment, be incorporated into the budgeting process for purchased patient services? The current budget for purchased patient services is flexed monthly for changes in enrollment by primary care market area, incrementing the area's budget for purchased patient services by 100 percent (more or less for enrollment increases and decreases, respectively) of the average cost per enrollee per month of a given enrollee type (e.g., Medicare, group).

- To create positive incentives for managing the purchased patient services budget, and to own the process, is it necessary to refine the budget process so bottom-up budgeting is done by determining service levels at the primary care market area? Budgeting for purchased patient services has moved to more decentralized budget setting and accountability, as noted above.

Information systems

The next set of issues concerning the management of purchased patient services for optimal cost and quality relates to the information systems

Table 8.2 Year 2 (1987) Utilization Management Status Report by District

Components	Region 1, District A	Region 2, District B	Region 2, District C	Region 3, District D	Region 3, District E	Region 3, District F
I. Preauthorization						
Admits						
Preadmit screening/authorization:						
• For staff M.D. admits	0%	100%	100%	90%	50%	100%
• For contract M.D. admits	*	100	100	50	100	80
Emergent/urgent notification/authorization	0	†	100	80	100	×
Preadmit discharge planning	Some%	100	75	20	80	90
Referrals						
100% referral review by purchased patient services coordinator/referral management system office						
• For appropriateness (location, term of referral, check against protocols/guidelines)	100	100	100	‡	90	100
• For medical coverage	10	100	100	100	100	100
Section chief review or designated M.D. review (second opinion)	35	100	§	40	‖	100
II. Concurrent Review						
Check service requested = service received	100%	100%	100%	For medical center only	100%	100%
Examination of bill (detailed review) prior to payment for nonprovided and noncovered services	100%	100%	100%	100%	80%	100%
Decertification (of inpatient)	Rehab	At primary regional hospital only	100%	At two medical centers only	¶	×
Discharge planning	Selected	No	Selected	Selected	Selected	One

Check against usual charge range	On request and special contingency	100%	100%	>$3000	>$500 ††	100%
Direct available services at HMO	Special contingency		‡‡			x

III. Retrospective Review

100% bill review (if not done earlier)	100%	x	100%	100%	x	100%
Audits (for appropriate admission)	Special projects					
Analysis by provider/trend data	General purchased patient services and special projects	80%‖‖	x	For one hospital only	¶¶	x
Compile utilization statistics	100%	***	100%	100%	100%	100%

x = Not yet implemented.
*For contract M.D. admits to HMO: 0% during backlog to other: 100%; rehabilitation (program not being implemented): 100%.
†Through designated coordinator.
‡Just about to begin 100% review.
§Differs between services of magnetic resonance imaging, lithotripsy, urology, ophthalmology, and cardiology.
‖Only if referral doesn't meet protocol.
¶The process is in place, no cases yet.
††Plus random checks at principal medical center in this district.
‡‡When M.D. gives prior approval or communication for district B, surgery, neurology; for district A, neurosurgery, nephrology, and some radiology procedures.
§§One hundred percent of bills greater than $3,000 are reviewed in principle (not sure of implementation).
‖‖Trend data is compiled every month. Analysis by the provider is ad hoc. They do not have computerized case management but do routinely monitor all backlogs manually by provider—100 percent.
¶¶Now all *designated* providers in the primary market area (district) and some others who are not used regularly.
***Monthly and quarterly reports.

that enable management to control and coordinate funds for purchased patient services. Historically, this HMO has not had information at the unit-of-service level on the fixed and variable costs associated with internally produced health services. Because the sale of services outside to non-HMO enrollees was and is a small part of this organization's business, there has not been a pressing need to develop internally generated service unit–specific marginal and average costs for pricing purposes. However, as the organization moves to make trade-offs between the internal versus external delivery of services, it has shifted to a service-specific, fixed and variable costing system. The budgetary decisions and management processes in place for the three-year period encompassed by this case study were not influenced by that information system (which is only now coming into the stream).

An important strategic factor is the design of information reports to track internal versus external costliness of services and to provide feedback for management decision making. Historically, the information on externally purchased services and outside referrals has been limited to claims *paid* in a particular period of time. The organization is now moving toward an accrual-based system, which would estimate the incurred expense by date of service (thus taking into account claims paid at a given point in time and *expected* claims to be paid in the future for a particular service, changes in referral volume, and the unit cost of referrals). One nuance in the transition from a claims-paid data system for reporting information on externally purchased services to a system based on incurred experience is the lag time in the development of a new system. As the HMO moves to a claims-incurred (accrual) data system, it temporarily loses the capacity to dip into the former claims paid system for purposes of management reporting. The short-term consequences of this loss for managing the delivery of outside services represent an important consideration for this case.

Another key strategic issue related to the information system concerns how the data are aggregated. Historically, the expenses associated with purchased patient services have been reported based on the location of the referring provider. If funds for purchased patient services are to be efficiently managed, decisions clearly have to be made regarding appropriate and efficacious utilization of resources by the primary care physicians responsible for individual enrollees and by specialty providers to whom the HMO staff decide to refer out specific cases. With dollars for purchased patient services managed at the level of the primary care market area medical center, costing for purchased patient services needs to be defined at those same levels, as well as relative to providers delivering externally purchased services.

System delivery models

The case analysis closes with a discussion of the alternative delivery models currently in place or being considered in this closed-panel HMO. Those six models are defined according to the degree of internal delivery versus external purchase for three types of services: inpatient services, specialty services, and primary care.

The predominant delivery model is one in which the majority of specialty and inpatient services are provided by the HMO's own professional providers and within organization-owned and organization-operated facilities. This model contains most primary care market area medical centers within the organization. Another prominent model, concentrated in some of the growth markets for enrollment within the urban corridor, is one in which some specialty and inpatient services are provided in-house, with some specialty and inpatient services purchased outside the organization. A third model present in one local market has specialty services provided within organization-owned facilities but inpatient care delivered through agreements with outside hospitals.

The fourth delivery model has most specialty and hospital services purchased outside the HMO, but with primary care strongly integrated within market area medical centers owned and operated by the HMO. A fifth model is one in which the HMO contracts for primary care, but specialty and hospital inpatient services are referred back to the organization's closed medical staff. Finally, in the newest growth market within the urban corridor, the organization will undertake (starting in year 4) to purchase primary, specialty, and hospital inpatient services through a network of providers in the local market.

Table 8.3 presents data that the analyst can examine to shed light on the question of the best delivery system model, subject to the environmental conditions in each of the three HMO regions and the primary care market areas within each of those regions. (The number identifying each area medical center [clinic] refers to which of the three regions the medical center is located in, and the letter appended to that number is simply a cross-reference for the author to identify the actual clinic in the raw data on which this table is based.) The expected expense in Table 8.3 is based on the age and gender distribution of the population using a given area medical center as its source of primary care and the average health care services cost per enrollee per year in each age and gender stratum. The expected expense does not take into account other factors that might influence cost (e.g., the staffing model, that is, how nurses or other midlevel practitioners are used, or the specific service mix of the clinic). Thus, the variance between the actual total and the expected expense in Table 8.3 must be carefully interpreted. Clinic 1J is

Table 8.3 Sampling of Expense Patterns by Delivery System Model in Year 3: Actual Expenses per Enrollee per Year

Expense Category	Sample Clinics (by region)				
	1C	3Q	3R	2L	1J
Total primary care	$ 150	$ 182	$ 199	$ 194	$ 186
Total specialty care	291	209	196	285	182
Specialty purchased patient services	36	50	62	220	20
Total outpatient mental health	26	17	17	14	10
Mental health purchased patient services	3	1	1	13	4
Total emergency	34	23	15	24	5
Emergency purchased patient services	2	21	14	22	1
Total inpatient	389	318	279	456	251
Inpatient purchased patient services	81	206	231	258	55
Total actual expense	1,211	1,036	991	1,274	893
Expected expense	1,199	1,024	1,015	1,143	1,114
Delivery system model	Internal specialty & inpatient	Mixed specialty & inpatient (some outside)	Internal specialty outside inpatient	Mostly outside specialty & inpatient	Outside (contract) primary care, internal specialty & inpatient

the only clinic with capitation reimbursement to physicians. Region 1 is the metropolitan area that constitutes the core for most of the HMO's potential population (and actual enrollment); region 2 captures the major adjoining suburban area; and region 3 represents a major extension into the newest growth markets in the HMO's north-south urban corridor.

In midyear 2 the director of purchased patient services produced the analysis of costs for purchased patient services in Table 8.4. The numbers illustrate the source of management's interest:

- Overall (HMO-wide), costs for purchased patient services exhibit almost a 4 percent unfavorable variance from budget for the year to date, with virtually all the variance attributable to PPPS.
- There are substantial differences in per-enrollee, per-month costs for purchased patient services associated with the delivery system models in place across the three regions. The costs for purchased patient services in region 3 and region 2 are substantially higher than district C in region 1. This difference reflects the presence of a focal, HMO-owned tertiary hospital in region 1 and in region 2, district B, respectively; the HMO has an exclusive contract with an inpatient specialty center in district D and a major community hospital in district F. Thus, costs for purchased patient services in those districts (with partial vertical integration of hospital and specialty care) are between the costs for purchased patient services of districts A and B and those of region 3, district E (the highest of all), where the HMO contracts with a designated hospital and with community specialty and primary care physicians.

Thus, as one examines these different delivery system models coexisting within the HMO, the logical first question is whether or not there are systematic cost differences (either in unit cost or volume of service) between these different delivery system models.

Going beyond that descriptive analysis, one might ask the normative question, Are the delivery models that have been chosen for specific geographic submarkets the best models given the environmental circumstances in that market? Here the organization has to ask itself about its contracting strategy and the extent to which it moves external providers up a ladder of risk in which those providers bear financial risk for potential inefficiency in unit cost and volume of service. The organization's general strategy has been to begin outside contracting with fee schedules negotiated to reflect the relative bargaining power of the HMO and the outside providers in a local market. Over time the HMO investigates the efficiency of those fee-for-service agreements and, where improvements are indicated, attempts gradually to move external providers up the ladder of risk. However, limited use has been made of

Table 8.4 First Six Months, Year 2 Purchased Patient Services Costs per Enrollee per Month

Region and District	Total			Medical Staff/PPPS			Hospital/Facility		
	Actual	*Budget*	*Variance*	*Actual*	*Budget*	*Variance*	*Actual*	*Budget*	*Variance*
1A	$ 7.44	$ 7.20	(3.47%)	$ 1.32	$ 1.35	2.22%	$ 1.90	$ 1.91	0.52%
2B	5.54	5.89	6.11	4.11	4.35	5.52	1.47	1.70	13.53
2C	32.95	33.83	2.60	11.75	12.51	6.08	11.54	11.19	(3.13)
3D	21.58	20.57	(4.91)	4.38	4.67	6.21	10.06	9.82	(2.44)
3E	35.06	35.33	(0.93)	20.42	20.24	(0.89)	7.88	9.03	12.74
3F	22.30	18.33	(21.65)	4.79	3.51	(36.47)	11.77	9.38	(25.48)
HMO Total	13.41	12.93	(3.63)	2.97	2.88	(3.69)	4.79	4.79	0.00

capitation contracting with either primary care providers or specialists in the community. Fixed per diem contracts for hospital inpatient services are in place in region 3.

Concluding Questions

1. Is there an integrated organizational approach that can be developed to link budget, incentive, accountability, and timely and accurate information? Can this approach serve as a kind of generic template for a closed-panel HMO wishing to implement more flexible staffing and contract structures?

2. What market factors govern the choice of tough versus soft contracting with outside providers for the delivery of specialty, inpatient, and primary care services?

3. What changes in the role of physician managers and their clinical professional colleagues need to be effected to manage the delivery of services outside the walls of the closed-panel HMO?

4. What delivery system models are likely to serve the interests of the HMO most effectively in providing appropriate access and quality of health services while simultaneously controlling cost and resource utilization?

Part **III**

Strategy Implementation and Reassessment

Marketing in a Buy-Right Environment

R. Scott MacStravic

St. Thomas Hospital is a 220-bed facility in a city of 60,000 people, the center of a metropolitan area with a population of 150,000. There are two other hospitals in the area, one with 125 beds and the other with 200. With recent inpatient utilization decreases, the average occupancy of hospitals in the area has slipped from 75 to 55 percent. St. Thomas has done only slightly better, with present occupancy at 60 percent.

The hospital's chief financial officer (CFO) has just produced a five-year forecast showing that the hospital's bottom line, which has declined from +8.0 percent a year ago to +3.6 percent in the recently completed fiscal year, will drop into the red in three years and stand at −3.8 percent by the fifth year. Tightened Medicare and Medicaid payments, a growing indigent care load, and competitive cost bidding among local purchasers are combining to push net revenues below expenditures. Cost-cutting measures have been implemented in each of the past five years, but now managers complain that there is simply no more fat left to cut.

In considering the causes of recent problems, the hospital has identified two primary categories—environmental factors it cannot do anything about by itself and market factors it can try to respond to. Chief environmental factors include governmental stinginess in paying for hospital services and a stagnant local economy with high unemployment and low-paid service workers who do not have health insurance coverage. The hospital supports both lobbying and economic development efforts in the country and in the state but feels it can do no more about these factors than it is already doing.

The chief market factor it has targeted for attention is the growing trend toward competitive contracting among local purchasers. The hospital has concluded that this trend will continue and that all local hospitals face an increasingly competitive and tenuous future. Not all the hospitals will survive, and St. Thomas is determined to be one that does. In the face of this reality, the hospital has decided it must abandon its tradition of low-profile operation among local hospitals and get down to some hardball competition.

The marketing department is enthusiastic about this change of policy, as it sees it as a signal of increasing importance for the marketing function, and looks forward to bigger and better budget allocations for its activities. Its new director, Kelly Fairchild, has up to now been excluded from top administration decisions and looks on the new environment as an opportunity to break into the upper echelons of power. There are now five top executives at the hospital, the CEO, the CFO, the COO, the chief nursing officer, and the chief physician officer. Fairchild aspires to becoming the hospital's first chief marketing officer on a pay level with these five.

With the marketing department having been only a part, and a minor part at that, in the hospital's past efforts aimed at the purchaser market, Fairchild begins by analyzing what approaches have been used and how well they have worked. She breaks down this analysis into three parts—marketing intelligence efforts, product and market development, and marketing communications.

Marketing Intelligence

Information developed by Fairchild's predecessor indicates that purchasers fall into five major categories: government (federal, state, and local), employers (principally the self-insured), unions (who control trust-fund health insurance programs), insurance companies (covering other employers and the general public), and managed care systems (HMOs, PPOs, etc.). Among government purchasers, thus far only Medicaid has engaged in competitive bidding; all other government purchasers allow beneficiaries to choose any hospital. These purchasers control their expenditures through limiting beneficiaries, reviewing utilization, and dictating payments, invariably well below the cost of even the most efficient providers.

St. Thomas has been one of those to secure and maintain a Medicaid contract ever since bidding began. Its historical commitment to serving the poor as well as those able to pay has kept it in this market, even as the other local hospitals have dropped out. This accounts in large part for St. Thomas's higher than average occupancy but does little for its financial health. It enjoys somewhat higher than average shares of worker compensation, local assistance and programs for handicapped children and other government agencies, though it loses money on all these patients as well.

The hospital had done well in the early years of Medicare's DRG payment system, ending up with bottom lines in the 9 to 12 percent range. This was due partly to the generally conservative and efficient practices of its medical staff, who manage patients with only the appropriate testing and treatment and minimize lengths of stay (LOSs). The hospital's low unit costs of operation are due primarily to its cadre of loyal, long-term, and efficient employees. It has avoided the need to use agency nurses, for example, while both of its peers have been saddled with this heavy expense under the shortage conditions that have prevailed in recent years.

It has not really attempted to exploit its low-cost position relative to other providers in the area in promotional efforts aimed at either the general public or local purchasers, even though its unit and case costs tend to be lower than another of the local hospitals that is promoting its lower than average prices in an aggressive advertising campaign. Up to now, St. Thomas has kept busy and kept its beds full by serving those in need, without deliberately going after patients. It enjoys a favored position in the mind of the poor and elderly in the area, maintained by its long tradition of service to both these segments.

It has not done as well in the employer, union, insurance, and managed care markets. Fairchild's analysis of market size and marketshares in the area indicate that St. Thomas has higher than average shares of nonpaying and dictated-payment patients, with lower than average shares of nongovernment, contract-payment patients (see Table 9.1).

Table 9.1 Payment Source Breakdowns

Payment Source	Percentage of Population	Percentage of Area Patient Days	Percentage of Patient Days at St. Thomas
Medicare	12	42	48
Medicaid or government	4	8	12
Self-insurance employers	15	9	6
Self-insurance unions	10	7	5
Insurance	20	15	10
Managed care	24	11	7
Uninsured	15	8	12

While the government-dictated payment and uninsured populations represent a total of 58 percent of all patient days in the market
(as opposed to only 31 percent of the population), they represent 72
percent of St. Thomas's patient days. This forces St. Thomas to do more
cost shifting to the remaining 28 percent of patient days. Unfortunately,
this cost shifting tends to make it even harder to get such patient days,
since greater cost shifting raises St. Thomas's prices competitively higher.
If the hospital cannot redress this balance soon, it may be unable to
compete at all in the competitive-bid market and find itself forced out of
business altogether.

St. Thomas has no systematic intelligence on the individual employers, insurance companies, and managed care organizations that control
the nongovernment market. Fairchild determines that the key to successful marketing to these purchasers is identification of and response
to the benefits they wish to obtain from selective contracting with area
providers. Low-cost health care is the obvious desideratum, but if that
were the only factor, then local providers would be in a commodity price
war, and Fairchild does not feel that St. Thomas could win in such a war
and still preserve its traditional mission of serving the unfortunate.

Fairchild engages a local market research firm to develop intelligence on the purchaser market, using combinations of personal interviews, focus groups, and surveys. She instructs the firm to identify
appropriate segments among these purchaser groups, focusing on differences in the criteria they use in selecting and retaining contract providers,
with special emphasis on factors other than price.

She also begins, in conjunction with the research firm, to develop
intelligence about St. Thomas's competitors. State utilization and cost
reports plus patient origin and destination surveys provide essential
hard data, while a community and purchaser survey will add the softer
intelligence on attitudes, preferences, and perceptions toward the three
competitors. Fairchild reviews the two competing hospitals' past advertising to get an idea of their strategies, noting the low-cost focus of one
hospital and the high-technology, sophisticated service capability focus
of the other.

She also begins to make personal sales calls on major purchasers in
the area, to introduce herself and begin developing working relationships
with them. She is set on implementing partnership strategies with as
many purchasers as possible, in which they will see and use St. Thomas
as a partner in their own efforts to have healthy, productive employees;
controlled health insurance expenditures; and whatever other outcomes
they aspire to that St. Thomas can help them achieve in ways that also
benefit the hospital and its mission.

These calls are initially intended to collect information and create initial impressions only; no real effort is made to sell anything to the purchasers. Initial contacts focus on identifying the true decision makers at each organization and on determining the roles that individuals play in making provider selection decisions. Interviews are used to identify the personal as well as organizational goals that motivate decision makers, to collect personal information as a basis for building dossiers on each. In subsequent efforts, Fairchild intends to develop a sales force that will continue this work.

As a result of the market research firm's investigation and Fairchild's own interviews, it is determined that purchasers are looking for the following outcomes in their selective contracting strategy:

- An ability to predict and control their expenditures for health insurance

- An assurance that they are getting value for money spent, that quality for the cost is as good as is available

- Confidence that their own costs are not being inflated by costs of other purchaser groups

- Assurance that their employees are happy with their health insurance coverage and with the providers they see under any limited provider option

- Assurance that their employees have adequate access to care sources, are using services when necessary and not when unnecessary

- Confidence that employees are being served in the most appropriate and cost-effective modes and settings for care and that the care for each is tailored to the individual needs of each

The research also revealed that the two competing hospitals have established fairly well-defined positions in the mind of local purchasers. One is viewed as the sophisticated, high-quality provider but with high costs. The other is seen as the low-cost provider but with questionable quality. St. Thomas does not have a definite position, being perceived as having good quality with an uncertain cost and focusing on serving the unfortunate. Local purchasers have contributed many times to fund-raising drives for St. Thomas in the past but have not thought of it as a particularly efficient business operation.

Local purchasers have made a number of changes in their health insurance programs over recent years in pursuit of desired outcomes. Among these changes are the following:

- Moved to self-funding and self-administration of plans (large employers only)
- Developed employee wellness promotion programs, including prevention and early detection screening as well as positive health activities
- Instituted or increased deductibles and copayments by employees
- Implemented or contracted for utilization reviews such as preadmission screening, second opinions before elective surgery, and ongoing and retrospective reviews for inpatient care
- Instituted specific incentives for employees to use and providers to offer less expensive modes of treatment, such as outpatient rather than inpatient care or medical rather than surgical treatment
- Contracted with lower cost providers on an exclusive or preferred provider basis
- Offered employees cafeteria benefit plans to reduce their health insurance liabilities

Fairchild knows from prior experience and from published literature that other purchasers around the country have also introduced such programs as employee information and counseling services intended to make employees more informed users of health services, including hot lines answered by doctors or nurses for advice any time of the day or night, or case management programs for high-use or high-cost cases in which extensive use of services over an extended period is likely, such as with chronic illness, serious accidents, and other disabilities.

While responding to purchasers' conscious, stated needs and wishes is an essential part of a successful marketing strategy, Fairchild is convinced that it is not always enough. The competition has access to the same information and may make it difficult for St. Thomas to develop and maintain a competitive distinction. Fairchild is convinced that employers will also respond favorably to programs that will increase the health and happiness of employees, thereby reducing absenteeism and turnover and promoting higher morale and productivity.

Programming

Fairchild's predecessor had suggested an aggressive discounting approach in going after the competitive-bid business. However, the CFO controlled negotiations with purchasers and tended to bid prices based on average costs rather than the marginal costs additional contract patient days would incur. As a result, St. Thomas has not done well in competitive bidding. The only strategy for gaining contracts suggested thus far has been to offer deeper and deeper discounts, well below average costs and even below marginal costs in many cases. There has been no ongoing contact with purchasers, only the annual judgment days when bids are solicited and winners announced.

Fairchild has decided that what St. Thomas needs is a Marketing Right strategy geared to the Buy Right environment of competitive bidding. However, she is convinced that focusing on cost alone is a self-defeating tactic. In the first place, St. Thomas is in a poor position to be and remain the lowest cost provider and still preserve its mission of serving the unfortunate, despite its generally low operating costs. Besides, any provider can match price in bidding, producing price wars that end up hurting everybody. In a recent example, the local low-cost hospital offered a 40 percent discount to gain a contract covering 2,000 employees and dependents.

Instead, Fairchild hopes to modify the selective contracting practices of purchasers so that they will select the best providers first, then negotiate prices with them that will be mutually rewarding. She aspires to creating and maintaining true working partnerships in which purchasers and St. Thomas are both working toward the same goals. To do that, she needs to be able to develop a significant competitive distinction that will justify and reward purchasers' adopting this partnership approach and selecting St. Thomas as a preferred partner.

She decides that the marketing distinction St. Thomas must be able to offer is the ability to monitor and report the quality, access, and efficiency it is able to offer and deliver to purchasers, together with a willingness to work with purchasers in continually balancing and enhancing these customer values. If St. Thomas can demonstrate high ability, patient satisfaction, good access, and acceptable prices, it will enable as well as encourage local purchasers to buy based on value (i.e., a combination of quality, access, and price) rather than price alone. Fairchild feels that with the right marketing approach to purchasers, the future of St. Thomas and its mission can be protected if not ensured.

Marketing Right

The Marketing Right strategy Fairchild works on has three major components:

- An ongoing market intelligence program that will continually assess and monitor purchaser knowledge, attitudes, and behavior and the reasons for them

- A marketing information program that will monitor and promote quality, satisfaction, access, and efficiency of services provided and the appropriateness of service use by purchaser beneficiaries
- An ongoing relationship management and communications program that will report on quality, satisfaction, access, efficiency, and appropriateness as delivered by St. Thomas over time

The key to this strategy is the ability to define, measure, monitor, manage, and report quality, satisfaction, access, efficiency, and appropriateness in ways that are meaningful to purchasers. Fairchild realizes that there are a number of approaches that might be used in accomplishing this. The hospital and its medical staff could develop the information components themselves, as the experts in the field, and persuade purchasers that these components address all their concerns. Outside organizations with prepackaged information programs could be investigated with a view to selecting one that seems most likely to satisfy the purchaser market.

Fairchild feels that neither of these approaches is truly a marketing or partnership way of meeting the challenge, however. Accordingly, she decides that the Marketing Right information system must be developed as a partnership effort involving both providers and customers. This approach will illustrate and demonstrate the partnership that Marketing Right involves and promote purchaser acceptance of the information and reporting system outputs, since purchasers will have helped to design them.

Others point out that there are some risks and costs involved with this approach. It is dangerous in that purchasers may push for information that will not make St. Thomas look as good as possible. Some information will point out to purchasers some of the warts and moles that the hospital has managed to keep largely hidden over the years. On the other hand, Fairchild feels that discovering negative information through the use of specific measures will give the hospital an opportunity to improve on the dimensions involved before purchasers even know how competitors measure up on those dimensions. Moreover, demonstrating a willingness to discover and respond to negative information should help build trust between purchasers and providers. Fairchild is hopeful that because St. Thomas really is a high-quality and low-cost provider, the risks involved in this approach will be minimal.

Communications

St. Thomas has not had any systematic communications strategy aimed at purchasers in the past. Its modest community and public relations efforts have been aimed primarily at the general public or at raising funds from local employers. Its advertising has been minimal, primarily involving announcements of various community health education programs, special screening activities, health fairs, and the like.

The other two hospitals have been far more aggressive in their advertising, focusing on their low-cost and high-quality positions, with the usual claims of being caring institutions thrown in. They have no systematic communications linkages with purchasers, relying on annual contracting wars as a basis for managing their relationships. The other hospitals have recruited some of the larger employer executives to their governing boards, however, as has St. Thomas.

Fairchild feels that purchasers are important enough in terms of their actual and potential lifetime contributions to St. Thomas's success and survival to warrant a continuing communications strategy. Her budget does not currently allow for a sales force; in fact, it was cut by 30 percent in this year's budget. She resigns herself to the necessity of being the primary ongoing communications link to purchasers, though she hopes to involve the CEO and other executives as much as possible in the relationship management effort. If the strategy pays off in significant contracts with purchasers, Fairchild is sure a sales force can be developed in the future.

The focus of the communications strategy will be on describing to purchasers what St. Thomas can deliver in the way of quality, satisfaction, access, efficiency, and appropriateness and then continually reporting what it has delivered. After starting with a reporting system jointly developed with local purchasers, the hospital will regularly update the indicators used in response to changes in its ability to monitor such indicators and to changes in what purchasers wish to keep track of.

The aim of this strategy is to persuade purchasers that St. Thomas is not simply a seller of services but a true partner with them in pursuing their goals. In this, St. Thomas already enjoys the reputation of being a mission-driven service organization more than a commercial enterprise. Fairchild is counting on this reputation being a positive trait and a meaningful foundation for establishing St. Thomas's position as an organization committed to worthwhile purchaser and public goals rather than its own success.

This strategy also promises to help protect St. Thomas against threats of removing its tax-exempt status. Other hospitals in the state, and indeed the other two hospitals in town, tend to be seen more and more as commercial enterprises. Their advertising efforts have occasionally gained them brief surges in marketshares for some services but have also affected their images in the community. Local purchasers tend to view them as businesses more than institutions, while St. Thomas still retains most of its reputation for commitment to service.

Fairchild believes that delivering benefits to local purchasers is a service to the community. While there are strong financial reasons for going after more of the nongovernment purchaser market, delivering quality, satisfaction, access, efficiency, and appropriate care to employees, dependents, and other beneficiaries is as much a part of the hospital's mission as is serving the unfortunate. She is convinced that the success that the hospital achieves in serving purchaser groups will be persuasive evidence to the general public of St. Thomas's excellence and service to the community.

On the other hand, Fairchild believes that purchasers will continue to be more interested in cost and efficiency than the general public. She decides that communications to purchasers will include a heavy emphasis on financial factors, while communications to the general public will focus on quality. Similarly, she decides that purchasers will be more interested in quality as measured across populations, where the general public will respond more to quality in personalized care for individuals.

Suggested Readings

Alexandra, L., and K. Barter. "Helping Employees Become Better Health Care Consumers." *Business and Health* (October 1985): 5–8.

Bachman, S., D. Pomeranz, and E. Tell. "Making Employers Smart Buyers of Health Care." *Business and Health* (September 1987): 28–34.

Butler, J. "GM's View on Purchasing High-Quality Providers." *Hospitals* (20 July 1987): 90.

Charles, J. "Using Informed Choice to Combat Health Costs." *Business and Health* (September 1987): 36–38.

Diamond, L. "Candid Clues for Buying Right." *Business and Health* (July 1988): 36–37.

Freeland, M. S., S. S. Hunt, and H. S. Luft. "Selective Contracting for Hospital Care Based Volume, Quality and Price." *Journal of Health Policy, Politics and Law* 12, no. 3 (Fall 1987): 409–26.

Iglehart, J. "Competition and the Pursuit of Quality: A Conversation with Walter McClure." *Health Affairs* 7, no. 1 (Spring 1988): 79–90.

Kenkel, P. "Seeking a Rational System." *Modern Healthcare* (4 November 1988): 64.

Koenig, R. "Comparison Shopping." *The Wall Street Journal*, 22 April 1988.

McClure, W. "Buying Right: The Consequences of Glut." *Business and Health* (September 1985): 43–46.

———. "Buying Right: How to Do It." *Business and Health* (October 1985): 41–44.

Schlossberg, H. "Pittsburgh Businesses Form 'Buy Right Council' to Drive Down Health Care Costs." *Marketing News* 24, no. 2 (22 January 1990): 9, 22.

Spencer, E. "Buying Quality Healthcare in the New Era of Medicine." *Health Industry Today* (September 1987): 36–41.

Geriatric Assessment Center

R. Scott MacStravic

Introduction

Georgetown Memorial Hospital is a 400-bed tertiary hospital in a community of 200,000, the major urban center for a county of 300,000. It also serves the six surrounding counties, none of which has a tertiary hospital of its own.

Roughly 30 percent of its admissions, 42 percent of its patient days, and 40 percent of its net revenues are derived from utilization by those 65 years of age and over. In spite of this, Georgetown has never had a specific strategy aimed at the elderly market segment. Its medical staff physicians lack enthusiasm for caring for the elderly and find Medicare regulations and procedures onerous and Medicare payment unsatisfying.

Recently, however, a physician trained in geriatric medicine, the first ever in the area, set up practice in town. Dr. Ames comes from a large university hospital in the East, where there has long been an extensive research, training, and service program aimed at the elderly. One of its nationally renowned programs is a geriatric assessment center (GAC) that offers a comprehensive assessment, treatment, and referral service for elderly with complex problems.

The purpose of the GAC is to identify the full range of medical, psychoemotional, and social challenges of each patient and then to develop plans for treatment that will provide the best possible combination of quality of care, quality of life, and reasonable cost for the patient. The university hospital's GAC also provided a case management service for local employers with significant retiree health insurance obligations.

Ames feels that the GAC program is an ideal way to begin the development of a systematic strategy for serving the elderly. He is convinced that the kind of program he was involved in back east will work equally well in Georgetown. He intends to develop research and training programs in geriatric medicine over the long run but feels that initiating a successful service program is the best way to start in this case.

Geriatric Assessment Center: Boutique Marketing Plan

Customers

The intended customers of the GAC are frail elderly persons with a variety of physical and mental problems. The frail elderly are looking for a more complete understanding of their problems and a more coordinated approach to dealing with them. They are eager to preserve their dignity and independence and to avoid being institutionalized if at all possible. National studies and a local survey indicate that of the 36,000 elderly in the county, roughly 4,000 are potential candidates for some version of the GAC program. In addition, roughly 2,000 more in the surrounding counties are potential prospects. This is a growing market as the numbers of aging people increase and the numbers of those over 85 and aged 75 to 84 increase faster.

Other customers for the GAC include the children of the frail elderly, particularly their daughters and daughters-in-law who tend to be left the responsibility for worrying about frail parents. With greater numbers of women in the workforce, their ability to care for frail elderly in the home diminishes and their ability to afford professional assistance increases.

Acquaintances, clergy, social agencies serving the aged, resident councils in retirement communities, and a variety of interested parties outside the family may also participate in identifying frail elderly prospects and in deciding whether and where to go for comprehensive assessment. Employers whose employees include people worried about frail parents may also be motivated to participate, even to stimulate employees to search for GAC services. Discharge planners at hospitals are also a potential source of referrals. Estimates are that 8 percent of elderly discharged from hospitals are good candidates for GAC services. Since referral would be postdischarge, planners at other hospitals may be less sensitive to losing patients, though the physicians involved may still be.

Physicians are a combination of customer and competitor. They may choose to refer their frail elderly patients to the GAC or decide that the GAC is trying to steal their patients from them. Internists and family and general practitioners serving the elderly are likely to have the greatest referral potential. Orthopedists, ophthalmologists, cardiologists, and neurologists may also refer a substantial number of patients if they are managing rather than simply consulting on frail elderly patients.

Attraction (based on what patients can learn prior to experience). The frail elderly are especially sensitive to convenience of access. The very conditions that make them prospects for the GAC limit their mobility and make them likely to seek out care at the nearest source, or where transportation is readily available. They are more likely to have traditional views of who should provide services and be attracted to mature, male physicians since that is what they are used to. They are particularly sensitive to the personal characteristics and behavior of providers. They are sensitive to the cost of GAC services, especially if they will be borne by their family.

Family members are looking for advice and assistance in dealing with what they probably see as an increasing problem. They will be sensitive to guilt feelings over any need to place their frail parents in a nursing home or other institution. They will appreciate actively participating in deciding what can and should be done about their frail parents, while also appreciating sharing the responsibility. They are more sensitive to the quality of assessment programs and to the availability of services to treat effectively whatever problems are identified. They are sensitive to the costs of GAC services but recognize that the costs of not diagnosing and treating frail elderly can become even more expensive later.

Third-party referral sources are mostly concerned with getting the needs of frail elderly met, feeling that at least something is being done. They are concerned about quality and cost but more with ensuring that problems are not being ignored. They may not wish to play an active role in selecting a GAC, though they can be good word-of-mouth allies. Prompt response is the key factor for this group.

Physicians are particularly sensitive to the possibility of losing patients to the GAC staff or to being criticized for failing to do what the GAC does. They may come to prefer to refer frail elderly patients if they see the GAC as helping them care for the patient. Specialists may refer frail elderly patients they have been seeing when they realize that their problems are too extensive.

Satisfaction (based on actual experience). Frail elderly patients are satisfied first through gaining a sense of confidence in the diagnoses, prognoses, and treatment recommendations they get from the GAC. If they discover that a condition they considered an inevitable consequence of aging can be ameliorated or cured, they can be delighted by their care. To the extent that they foresee gaining in quality of life, they should be satisfied by the GAC service. Being able to avoid institutions is a key factor for most.

The family wishes to be assured that their frail parent is in the best of hands. They want to be kept thoroughly and promptly informed as diagnoses are made and to participate in making treatment and habitation choices. They would prefer to enjoy freedom from worry or burdensome responsibility for their parents and to avoid feeling guilty about any necessary arrangements that must be made for the good of the patient.

Third parties are satisfied primarily by knowing that the frail elderly person they were concerned about is in good hands. They may appreciate knowing what arrangements have been made and hearing any good news that emerges from the assessment. Both their involvement and their concern are likely to be shorter in duration than that of family members, but satisfying them may lead to future referrals.

Primary physicians wish first to feel confident they will retain or regain their patient and not be embarrassed by anything that is told to the patient or family during the assessment. They are satisfied by the same factors that they generally enjoy in relations with referral specialists. Specialists who refer patients for management also want to be kept informed. Key is making clear to any physician referring a patient what will happen during and after the GAC experience and making sure that is what the referring physician had in mind.

Competition. Since there is no other GAC in the area, the competition is all other arrangements that patients, family members, referral sources, and physicians make to diagnose and treat frail elderly patients. Since the GAC has the only gerontologist in town, it enjoys a competitive distinction, and gerontologists are hard to find. Moreover, the comprehensive specialized medical staff and technologies available at Georgetown offer a superior backup for the GAC that other hospitals cannot duplicate.

On the down side is that Georgetown does not enjoy a reputation as a warm, caring institution, as much as it is seen as a technologically superior one. People may prefer to go to their personal physician, someone they know and trust. The GAC may be seen as a place for only the very seriously ill, and many elderly or their family may see it as a place of last resort if its role and program are not communicated properly.

As a brand new service previously unavailable in the area, the GAC has the challenge and the opportunity to define what it is in the public mind. It can offer one-stop convenience in addition to specialized, comprehensive quality. Its price will be a major factor for those whose insurance does not cover the costs. Its superior benefits will satisfy the various customers it wishes to attract.

Payment. Insurance companies in the area represent mixed potential regarding GAC services. They generally do not cover routine physical examinations, but they may be persuaded that GAC programs save them money in the long run. With one local company covering 45 percent of the elderly market, there is a clear market leader and high-leverage customer to deal with.

Medicare will pay for GAC services under Part B but does not consider the inpatient stay essential. As a Part B service, the GAC is subject to deductibles and copayment, though 90 perent of the elderly in this market have supplemental insurance as well. At present, Medicare is not interested in the possibility that GAC programs save money in the long run.

The greatest interest may come from the IPA-model HMO in the area. It covers 45 percent of the elderly in a capitation, risk-sharing contract for Medicare. If it sees the GAC as a way to prevent or reduce subsequent utilization and expenditures, it may cover its costs and even actively promote its services for appropriate patients. This HMO is a key customer for successful development of the GAC.

The GAC program

Product. The basic service of the GAC is a comprehensive assessment of the physical, mental, and social condition of frail elderly patients, including diagnoses, prognoses, and treatment and habitation recommendations. The benefits to patients arise from the scope of the assessment; the accuracy, completeness, and usability of the information and test results produced and provided; and the integrated plan for treatment and habilitation that emerges. By identifying early stages of some conditions and noting the interaction of conditions and current medications, the GAC can often cure or reduce the severity of conditions, thereby improving the quality of life and preventing or postponing future problems.

The family members gain a fuller appreciation of the capabilities, limitations, and prospects for their loved ones and a stronger basis for making habilitation decisions. They can avoid or temper guilt feelings over necessary steps. They can also enjoy the increased or preserved capabilities of the frail parent and avoid or postpone the deterioration that often occurs when conditions are not fully identified, understood, and treated.

In response to concerns of family, physicians, and purchasers, the GAC program will be offered in a variety of mixes of inpatient and outpatient modes and involve different lengths of time, and different tests and procedures, depending on the health status and living arrangements of each patient. This variation will enable the GAC to promote its ability to tailor each care experience to each patient, rather than offering only a single, lockstep, standard experience for all. Decision makers will thus be offered choices and the ability to participate in designing the care experience for each patient, thereby promoting greater confidence in the GAC as committed to the patient rather than to payment.

Place. The GAC itself is located on the first floor of the hospital, with its own entrance and nearby parking. Family members can bring the patient to the door and have an attendant park their car rather than have to leave the patient. The entrance and all rooms in the GAC are wheelchair accessible. The hospital has acquired a van to transport those patients who can make no other arrangements. The van will go to the patient's home for pickup and return on discharge.

The facility is decorated in warm colors, is kept warm and quiet with carpeting and drapes, and has comfortable furniture. Signs in large letters are provided to help patients navigate within the unit. Equipment is kept out of sight except when being used, to reduce patient anxiety. Staff wear identifiable uniforms and name tags with names printed in large letters. Elderly volunteers, in addition to the patients' own family members, help GAC patients find their way about the unit.

Admission to the GAC unit can be arranged for any day of the week and any time of day, though morning and evening are preferred and promoted. For patients in outpatient phases of the program, specific tests can be obtained at a number of laboratory locations or through their own doctors' offices. The GAC staff coordinates such tests to maintain quality while facilitating access for the patient and promoting satisfaction for physicians. Flexibility of place is part of the customization process.

Price. Given the price sensitivity in the market, the charges for the GAC are flexible, based on how long a stay is needed and how many tests are required. The cost of the overnight stay is set at a level competitive with local hotels. Family members are encouraged to stay with the patients overnight. This practice saves on staffing costs, helps the patient cope, and makes the family members feel better in many cases. Family members and patients are encouraged to participate in deciding on further tests and procedures, especially when they will bear much or all of the costs.

Promotion. A special promotion strategy has been developed for each customer segment. Individual sales calls will be made to local insurers, especially the HMO, and to local physicians. A series of educational programs, guided tours, and speakers bureau programs will be provided for third-party referral sources. Speakers bureaus, public service announcements (PSAs), publicity, and paid advertising will be aimed at patients and their families.

An initial media blitz will be used to promote awareness of the GAC as a new program. A grand opening will be held, with a renowned speaker invited to discuss problems and programs for the frail elderly and their families. Newspaper, television, and radio PSAs and publicity will be used in addition to advertising. A direct mailer will be used to promote the grand opening. Representatives of high-leverage referral sources will be invited.

A major component of promotion is a community outreach effort by volunteers, including former patients of the GAC and their family members where possible. These volunteer outreach workers use a networking approach to identify prospects and referral sources. In addition, patients and their family members are regularly contacted following discharge to check on the progress of patients' and encourage them to mention the GAC to friends and acquaintances. Both outreach volunteers and former clients are supplied with brochures to distribute.

The qualifier or grabber for advertisements will be, "Before you Consider a Nursing Home . . . " and its theme that frail elderly persons and their families should try the GAC assessment before they resign themselves to placement in a nursing home. The body of the advertisement will cite statistics (initially from national studies, eventually from the GAC itself) showing increased longevity, independence, and quality of life for comprehensively assessed and treated patients. The hook will be an invitation to write or call for additional information or to make an appointment. The signature will be "Georgetown Community Hospital Geriatric Assessment Center—The First Resort for Frail Elderly." This will be tied in with copy indicating nursing home placement as a last resort.

After the GAC is well under way, a combination of slice-of-life stories based on actual cases and testimonials of actual patients will be used to supplement statistics. Advertisements aimed at adults with frail elderly parents will focus on the loss of freedom that occurs with a frail elderly parent to worry about and how that freedom can be regained through the use of the GAC program. Advertisements aimed at referral sources will describe personal cases appropriate for the GAC with the grabber, "Does this sound or look like someone you know?" and describing how the GAC can address the problems cited in each case.

Evaluation. One evaluation consists of checking on patients referred and admitted to the GAC to find out how they happened to come and where they heard about the program. Personal referral sources are recorded and followed up with thank-you contact and progress reports (where permitted) and sent brochures. Media sources are recorded for compilation and comparison to expenditures.

People calling in, coming to the grand opening, or writing for information will be logged by media or other sources used to learn about the GAC. Those attending the opening will be asked about it. People calling in will be asked the same thing. Coupons entitling their users to a free brochure are coded to indicate where and when they appeared. People writing in on their own are given a different internal box number to write to, varying by where the advertisement or story appeared.

A before survey has been done as part of the planning for the GAC, indicating what circumstances people feel are appropriate for GAC services, what levels of awareness exist relative to sources of care, preferences for sources, and intention to use GAC-type services. An after survey will be conducted to monitor awareness, preference, and intention changes following the media blitz. A panel approach will be used for the two surveys to avoid sampling differences affecting the results. Respondents will be asked recall and recognition questions in addition to repeats of the before survey questions.

The primary revenue and profit evaluation will be based on the number of people using the GAC and the revenues and expenses generated through room, testing, and counseling charges. Since this revenue is all marginal for the hospital, a marginal revenue and cost analysis will be used. Since the GAC is an elective program, appointments will be scheduled to minimize volume fluctuations and ensure that waits are short. This practice should keep costs lower. The calculated break-even volume is eight admissions a week, or 400 per year, assuming an average five-day LOS in the inpatient unit, requiring only a 10 percent share of the total prospects in the county or 7 percent counting out-of-county prospects.

A secondary evaluation will be based on tracking the GAC patients following assessment to determine what additional utilization and revenue they generate for the hospital through the use of subsequent inpatient and outpatient services. The utilization of medical staff members will also be tracked, even when it results in no hospital revenue, to monitor and report the program's contribution to member physicians. These will be compared to estimates of what would have been the case without the GAC.

A tertiary evaluation will be done based on the calculated effect of the GAC promotion and program on the hospital's share of the elderly market overall. This will be correlated with the before and after survey results. Only a portion of any share increase with its revenue and profit consequences will be attributed to the GAC effort, given other marketing and promotion efforts aimed at the same segment.

A further evaluation will focus on the impact of the GAC program and promotion effort on the awareness, attitudes, intentions, and behavior of the secondary markets incorporated in the overall GAC strategy— the general public, purchasers, physicians, and other referral sources. Since these are markets for far more than the GAC program, it is hoped that the GAC will improve, or at least not damage, the hospital's position with its other significant markets.

Suggested Readings

Marketing concepts and techniques

Albrecht, K., and R. Zemke. *Service America: Doing Business in the New Economy.* Homewood, IL: Dow Jones-Irwin, 1985.

Kotler, P., and R. Clarke. *Marketing for Health Care Organizations.* Englewood Cliffs, NJ: Prentice-Hall, 1987.

MacStravic, R. S. *Managing Health Care Marketing Communications.* Rockville, MD: Aspen, 1986.

Geriatric assessment centers

Aging and Long Term Care. "Geriatric Assessment Examined." (November– December 1986): 3–4.

Bowe, J. "Geriatric Center Closes the Loop in Delivery of Care." *Today's Nursing Home* (October 1984): 6–7.

Doyle, M., and M. Milligan. "One Hospital's Initiatives Meet Health Care Needs of Elderly." *Aging and Long Term Care* (September–October 1986): 4.

Dwight, M. "Is Your Hospital Ready to Market Geriatric Services?" *Health Management Quarterly* (Fall–Winter 1985): 1–5.

Modern Healthcare. "Geriatric Unit Could Cut Nursing Home Use—Report." (15 February 1985): 150.

The elderly

Blazer, J., and T. Rynne. "The New Senior Market." *Healthcare Executive* (March– April 1987): 18.

Dychtwald, K., and M. Zitter. "Blueprint for Hospitals in an Aging Society." Series. *Healthcare Forum* (1987).

Healthcare Marketing Report. "The Elderly: A Growing Market for Healthcare Services." (October 1987): 1–2, 7.

Newbold, P. "Preparing for Life's Third Age." *Healthcare Executive* (March–April 1987): 14.

Capitated Medicaid and St. Joseph's Hospital

Bradford Kirkman-Liff

Purpose of the Case

This case study presents the initial reactions of St. Joseph's Hospital and Medical Center, a large nonprofit hospital in Phoenix, Arizona, to the creation of a competitively bid, prepaid, managed care Medicaid program in 1982. It also presents the events in the first year of the Medicaid experiment and the subsequent reactions of the hospital. It illustrates the diverse set of issues that a hospital faces when it moves toward greater vertical integration in health care.

St. Joseph's Hospital and Medical Center in the Summer of 1982

St. Joseph's Hospital and Medical Center was founded in 1895 as the first hospital in Phoenix, Arizona, when the state was still a U.S. territory. In 1982 it was one of five hospitals founded, owned, and operated by the Sisters of Mercy, headquartered in Burlingame, California. Each of the five institutions was financially independent from the others and from the Sisters of Mercy.

This article has been reprinted from *Journal of Health Administration Education* Vol. 8, no. 4 (Fall 1990), with permission of the Association of University Programs in Health Administration.

In 1982 St. Joseph's Hospital and Medical Center operated 626 beds and was one of the two tertiary hospitals in Phoenix. At that time the hospital employed more than three thousand persons, and over one thousand private and staff physicians and residents were associated with the hospital. The hospital campus contained four separate buildings with approximately 622,000 square feet of floor space located on 23 acres of land in the uptown central business area of Phoenix.

Over 26,000 patients were admitted annually, with more than 25,000 persons seen in the emergency department. Over 40,000 outpatients were serviced through the ambulatory care clinics. In 1981 the hospital had an occupancy rate of 80.6 percent, with an average length of stay of 7 days. The hospital had recently completed a large facility renovation and expansion project. This included the construction of an outpatient services building, containing an ambulatory surgery facility, a large family medicine residency program center, and other outpatient care activities. Table 11.1 presents the 1981 balance sheet; Table 11.2 presents the 1981 statement of revenue and expenses; and Table 11.3 presents a summary of the financial ratios of St. Joseph's Hospital and Medical Center for 1981.

Besides providing inpatient care in the basic services of medicine, surgery, pediatrics, obstetrics and gynecology, and psychiatry, the hospital served as a tertiary care referral center and offered the following specialized services.

Barrow Neurological Institute (BNI)

BNI provides not only care and treatment of patients with neurological disorders and injuries but also education and research in the neurological science. BNI is Arizona's designated center for treatment of head injuries. Established in 1962, and now organized into six divisions, it is one of only three neurological institutes on the continent not connected with a university.

Cardiovascular services department

This department includes a cardiac catheterization laboratory, a cardiovascular diagnostic laboratory, a coronary care unit, an intensive care unit, and surgical suites. It is one of three such facilities in Phoenix.

Radiation oncology department

This department features a multidisciplinary, highly individualized approach to cancer treatment, providing consultation and treatment of both inpatients and outpatients for all types of cancer. It also conducts an

Table 11.1   Balance Sheet for St. Joseph's Hospital and Medical
Center, 1981

Assets		*Liabilities and Fund Balances*	
Current Assets		Current Liabilities	
Cash	$ 123,805	Current portion of	
Accounts receivable, less		long-term debt	$ 20,000
allowance for doubtful		Accounts payable	1,529,969
accounts of $2,185,604	12,324,448	Accrued liabilities	3,202,287
Supply inventories	974,417	Payable to	
Prepaid expenses	116,909	intermediaries	2,777,645
Total current assets	13,539,579	Total current liabilities	7,529,901
Investments	15,933,835	Construction liabilities	3,586,567
To be paid from trust		Long-term debt	86,184,472
fund assets	3,586,567		
Endowment fund assets	2,104,281	Other liabilities	1,200,188
Trust fund assets	25,768,521	Fund Balances	
		Unrestricted fund	43,323,583
Other assets	3,215,176	Restricted funds	2,760,990
Gross property, plant and		Endowment fund	2,104,281
equipment	108,132,953	Total fund balances	48,188,854
Less accumulated			
depreciation	22,004,363		
Net PPE	86,128,590		
	146,689,982		146,689,982

ongoing education program. This department is housed in a one-story,
5,200-square-foot building attached to the main hospital building.

Division of reproductive medicine (DORM)

DORM integrates and coordinates patient care in high-risk pregnancies
in the prenatal, neonatal and postpartum stages. DORM has played an
important role in the establishment of each of two statewide programs:
the Arizona Newborn Intensive Care and Transport Program and the Arizona Maternal Transport Program. The hospital is one of four hospitals
in the state participating in these programs.

   The Sisters of Mercy, as owners of the hospital, had a direct and
clear influence on the mission and values of the organization, as seen
in the long history of involvement with indigent ambulatory care by St.
Joseph's Hospital. In 1982 the hospital operated four charity/teaching

Table 11.2 Statement of Revenues and Expenses for St. Joseph's
Hospital and Medical Center, 1981

	Amount	*Percentage*
Operating Revenue		
Routine inpatient services	$30,291,220	33.3
Ancillary inpatient services	51,837,751	57.1
Outpatient services	8,696,801	9.6
Gross patient revenue	90,825,772	100.0
Less deductions from patient revenue		
Charity	2,548,050	2.8
Contractual and other allowances	11,179,352	12.2
Provision for doubtful accounts	2,415,139	2.7
Total deductions	16,142,541	17.7
Net patient revenue	74,683,231	82.3
Research grant revenue	410,119	.4
Other operating revenue	1,721,144	1.9
Total operating revenue	76,814,494	84.6
Operating Expenses		
Salaries and wages	35,104,189	38.6
Employee benefits	5,407,078	5.9
Medical fees	4,713,466	5.2
Supplies and services	20,899,770	23.0
Insurance	1,137,141	1.3
Depreciation	2,934,395	3.2
Interest	1,443,126	1.6
Total operating expenses	71,639,165	78.8
Operating revenue over operating expenses	5,175,329	5.7
Nonoperating Revenue	2,507,964	2.8
Excess of Revenue over Expenses	7,683,293	8.5

clinics with salaried physicians. These clinics provided services in repro-
ductive health, pediatrics, family medicine, and internal medicine. Care
was provided on a reduced or no-fee basis to low-income residents of
the area served by the hospital.

There were some minor problems at the newly opened facility.
Patient visits had declined, especially in the Family Medicine Practice
Center. The location of the center within the larger ambulatory care

Table 11.3   Summary of Financial Ratios for St. Joseph's Hospital and
Medical Center, 1981 and 1982

	1981	1982
Current ratio	1.80	1.76
Accounts Receivable		
Collection period in days	56.0	55.0
Bad debt ratio	.026	.028
New working capital per bed	$5,724	$4,652
Debt ratio (debt/equity)	1.9	1.7
Revenue per dollar of working capital	$23.78	$33.36
Net fixed assets per bed	$137,586	$157,397
Net profitability	.101	.043
Return of equity	.179	.085
Inpatient revenue per stay	$3,251	$3,888
Inpatient revenue per day	$467	$548
Costs per stay	$2,836	$3,799
Costs per day	$407	$535

facility made it difficult for patients to find the Family Medicine Practice
Center. It was no longer directly visible from the street, and it was also
difficult to find parking. Nonetheless, the development of the ambulatory
care center gave St. Joseph's Hospital and Medical Center the potential to
operate as a complete health care campus, providing a vertical spectrum
of care.

Maricopa County Health Care Marketplace in 1982

Maricopa County and Phoenix in the 1980s were among the fastest-
growing counties and cities in the United States. The population had
grown by 55.4 percent between 1970 and 1980, and in 1982 the county
population was approximately 1,600,000. Some 14 percent of the population was Hispanic, 3 percent was black, and 2 percent was Native
American. The 1982 midyear unemployment rate was 8.8 percent, as
compared with 10.5 percent for the United States as a whole.

Hospitals

There were 4.2 hospital beds per 1,000 population in the county. Utilization rates were slightly lower than the average for the U.S.: in 1981
there were 992 patient days per 1,000 population, and 171 admissions

per 1,000 population. Patient days had been sliding downward since
1975, when the rate was 1,027 patient days per 1,000 population. Data
on beds, patient days, admissions, and occupancy for all hospitals in
Maricopa County in 1981 is displayed in Table 11.4.

The health care marketplace in Phoenix was marked by a high
degree of interorganizational rivalry and competition in the 1980s. The
major rival of St. Joseph's Hospital was Good Samaritan Hospital and
Medical Center, a 770-bed tertiary hospital located about two miles from

Table 11.4 Beds, Patient Days, Admissions, and Occupancy for All
Hospitals in Maricopa County, 1981

Facility	Licensed Beds	Patient Days	Admissions	Percentage of Occupancy	Average Length of Stay (Days)
Walter O. Boswell Memorial	271	81,119	9,681	81.9	8.4
Valley View Community	56	12,180	1,629	59.6	7.5
Wickenburg Community	34	5,304	864	42.7	6.1
John C. Lincoln	282	71,409	12,289	69.4	5.8
Scottsdale Community	34	7,475	1,204	60.2	6.2
Scottsdale Memorial	340	101,591	16,539	81.9	6.1
Maryvale Samaritan	256	56,713	8,918	60.7	6.4
Phoenix Baptist	231	72,500	11,649	86.0	6.2
Phoenix General	301	65,474	9,591	59.6	6.8
Humana Phoenix	314	63,801	10,195	55.7	6.3
Good Samaritan	695	199,320	27,781	78.6	7.2
Maricopa Medical Center	549	136,557	19,252	67.9	7.1
Phoenix Memorial	160	38,980	5,765	66.7	6.8
Phoenix Community	50	11,780	2,089	64.5	5.6
St. Joseph's	626	175,796	25,262	80.6	7.0
St. Luke's	420	114,205	10,912	74.7	10.5
Tempe St. Luke's	110	15,480	2,705	38.6	5.7
Chandler Community	42	11,455	2,152	74.7	5.3
Desert Samaritan	273	87,688	16,239	88.0	5.4
Mesa General	105	25,941	4,236	67.7	6.1
Mesa Lutheran	296	90,583	13,942	83.7	6.5
Glendale Samaritan	52	14,104	2,383	62.3	5.9
Camelback Phoenix	89	25,072	1,226	77.2	20.5
Camelback Scottsdale	74	16,329	838	60.5	19.5
Total	5,670	1,500,856	217,341	72.9	6.9

St. Joseph's. (The third tertiary hospital in the state was located at the medical school in Tucson, 125 miles away.) Good Samaritan was the flagship institution of Samaritan Health Service, the major multihospital system in Arizona. Both St. Joseph's and Good Samaritan operated open heart surgery programs, cardiac and neonatal ICUs, oncology centers, renal dialysis centers, and genetic counseling services. The institutions viewed themselves as in constant struggle to be seen as the premier health institution in the state.

The State of Arizona's refusal to participate in Medicaid had resulted in the development of a strong county health department in Phoenix. The Maricopa County Department of Health Services operated Maricopa Medical Center (a 549-bed hospital) and a network of 13 primary care sites. The facilities were located in or near low-income neighborhoods and were staffed by bilingual providers.

HMOs

Only two HMOs were operating in Phoenix in 1982; each had approximately 15,000 members. The Arizona Health Plan (AHP) was started in 1972 by Connecticut General, an insurance company based in Hartford, Connecticut. The competitor was INA Health Plan (INA), which was started by Arizona Blue Cross-Blue Shield in 1972 as ABC HMO. When this HMO encountered financial difficulties, it was purchased and renamed by the Insurance Company of North America, based in Philadelphia, Pennsylvania. The two HMOs had been federally qualified since 1978. As neither HMO owned or operated its own hospital, each contracted with various nonprofit hospitals in the community for inpatient care. The two HMOs used a combination of discounted charges and per diem rates to pay their contracting hospitals. As such, the hospitals viewed the HMOs as patient referral sources. The physicians in both plans were salaried employees.

The parent companies of AHP and INA had announced plans for a merger in early 1983, and there was speculation that the two HMOs would be merged into one plan, with a total enrollment of more than 150,000 members. If no new HMOs entered the Phoenix market, antitrust considerations might have required one of the parent firms to sell one of the HMOs, as such a merger would then have resulted in no inter-HMO competition. However, various efforts were underway in the Phoenix community to create new HMOs. It was anticipated that the AHP and INA merger would create a "price umbrella" under which new HMOs could successfully compete. These efforts focused on the development of Independent Practice Association ("open panel") HMOs, as both AHP and INA were staff model plans.

There were approximately 2,910 physicians in active practice in Maricopa in 1982. Table 11.5 provides more detailed information on the supply of physicians. The distribution of medical staff within St. Joseph's Hospital generally mirrored the county distribution, except for an underrepresentation of family medicine physicians.

The AHCCCS Program: Structure and First-Year Bid Process

In 1982 the state of Arizona initiated a program of statewide competitive bidding for capitated contracts with health plans that were to enroll Medicaid patients. Arizona had not participated in Medicaid prior to this, and indigent patients had been served by county health department clinics and hospitals. (Competitive bidding was not used by the county health department in its contracts for acute medical care services. The county health department used competitive bidding as part of the contracting process for nursing home services for long-term care patients.)

The Arizona Health Care Cost Containment System (AHCCCS, pronounced "access") was intended to provide an acceptable level of quality health care to the Medicaid population while controlling costs through creation of a competitive market for indigent care. The program was also expected to stimulate the formation of new health maintenance organizations that would serve the non-Medicaid population.

Table 11.5   Practicing Physicians in Maricopa County, 1982

| | Form of Practice | | | |
| | | Hospital-Based | | |
	Office-Based	Residents	Full-Time Staff	Total
General practice or family medicine	420	65	15	500
Internal medicine	250	130	20	400
Obstetrics/gynecology	160	45	5	210
Other medical specialties	335	45	20	400
Surgical specialties	565	80	20	665
Other specialties	525	90	120	735
Total	2,255	455	200	2,910

The legislation creating AHCCCS contained six major mechanisms for restraining health care costs while, at the same time, ensuring that appropriate levels of quality health care services were provided to eligible persons in a dignified fashion. Each of these items was designed to contribute to the establishment of a health care financing system that would be less expensive than conventional fee-for-service systems that lack such devices. The mechanisms were:

1. primary care physicians acting as "gatekeepers" (case managers)
2. prepaid capitated financing
3. competitive bidding process
4. patient cost sharing (involving small copayments)
5. limitations on freedom-of-choice of hospitals, physicians, and other providers
6. capitation of the state by the federal government (federal contribution would be prospectively determined and based on a cost per recipient, rather than retrospectively determined from fee-for-service costs)

Request for proposals

One of the first activities of the program was issuance of a request for proposals (RFP) by the administrator of AHCCCS on July 2, 1982. Bids were due on August 6, and contracts resulting from this request for proposals would be effective for one year from October 1, 1982. The bidding process would be repeated for contracts to resume or begin on October 1, 1983. The RFP from the administrator of AHCCCS was a lengthy document that specified the procedure for bidding and detailed specifications for the services to be offered on a prepaid, capitated basis for the first year of the program. The RFP also contained previously unreleased information concerning the procedures and policies of the program.

Priorities in bidder selection

The RFP made it clear that priority in the contract award process would be given to proposals from full-service providers. However, it was anticipated by some providers that partial-service providers offering service for prepaid capitation payments would be awarded contracts and that the AHCCCS administrator would link such providers to networks providing the full range of services. Potential partial-service providers, such as hospitals, were encouraged at public meetings to develop networks in advance of the bidding and to submit full-service bids.

Members

There were three major categories of potential AHCCCS members. First, there were the categorically needy, who would be eligible for AHCCCS due to their eligibility for other welfare programs. The state would receive substantial federal funding for this population. This category would be composed of recipients of Aid for Families with Dependent Children (AFDC) and Supplemental Security Income (SSI) benefits. The SSI population includes aged, disabled, and blind beneficiaries. Second, there were the medically needy and medically indigent, who would be eligible for AHCCCS due to their low incomes. The state would receive no federal funding for this population. However, some of the medically needy and medically indigent would be Medicare recipients, and the contractors would receive payment for Medicare-covered services from HCFA. Finally, the program included the potential offering of the AHC-CCS contractors to state, county, and private employees. If desired by employers, full-service AHCCCS contractors would be included among the other HMOs offered to employees during the normal open enrollment period. The state, county, and private employee groups would not be subsidized by the program: they and their employers would share in the full cost of the capitation. The rationale for including these nonindigents in the program was threefold. (1) Inclusion of state, county, and private employees in the program would make participation in AHCCCS more attractive for HMOs and hence stimulate more competition for contracts, which would result in lower costs. (2) The inclusion of a private sector population in the contracted plans would provide a barrier to providing lower-quality care and service for the low-income groups. (3) The costs of coverage under AHCCCS were expected to be substantially lower than that available from conventional insurers. This would reduce state and county government employee benefit costs and would also make health insurance affordable for small employers.

Services

The services to be provided under the contract included hospital inpatient, outpatient and emergency room services, and physician services (surgery, anesthesia, inpatient visits, office visits, and obstetrics), as well as lab, X-ray, pharmacy, emergency mental health (forty-eight hours of confinement for acute psychotic episodes), emergency dental, and other services (ambulance, medical supplies, nursing services). Certain services were excluded from AHCCCS coverage: family planning, abortions, cosmetic surgery, experimental transplants, long-term care (nursing home,

home health, hospice and other associated services), and nonemergency mental and dental services.

Choice

In order to stimulate high quality, enrollees would be allowed to choose their own contractors and would be allowed to switch contractors once a year. Enrollees would not have to pay any monthly fees for their coverage (although they would have to pay some copayments for actual use of services). This lack of cost sharing meant that enrollees would have no financial risk for their choice of contractor. Those enrollees who did not express a preference would be assigned by the AHCCCS administrator to the lowest-cost contractor until that provider's capacity was filled.

Contractor service areas

Respondents to the RFP were required to bid prepaid capitation rates and total capacity by geographical area. Bidders could choose to offer capacity either statewide or by geographical area. In preparing capacity bids, potential contractors were to indicate the geographical areas to be served and the maximum number of enrollees that the bidder wished to serve in each specific geographical area. The bidder could not, however, specify the number of enrollees to be served by category of eligibility. In other words, a bidder could not bid for a maximum number of recipients in each welfare category in an area; it could limit only the total number of recipients in an area. A geographical area could be a portion of a county, an entire county, or multiple counties. If the geographic region of service was smaller than a county, the bidder was to designate the service area by providing United States Postal Service zip codes as geographic area delineators. Contractors had no assurances that they would be awarded their full capacity of enrollees.

Gatekeeper system

Each full-service contractor was to be responsible for developing its own gatekeeper system. Each enrollee would be required to select or be assigned to a primary care physician who would have to be a family or general practitioner, a pediatrician, a general internist, or an obstetrician/gynecologist. The primary care physician would serve as case manager for assigned enrollees and, except for emergency treatments, would approve all care and referrals.

Utilization control and quality assurance

Contractors were responsible for developing their own utilization control and quality assurance programs, which would be subject to the approval of the administrator. These programs would be expected to include peer review programs, utilization control programs, and utilization statistics reporting systems. Contractors were expected to develop preadmission certification, concurrent review, and early discharge planning programs, as well as outpatient surgery and testing, second opinion, and same-day-as-surgery admission programs.

Copayments

AHCCCS legislation prescribed that nominal copayment fees (between $.50 and $1.00) be charged to certain members for certain services rendered by providers. Potential contractors were required to adjust capitation rate bids for required copayments and for any optional copayments that they chose to require.

Reinsurance

While the AHCCCS program of prepaid capitated networks was designed for risk and cost sharing between contractors and AHCCCS, providers were allowed to seek outside sources for limited amounts of reinsurance coverage. However, such reinsurance coverage could not reduce the contractor's liability below $5,000 per member during any consecutive twelve-month period beginning at the date of enrollment of the individual members. AHCCCS announced plans to provide reinsurance for contractors whose costs surpassed $20,000 for emergency and inpatient services for one individual. Aggregate stop-loss coverage might be available for some contractors (most likely small and rural contractors), but the AHCCCS administration could not provide any specific details about this coverage. Based on studies done by the administrator's actuaries it was estimated that 4 percent of the AFDC enrollees, 2 percent of the SSI and medically indigent and medically needy with Medicare, 8 percent of the medically indigent and medically needy without Medicare, and 2 percent of the state, county, and private employees would have health care expenses in excess of $20,000 per year per individual.

Deferred liability

AHCCCS stated that enrollment in a prepaid capitated plan would not become effective for individuals who were hospital patients at the time of enrollment until such individuals were discharged from hospitals. AHCCCS would be financially responsible for services provided to such enrollees from the time of eligibility determination until the effective date of enrollment (date of discharge). Contractors under the AHCCCS program would not be responsible for the costs of care for such enrollees until the enrollee was discharged from the hospital.

Proposal evaluation

A two-step process would be used to select successful bids. First, the acceptability of potential contractors to the AHCCCS program would he determined. Second, the potential contractors determined to be acceptable would be ranked on the basis of objective criteria. These determinations would be made on a county-by-county basis. Contracts would be awarded to the highest-ranking bidders, by county and by descending ranking until the AHCCCS requirements of each county were met.

Acceptability

An acceptable proposal would have to demonstrate the bidder's ability to adequately and responsibly provide the proposed service to AHCCCS enrollees at a reasonable cost. Because acceptability would represent the minimum requirements for any potentially successful bidder, the proposal would have to show that the bidder was acceptable in all of the following areas:

Technical: The bidder must be qualified to provide the proposed services and to be experienced in these areas. The bidder must have adequate physical facilities, equipment, and professional staff to provide the proposed level of service.

Price: The Director may reject any bid at a price that is unreasonable when compared to the benefits offered or that would endanger the solvency of the AHCCCS Fund.

Legal: The bidder must be an entity able to contract with the State and to contract with other entities as necessary. The bidding entity must be legally responsible in the event of litigation.

Management: The bidder must be able to effectively and efficiently provide the proposed services. It must have appropriate management structures, experienced personnel, and adequate information systems.

Finance: The bidder must be financially viable and have adequate resources relative to the proposed level of risk. It must be clear that the bidder can finance the facilities and operating expenses associated with a successful AHCCCS bid. While no specific financial resource requirement will be used, all bidders and particularly new organizations must have well-thought-out financial plans that demonstrate financial sophistication and ability.

Ranking

The rankings would be based on price, delivery system characteristics, and administrative simplicity. First, the bids offering the lowest prices would be favored, all other things being equal. Second, the bids that offered delivery systems with greater accessibility would be favored, all other things being equal. Third, because the state would have substantial and significant costs associated with AHCCCS administration, those programs that require less state involvement would be favored. The number of providers and the nature of the contractual relationships and proven organizational effectiveness would be considered, as more complex delivery organizations could separate control from responsibility and lead to problems in quality of service. This was taken to mean that already existing staff model HMOs would be preferred to newly created IPA or network model plans.

Available actuarial data

AHCCCS administration provided data to assist potential bidders in the preparation of bids because directly applicable historical utilization and cost experience data were not available and because many of the available data sources that existed within the state were felt to be unreliable. The information represented a consolidation of what was believed to be the most consistent, reliable sources available, based on the judgment of the administrator's actuaries after reviewing available data. Bidders were cautioned to make their own decisions as to the reliability of this information.

Sources of data

Three major sources of utilization and claims experience were available. Medicaid fee-for-service experience from Texas, New Mexico, Colorado, California, and Nevada was available in varying amounts of detail. In addition to the fee-for-service data from other states' Medicaid programs, studies were conducted in several counties in Arizona to determine costs of the counties' health programs. The final general source of data considered came from experience of California's prepaid health plans in covering MediCal eligibles. This source of data had perhaps the greatest amount of available detail regarding categorically needy individuals. It also gave some indication of the potential savings for mature, well-run alternative delivery systems. The levels shown were considered reasonable for newly formed provider organizations that could achieve medical cost savings comparable to well-managed IPA model HMOs and beginning closed-panel HMOs. Table 11.6 contains these utilization estimates, and Table 11.7 contains estimates of potential eligibles.

Based on the available data, bidders were told to anticipate that 70–75 percent of the AFDC population would be children, with the majority of the remaining population being younger female adults. They were also told to expect that the medically needy and medically indigent populations that were not eligible for Medicare (but were eligible for AHCCCS) would differ from the AFDC because many more two-parent families would be included in the former. This would result in a population that would be roughly 50 percent adults and 50 percent children. Men would comprise 40–45 percent of the adult portion of this population.

St. Joseph's View of AHCCCS in the Summer of 1982

In the view of senior managers, there were five possible benefits to participating as a direct bidder in AHCCCS. First, they would gain experience with the HMO concept. Although there was only one operating HMO in the Phoenix market, HMOs were becoming a more dominant force in health care nationwide. Participating in AHCCCS could give them the needed learning experience in order to establish a hospital-controlled HMO, possibly in partnership with their medical staff.

Second, they could use the existing excess capacity to obtain more funding for their charity clinics. These clinics had excess capacity to handle more patients, and as the physicians were on salary, there would be very little additional direct monetary cost. There was also a fear that the clinics could lose so many patients to AHCCCS that their viability as teaching programs would be threatened. Participation would bring in additional revenue and more teaching material.

Third, the managers thought that the reinsurance aspects of the program for catastrophic cases could result in the hospital receiving direct payments from AHCCCS on a fee-for-service basis. Given the hospital's traditional markup and profit margin, such revenues would be welcome. However, it was not clear whether the hospital would receive the full traditional markup on these contracted patients.

Fourth, by contracting as an AHCCCS plan they would capture a portion of the AHCCCS population and could control and funnel the referrals to their own institution. This would strengthen the existing specialties services and provide additional patients for the specialists affiliated with the hospital.

Table 11.6 Estimated Utilization Ranges by Enrollment Category (Annual Rates per 1,000 Members)

Enrollment Category Type of Service (Unit)	AFDC	Aged and MI and MN with Medicare	Disabled	Blind	MI and MN without Non-Medicare
Hospital inpatient (day)	400–600	2,200–2,800	2,400–3,000	2,100–2,700	450–700
Hospital OP and ER (visit)	150–250	400–500	700–900	500–600	175–290
Physician services					
Surgery (procedure)	340–420	600–750	625–775	660–800	400–475
Anesthesia (case)	40–60	60–80	65–85	70–90	45–70
Inpatient visits (visit)	475	2,075	2,225	2,000	550
Office visits (visit)	3,450–4,250	4,630–5,630	4,900–5,900	4,700–5,700	4,000–4,900
Obstetrics (case)	30–35	—	2–4	—	35–40
Misc. medical (procedure)	1,150–1,450	2,420–2,960	2,450–3,050	2,300–2,800	1,325–1,675
Lab (procedure)	2,250–2,750	4,250–5,250	5,000–5,800	3,800–4,600	2,600–3,150
X-ray (procedure)	525–625	1,000–1,300	1,000–1,200	900–1,100	600–720
Emergency mental health (visit)	125–175	50–100	500–700	250–300	145–200
Pharmacy (script)	3,500–4,200	16,000–17,500	16,500–18,000	13,500–16,500	4,000–4,800
Emergency dental (visit)	180–200	190–230	215–265	165–200	190–230
Other (service)	75–125	400–600	1,000–1,300	1,250–1,750	90–150

Table 11.7 Estimates of Potential Eligibles

Area	AFDC	SSI	Total AFDC/SSI	Medically Indigent/Needy	Total
Maricopa	29,904	13,304	43,208	35,592	78,800
Arizona Total	61,661	29,420	91,081	123,878	214,959

Fifth, participation in AHCCCS would allow the institution to fulfill its mission to provide care to the poor. The chief financial officer and the Sisters on the board of trustees of the hospital had a strong belief in this mission. In the past the hospital had to work very hard to find the resources to operate its programs targeted at low-income groups. Now they had the opportunity to provide comprehensive, coordinated care to this population, paid for with public funds. The potential profits from an AHCCCS contract could in turn be used to expand their services for those low-income individuals who were not deemed eligible for AHCCCS membership. The hospital could use the public program to cross-subsidize the charity programs. Since the eligibility levels were substantially below the federal poverty line, it was expected that many of the poor would not be members of the program.

There were substantial perceived risks of bidding. The major concern was financial: could an institution make money on the contract? It was expected that the reimbursement would be less than the full charges that would normally be charged to patients. However, due to contractual discounts, fewer and fewer patients in the general public were paying full charges. The important concern was the possibility that the actual costs for care would be substantially greater than the capitation. Despite the provision of estimated utilization rates by the state, there was no available actuarial data on the health care utilization patterns of the poor in Arizona.

There also was a concern about the willingness of the state to cooperate with contractors. The managers at St. Joseph's Hospital did not think that AHCCCS would necessarily view contracting as a win-win situation. Rather, they felt that AHCCCS would take a more adversarial stance, demanding the lowest possible rates, refusing to help if a plan ran into financial problems, and unwilling to pay higher rates, even though that might mean that the program would be more stable. The short time period between the release of the RFP and the response date was indicative of the hurried nature of the program's implementation. AHCCCS had indicated publicly that the bid deadlines could not be changed.

Another risk involved the targeted population. There was a strong risk of adverse selection. As enrollees would have the opportunity to pick their provider, those with the most past experience with the medical care system would be more likely to select a known, high-quality institution than a less well known institution. Such potentially high-cost patients could quickly fill the provider's enrollment capacity, leaving it without enough low-cost patients to balance the revenues. The institution would in this way experience adverse selection.

The contract requirement to establish a quality assurance and utilization review program was also of some concern, as St. Joseph's Hospital did not have a formal utilization review program and the quality assurance effort was focused on inpatient care, especially surgery.

A last issue involved copayments and benefits. Was the contractor to refuse to provide care if a patient did not have the copayment, or was the contractor required to provide the care and then bill the patient for the copayments? The benefit structure of the program was very confusing. Was the contractor to refuse to provide those services that were excluded from the benefits, even if a patient had clear clinical needs for those services, or was the contractor required to provide the care but bill the patient for the costs of those services?

Year One Decision by St. Joseph's Hospital

After some initial discussions, a consensus emerged among the managers that the overall uncertainty about the program and the short time frame for a response to the RFP made it impossible for them to decide to participate in the program as a direct contractor. The administration of St. Joseph's Hospital assumed that AHCCCS contractors would be reputable firms. They expected the state to do a careful job of selecting the contractors and monitoring their activities. The administration felt that the hospital would be better off as a subcontractor to the intermediaries, receiving payment for hospital care on a fee-for-service basis. In this way it would avoid taking risks, while still receiving AHCCCS revenues. A decision was made to negotiate subcontracts with whichever winning bidders approached the hospital, on a discounted fee-for-service basis.

Results of Bidding in the First Year of AHCCCS

Five organizations submitted full-service proposals to AHCCCS to serve indigent in Maricopa County. The bids were all judged to be too high, and bidders were asked for "voluntary price reductions," as state procurement law prohibited negotiations between AHCCCS and the bidders.

All five bidders received contracts after submitting lower bids. Table 11.8 displays the original and revised bids for the different categories of AHCCCS members.

Arizona Family Physicians, later to be known as Arizona Physicians IPA (APIPA) received contracts in all fourteen Arizona Counties, including Maricopa County. The plan was created by a group of family medicine physicians based in Phoenix, solely to bid for AHCCCS contracts. The plan operated primarily on a discounted fee-for-service basis, with some capitation of gatekeepers who had large patient rosters. It was the only statewide plan in the program, and it offered to provide care to 120,000 members in Maricopa County, a figure greater than the estimated total participants in the county.

Health Care Providers (HCP) received contracts in Maricopa and adjoining Pinal counties. The plan was organized by two ophthalmologists, was based in Phoenix, and like APIPA was created solely to bid for AHCCCS contracts. It operated on a discounted fee-for-service basis with

Table 11.8   AHCCCS Bidders and Prices for Maricopa County, Contract Year One (10/82–9/83)

	Categories					
Bidder	Composite	AFDC	Aged	Disabled	Blind	MN/MI
Arizona Family Physicians						
Original	75.26	64.18	45.31	155.88	137.86	69.51
Revised	70.79	55.05	45.31	149.31	129.74	69.51
Health Care Providers						
Original	95.59	79.40	54.51	195.28	177.19	91.90
Revised	83.83	61.14	50.08	182.53	165.05	85.58
Maricopa County Department of Health Services						
Original	87.53	55.31	59.79	125.56	96.21	116.38
Revised	83.22	54.30	59.79	125.56	96.21	100.69
Arizona Health Plan—INA Health Plan of Arizona						
Original	97.56	60.00	52.17	182.15	173.91	121.76
Revised	90.75	56.11	49.20	164.72	163.41	114.10

a panel of primary care physicians. It offered to provide care to 95,000 members in Maricopa County.

Maricopa County Department of Health Services received a contract through a health plan created to bid for AHCCCS services. Known as Maricopa Health Plan (MHP), it was organized as a unit of the county health department and operated through contracts with the Maricopa Medical Center for inpatient care and with the existing county primary care centers for ambulatory care. It offered to provide care to 105,000 members. The plan was managed by Health America, under a multiyear contract, with the management eventually to be assumed by the county health department.

Arizona Health Plan and INA Health Plan, the two existing HMOs in Maricopa County, submitted separate proposals with identical prices, as the two plans were coordinating their activities in preparation for merger. For all purposes, they were seen as one contractor. The owners of the plans had received antitrust clearance for the merger and therefore could coordinate their prices prior to the merger. Each plan offered to enroll 2,500 AHCCCS members.

Eleven other health plans received AHCCCS contracts to serve clients in other counties. Most of these plans were created by local hospitals and physicians specifically to bid for AHCCCS contracts; they served the population in a single rural county.

St. Joseph's Experiences with the AHCCCS Program in 1982 and 1983

The institution contracted with two AHCCCS plans (Arizona Physicians IPA and Health Care Providers) to provide inpatient care on a discounted fee-for-service basis. In order to assure continuity of care, the hospital also entered into a subcontract with the Maricopa Health Plan to provide outpatient care to AHCCCS patients who were already receiving care through the clinics. The discounts were not deep, and there remained reasonable profits in these arrangements. These contracts called for no vertical integration between St. Joseph's Hospital and the three AHCCCS plans. St. Joseph's was to receive payment for providing services to the plans' members, as with any other insured group.

St. Joseph's Hospital was not unique in this approach. In 1982 almost all of the private, nonprofit hospitals in Maricopa County decided to subcontract with AHCCCS plans. None developed their own plan. All of the hospitals expected to be paid rates that were close to their full charges and wanted to avoid the risks of participating as a contractor.

None of the hospitals expected to receive sufficient entrepreneurial profits from participating as a bidder to make owning a plan worthwhile. As in the case of St. Joseph's Hospital, none of the other Phoenix hospitals had experience with managing an HMO.

It rapidly became apparent that the expectations of the managers at St. Joseph's Hospital were incorrect. The first year of AHCCCS was a very difficult period for the state, the program, the health plans, the participants, and the subcontracting providers. Enrollment grew beyond initial projections, resulting in a deficit in the state budget. Confusion between program administration, the contracting health plans, and the subcontracting physicians and hospitals led to a small number of unfortunate cases of uncoordinated and inadequate care. These were publicized in the local media. In order to avoid more of these incidents, the contracting health plans and their subcontractors frequently provided services to individuals who were in the process of seeking eligibility for AHCCCS. If the patient's eligibility application was eventually rejected, however, the plans could not recoup such care costs from future capitation, and subcontractors might not receive reimbursement.

These problems had negative impacts on St. Joseph's Hospital. Arizona Physicians IPA and Health Care Providers were very slow in paying their bills. Legal battles with these plans over payment started after the first four months of the program. The experience with these plans was generally felt to be unfavorable. There were concerns over the effectiveness of the quality assurance and utilization review activities of these plans. At the same time the AHCCCS administration itself was slow to pay the bills for the fee-for-service patients who were hospitalized at St. Joseph's as AHCCCS members.

Overall, in 1982 the hospital had an 76.6 percent occupancy, with an average length of stay of 7.1 days. Table 11.9 presents the 1982 balance sheet, Table 11.10 presents the 1982 statement of revenue and expenses, and Table 11.3 presents a summary of the financial ratios of St. Joseph's Hospital and Medical Center for 1982. Between 1981 and 1982 the hospital experienced substantial increases in its operating expenses, especially in personnel costs, and these translated into large rate increases. However, the overall profitability of the hospital declined.

Other Changes in the Maricopa County Health Care Marketplace

Phoenix, like the rest of the country, was recovering from the recession. The midyear unemployment rate was 6.0 percent, as compared with 8.8

Table 11.9 Balance Sheet for St. Joseph's Hospital and Medical
Center, 1982

Assets		*Liabilities and Fund Balances*	
Current Assets		Current Liabilities	
Cash	$ 170,593	Current portion of	
Accounts receivable, less		long-term debt	$ 57,325
allowance for doubtful		Accounts payable	2,020,925
accounts of $2,439,047	13,946,478	Accrued liabilities	3,808,030
Supply inventories	990,033	Payable to	
Prepaid expenses	151,207	intermediaries	2,787,726
Total current assets	15,258,311	Total current liabilities	8,674,006
Investments	16,852,032	Construction liabilities	1,052,116
To be paid from trust			
fund assets	1,052,116	Long-term debt	86,525,398
Endowment fund assets	2,182,441	Other liabilities	1,232,351
Trust fund assets	14,296,036	Fund balances	
		Unrestricted fund	47,586,765
Other assets	2,834,535	Restricted funds	2,700,896
Property, plant and		Endowment fund	2,182,441
equipment	125,167,031	Total fund balances	52,470,102
Less accumulated			
depreciation	26,636,413		
Net PPE	98,530,618		
	149,953,973		149,953,973

percent for the U.S. as a whole. Data on beds, patient days, admissions, and occupancy for all hospitals in Maricopa County in 1982 is shown in Table 11.11.

The two operating HMOs had merged into a single plan, renamed CIGNA Healthplan, with more than 175,000 members and thirteen primary care centers. CIGNA continued to employ physicians on a salary basis and used a combination of discounted charges and per diem rates to pay contracting hospitals. No additional HMOs appeared in the Phoenix market in the year since the start of AHCCCS, although some of the AHCCCS plans indicated that they might develop non-AHCCCS programs. One Tucson-based plan, Intergroup, was rumored to be planning an expansion into the Phoenix market. Intergroup in Tucson capitated multispecialty groups for ambulatory care and established shared risk pools with these groups for the costs of hospitalization.

Table 11.10 Statement of Revenues and Expenses for St. Joseph's
Hospital and Medical Center, 1982

	Amount	*Percentage*
Operating Revenue		
Routine inpatient services	$ 34,766,399	32.7
Ancillary inpatient services	61,109,002	57.5
Outpatient services	10,378,101	9.8
Gross patient revenue	106,253,502	100.0
Less deductions from patient revenue		
Charity	2,798,277	2.6
Contractual and other allowances	9,017,319	8.5
Provision for doubtful accounts	3,068,185	2.9
Total deductions	14,883,781	14.0
Net patient revenue	91,369,721	86.0
Research grant revenue	573,099	.5
Other operating revenue	2,138,118	2.0
Total operating revenue	94,080,938	88.5
Operating Expenses		
Salaries and wages	44,058,215	41.5
Employee benefits	7,500,387	7.0
Medical fees	5,130,499	4.8
Supplies and services	26,153,024	24.6
Insurance	1,176,920	1.1
Depreciation	4,764,137	4.5
Interest	4,898,434	4.6
Total operating expenses	93,681,616	88.1
Operating revenue over operating expenses	399,322	.4
Nonoperating Revenue	3,683,649	3.5
Excess of Revenue over Expenses	4,082,971	3.8

The AHCCCS Program: Second-Year Bid Process

In the summer of 1983 the administrator of AHCCCS issued a second
request for proposals seeking bids from health care organizations to
serve indigent for the next two-year period. Key policy decisions during
the early months of 1983 affected the development of the AHCCCS
administration's request for proposals. Among those policy decisions
were the following:

Table 11.11   Beds, Patient Days, Admissions, and Occupancy for All
Hospitals in Maricopa County, 1982

Facility	Licensed Beds	Patient Days	Admissions	Percentage of Occupancy	Average Length of Stay (Days)
Walter O. Boswell Memorial	355	89,575	10,632	69.1	8.4
Valley View Community	104	13,107	1,606	45.2	8.2
Wickenburg Community	34	4,507	838	36.3	5.4
John C. Lincoln	282	72,914	12,272	70.8	5.9
Scottsdale Community	34	7,621	1,226	61.4	6.2
Scottsdale Memorial	350	100,574	17,101	78.3	5.9
Maryvale Samaritan	256	59,972	9,104	64.2	6.6
Phoenix Baptist	231	69,526	11,538	82.5	6.0
Phoenix General	301	67,201	9,847	61.2	6.8
Humana Phoenix	314	65,905	10,679	57.5	6.2
Good Samaritan	770	198,275	33,081	70.8	6.0
Maricopa Medical Center	559	130,366	19,064	63.9	6.8
Phoenix Memorial	160	38,804	6,069	66.4	6.4
Phoenix Community	50	13,719	2,376	75.2	5.8
St. Joseph's	626	175,050	24,661	76.6	7.1
St. Luke's	280	63,903	8,207	63.1	7.8
Tempe St. Luke's	110	15,757	2,741	39.2	5.7
Chandler Community	42	11,469	2,146	69.0	5.3
Desert Samaritan	273	90,425	16,284	90.7	5.6
Mesa General	105	24,421	4,059	63.7	6.0
Mesa Lutheran	325	98,511	13,950	80.6	7.1
Glendale Samaritan	62	13,279	2,606	58.7	5.1
Camelback Phoenix	89	24,874	1,118	76.6	22.2
Camelback Scottsdale	81	20,250	928	68.9	21.8
St. Lukes Behavioral	150	47,375	2,134	86.5	22.2
Total	5,943	1,517,380	224,267	70.1	6.8

Bids from partial-service providers would not be solicited under
the RFP.

Bids for nonsubsidized groups (state, county, and private employees) would not be included in the RFP. However, only those bidders
awarded contracts for subsidized groups would be eligible to participate
in any subsequent procurement for nonsubsidized groups under AHC-
CCS. This decision was prompted by the unwillingness of state, county,

and private employers to offer AHCCCS plans to their employees during open enrollment, due to the turmoil during the first year of the program.

The individual stop-loss level, or deductible, for AHCCCS-provided reinsurance would remain at $20,000 per member per year; however, contracting health plans would now be liable for 10 percent coinsurance on all costs in excess of the deductible. AHCCCS reinsurance coverage would be provided for 90 percent of emergency and inpatient costs over $20,000 per member per year. AHCCCS contractors in the first year had been unable to obtain commercial reinsurance for the costs between $5,000 and $20,000 per member per year. Plans would therefore be at risk for the first $20,000 of each member's costs, and for 10 percent of all costs over $20,000.

Contracts would be for one year from October 1, 1983, and would be renewable at the option of both parties for one additional year.

Bidders on the RFP were now required to provide services to on-reservation Native Americans who chose to leave the reservation to receive health care services through AHCCCS. These services would be paid for on a capped fee-for-service basis, with the AHCCCS administration establishing the upper allowable fee level. This feature was included because AHCCCS was required by federal court rulings to provide care to eligible Native Americans who needed services that were not available on the reservation. This population group was not included as part of the prepaid capitation population, however, because of uncertainty about the rate at which they would leave the reservation to use AHCCCS contractor services, and because the potential utilization levels of those who might want to enroll were difficult to predict due to their ability to obtain free care through the Indian Health Service.

There were also other policy positions relating to enrollment policy and assignments that would impact on the development of proposals and bid prices. Bidders were instructed to develop bid rates to reflect the following enrollment policy decisions:

Members who did not choose another provider would remain with the current plan if the plan received a new contract.

Members who did not select a contracting health plan within the prescribed time frames (thirty days for categorical members, two days for the medically indigent/medically needy members) would be assigned to the lowest bidder in the service area. This would reduce the potential for adverse selection by high-cost enrollees: it was therefore expected that this would assure the submission of reasonable low bids. Without "auto-assignment," established plans like CIGNA would attract a disproportionate share of enrollees with preexisting conditions and would have to raise their rates or withdraw from the program. The implementation of a revised open enrollment process was expected to help offset selection risks. This would create a more level playing field for all bidders. At the same time, once a year members would be allowed the opportunity to leave a plan with which they were not satisfied.

Newborns would be covered for the first month of life under the mother's capitation payment.

New members would be enrolled in a contracting health plan even though they might be hospitalized on the effective date of enrollment. Except in a limited number of situations the contracting plan would be financially responsible for the care of these hospitalized new enrollees.

St. Joseph's View of AHCCCS in the Summer of 1983

The announcement of the second AHCCCS request for proposals resulted in a reconsideration of the hospital's participation. In addition to the advantages perceived from the first year's experience, participation had other perceived benefits. First, a direct contract would eliminate the problem of slow payment by other plans. It was felt that this would improve cash flow, as the hospital would receive up-front capitation prior to admissions, rather than having to wait six months for payments.

Second, there was a concern that the changes in patient referral patterns outside of St. Joseph's could be permanent if action were not taken. Despite their contracts with St. Joseph's Hospital, Arizona Physicians IPA and Health Care Providers were using the Samaritan Health System hospitals almost exclusively. This happened because most of the specialists associated with these two plans were on the staff at the Samaritan Health System hospitals. The contracts between St. Joseph's Hospital and the two plans did not specify some minimum level of use, as St. Joseph's had expected that the plans would send the hospital a reasonable volume of patients. In fact, St. Joseph's Hospital was losing patient days. Direct control would restore former referral patterns.

Third, they felt that AHCCCS, if viewed on a marginal revenue and marginal cost basis, was likely to be profitable. That is, the additional revenue that AHCCCS would bring in would be greater than the short-run marginal costs of providing the care. The hospital had sufficient excess capacity that AHCCCS patients would not crowd out more profitable patients. It was expected that the short-run variable costs would be covered by the contract and that any contribution to the institution's fixed costs would be better than no contribution.

Fourth, the medical staff of the hospital was concerned that the AHCCCS contractors and their physicians were involved in medical decisions that should be left to the hospital-based physicians. Some physicians felt that the quality of care for the indigent patients would be improved if St. Joseph's became a direct AHCCCS subcontractor. The development of an AHCCCS plan would give the institution more control over how care would be provided to AHCCCS patients.

Fifth, a group of patients frequently seen in the hospital's charity clinics was alternately gaining and losing AHCCCS eligibility. When they lost eligibility, the hospital provided care without reimbursement; when they gained eligibility, they went to other providers, who were receiving AHCCCS capitation. Participation would result in some reimbursement for this patient care.

Last, the Family Practice Center continued to have a shortage of patients, and AHCCCS clients could be served in the existing facility. There was capacity for 1,000 to 1,500 new patients.

However, the major concern from the first year remained. Could an institution make money on the contract? Would costs be less than reimbursement? No financial reports were available on the existing plans to indicate the potential losses; certainly the slow payments indicated that APIPA and HCP were in serious financial difficulty.

Within the organization support for participation was divided. The director of the Family Medicine Practice Center was a strong advocate of bidding, as participation would bring in more patients to the family medicine practice. The physicians in the Mercy Care Clinics were ambivalent. A successful bid could bring in more patients and revenues, but it would mean that the physicians would have to assume a gatekeeper role, and this would be their first experience at working within a managed-care program. Their active cooperation in the program was essential to its success, as these physicians were all primary care physicians and would be very active in caring for AHCCCS enrollees.

Some of the specialists associated with the hospital opposed bidding, fearing that care for AHCCCS' patients would dominate the institution. A majority of the medical staff were not enthusiastic about serving AHCCCS patients, due to the slow payment of their fees by other plans. Overall, only a small number of physicians were involved in some of the decisions, such as how residents would be involved in the program and how private physicians would treat and be reimbursed for AHCCCS patients. Though the physicians were consulted, their views on whether to bid were not binding. The managers expected that most of the care for AHCCCS enrollees would be provided by the staff of the primary care clinics, with the infrequent specialist care paid on a fee-for-service basis.

The board of trustees of the hospital was very much involved in the decision to bid. There were many conversations with individual board members, presentations were made to the board finance committee, and the matter was discussed at three different meetings of the full board. There was some reluctance to participate, due to the novelty of the concept, but it was seen as a way to support the Mercy Care Clinics and other ambulatory care activities. The board was kept informed of the program through written reports provided on a monthly basis.

Year Two Decision by St. Joseph's Hospital

The overall decision to bid was made by administrators. After gaining board approval, the decision to bid went to the corporate headquarters in California for final approval.

The initial strategy to construct the bid focused on estimating a competitive bid price, because the program was putting a great deal of pressure on the plans to have low bids. A consulting firm was employed to examine the patient utilization data provided by the program. They backed into the cost estimates by first estimating a competitive bid, and then dividing through by the utilization rates provided by the program to derive an approximate cost per unit of service that would on paper justify the final bid price. This approach was acceptable, as the hospital would not actually pay these supposed average costs, but in fact would only incur marginal costs for most of the services.

The primary care physicians expected to participate in the program were already on salary. If an AHCCCS contract was obtained, the plan would pay the clinics on a fee-for-service basis, and the clinics would use these funds to pay the salaries. The amount of fee for-service payments to parties outside of St. Joseph's would be small, as this would only be for specialist and ancillary services, estimated to be no more than 20 percent of the total costs. As the expected enrollment of the plan would only be 2,000 members, the hospital used various rules of thumb to estimate the costs: 15 percent of the AHCCCS bid would go for administrative costs, 40 percent would go to the hospital services, 20 percent to specialists and ancillary services, and 25 percent to primary care.

Using this strategy St. Joseph's Hospital Medical Center submitted a response to this RFP, using "Mercy Care Plan" as the name for their AHCCCS plan. They offered a capacity of 2,250 members, in order to minimize the potential risk of economic losses if the price turned out to be less than the actual short-run marginal cost. They estimated that the 2,250 members would include 945 AFDC members, 135 aged and medically indigent and medically needy with Medicare members, 90 disabled and blind with Medicare members, 180 disabled and blind without Medicare members, and 900 medically indigent and medically needy (without Medicare) members.

Results of Bidding in the Second Year of AHCCCS

The AHCCCS administration judged the submitted bid prices of all vendors in Maricopa County to be too high and requested voluntary price reductions. The revised bids were again rejected by the program, and a completely new second round of bidding was ordered. The institution's managers complied with this request, by slightly modifying their original "backed-into" bids. Table 11.12 presents the estimated utilization, utilization rates, costs per unit of services, and service costs used to calculate the second set of bids. The AHCCCS administration then asked for further price reductions, and St. Joseph's administration decided to lower its prices a third time in order to obtain participation in the program. St. Joseph's bids were then accepted in all but one category, and a contract for 2,250 enrollees was awarded for a one-year period, with an option for a one-year renewal. Table 11.13 presents the initial bids from St. Joseph's Hospital, the revised bids after the first voluntary price reduction, the new bids after a second round of bidding was ordered, and the final payment rate. Table 11.14 displays the final payment rates for the other bidders in Maricopa County.

Concluding Comments

The creation of the AHCCCS program confronted the managers of St. Joseph's Hospital and Medical Center with a unique opportunity that entailed substantial risk. The financial and organizational challenges posed by AHCCCS can be framed as three sets of questions.

The first set focuses on the financial and economic considerations that were foremost in the minds of the managers concerned. AHCCCS offered a capitation contract that would provide fixed revenues for an undefined volume of services: a risky situation that will confront increasing numbers of managers throughout the U.S. in the next decade. An assessment of this situation can provide insight into similar contracting situations.

The second set of questions considers the decision process within the hospital in each of the two years. The concern in these questions is not the appropriateness of the decision to participate as a subcontractor in the first year and to bid directly in the second year of the program. Rather, the focus is on the way in which the decisions were made, involving different levels of participation by physicians and board members.

The third set of questions asks the reader to extrapolate and anticipate difficulties that might arise from participation in a capitated Medicaid program.

Table 11.12   Capitation Rate Calculation, 1983 Second Bid

AFDC Members Service Category	Projected Total Utilization for 945 Members	Utilization Rate for Service per Member per Month	Cost per Unit of Service	Service Cost per Member per Month
Hospital inpatient	378	.03333	$550	$18.33
Hospital outpatient and emergency	189	.0167	83.58	1.39
Physician services				
Surgery	321	.0283	600	16.98
Anesthesia	47.25	.0042	120	.50
Inpatient visits	378	.03333	35	1.17
Office visits	3,260	.2875	20	5.75
Obstetrics	30.7125	.0027	650	1.76
Miscellaneous	1,228.5	.1083	10	1.08
Laboratory	2,126	.1875	7.25	1.36
X-ray	495	.0437	31.20	1.36
Pharmacy	3,260	.2875	2.75	.79
Emergency mental health	141.75	.0125	72.13	.90
Emergency dental	1,969.4375	.1737	52.62	9.14
Other	342.5625	.0302	49.12	1.48
Total gross capitation bid per member per month (PMPM)				61.99
Less: Adjustments				
for copayments				.52
for coordination of benefits recoveries				1.19
for value of services reinsured by AHCCS				3.47
Medicare				—
Net health care capitation per member per month				56.81

Aged and Medically Indigent and Medically Needy with Medicare Members Service Category	Projected Total Utilization for 135 Members	Utilization Rate for Service per Member per Month	Cost per Unit of Service	Service Cost per Member per Month
Hospital inpatient	337.5	.2083	$568	$118.32
Hospital outpatient and emergency	60.75	.0375	83.58	3.13
Physician services				
Surgery	91.125	.0563	900	50.67
Anesthesia	9.45	.0058	200	1.16
Inpatient visits	253.125	.1563	35	5.47
Office visits	692.55	.4275	20	8.55
Obstetrics	—	—	—	—
Miscellaneous	1,363.15	.8415	48	40.39

Continued

Table 11.12 Continued

Aged and Medically Indigent and Medically Needy with Medicare Members *Service Category*	*Projected Total Utilization for 135 Members*	*Utilization Rate for Service per Member per Month*	*Cost per Unit of Service*	*Service Cost per Member per Month*
Laboratory	641.24	.3958	7.25	2.87
X-ray	155.25	.0958	89.85	8.61
Pharmacy	2,261.25	1.3958	6.50	9.07
Emergency mental health	10.125	.0063	72.13	.45
Emergency dental	71.55	.0442	224.74	9.93
Other	74.25	.0458	36.36	1.67
Total gross capitation bid per member per month (PMPM)				260.29
Less: Adjustments				
for copayments				2.16
for coordination of benefits recoveries				2.28
for value of services reinsured by AHCCCS				5.69
Medicare				170.65
Net health care capitation per member per month				79.51

Disabled and Blind with Medicare Members *Service Category*	*Projected Total Utilization for 90 Members*	*Utilization Rate for Service per Member per Month*	*Cost per Unit of Service*	*Service Cost per Member per Month*
Hospital inpatient	290	.2685	$ 717	$192.52
Hospital outpatient and emergency	72	.0667	83.58	5.57
Physician services				
Surgery	70	.0648	1,250	81.00
Anesthesia	6.75	.0063	250	1.57
Inpatient visits	182.25	.1688	35	5.91
Office visits	486	.45	40	18.00
Obstetrics	.27	.0003	700	.20
Miscellaneous	302	.2796	90	25.16
Laboratory	486	.45	18	8.10
X-ray	99	.0917	89.85	8.24
Pharmacy	1,620	1.5	11.50	17.25
Emergency mental health	54	.05	75	3.75
Emergency dental	56.60	.0524	294.68	15.44

Continued

Table 11.12   Continued

Disabled and Blind with Medicare Members Service Category	Projected Total Utilization for 90 Members	Utilization Rate for Service per Member per Month	Cost per Unit of Service	Service Cost per Member per Month
Other	109.125	.1010	52.47	5.30
Total gross capitation bid per member per month (PMPM)				388.01
Less: Adjustments				
for copayments				1.33
for coordination of benefits recoveries				1.55
for value of services reinsured by AHCCCS				7.76
Medicare				263.85
Net health care capitation per member per month				113.52

Disabled and Blind without Medicare Members Service Category	Projected Total Utilization for 180 Members	Utilization Rate for Service per Member per Month	Cost per Unit of Service	Service Cost per Member per Month
Hospital inpatient	486	.225	$585	$131.63
Hospital outpatient and emergency	144	.0667	83.58	5.57
Physician services				
Surgery	126	.05833	950	55.41
Anesthesia	13.5	.0063	120	.75
Inpatient visits	364.5	.1688	35	5.91
Office visits	972	.45	40	18.00
Obstetrics	.54	.00025	700	.18
Miscellaneous	495	.2292	60	13.75
Laboratory	972	.45	7.25	3.26
X-ray	198	.0917	89.85	8.24
Pharmacy	3,105	1.4375	2.75	3.95
Emergency mental health	108	.05	72.13	3.61
Emergency dental	99	.0458	212.65	9.74
Other	218.25	.1010	33.46	3.38
Total gross capitation bid per member per month (PMPM)				263.38
Less: Adjustments				
for copayments				1.84
for coordination of benefits recoveries				1.05
for value of services reinsured by AHCCCS				33.45
Medicare				—
Net health care capitation per member per month				227.04

Continued

Table 11.12 Continued

Medically Indigent and Medically Needy without Medicare Members Service Category	Projected Total Utilization for 900 Members	Utilization Rate for Service per Member per Month	Cost per Unit of Service	Service Cost per Member per Month
Hospital inpatient	562.5	.0521	$568	$ 29.59
Hospital outpatient and emergency	225	.0208	87.50	1.82
Physician services				
Surgery	427.5	.0396	900	35.64
Anesthesia	58.5	.0054	120	.65
Inpatient visits	461.25	.0427	35	1.49
Office visits	4,421.25	.4094	20	8.19
Obstetrics	33.75	.0031	700	2.17
Miscellaneous	1,485	.1375	48	6.60
Laboratory	2,868.75	.2656	7.25	1.93
X-ray	663.75	.0615	89.85	5.52
Pharmacy	4,421.25	.4094	2.75	1.13
Emergency mental health	173.25	.0160	72.13	1.16
Emergency dental	1,350	.1250	85.91	10.74
Other	247.5	.0229	45.58	1.04
Total gross capitation bid per member per month (PMPM)				107.67
Less: Adjustments				
for copayments				1.92
for coordination of benefits recoveries				1.08
for value of services reinsured by AHCCCS				6.03
Medicare				—
Net health care capitation per member per month				98.64

These sets of questions are enumerated below.

Analysis of AHCCCS Contracts

1. As presented by the state to potential bidders in 1982, was the AHCCCS program a desirable business venture? Was AHCCCS a desirable medical care opportunity? Consider this question from the perspective of the managers at St. Joseph's, and clearly describe both your business and medical care criteria.

2. As presented by the state to potential bidders in 1983, was the AHCCCS program still (if ever) a desirable business venture? What were the implications of the various contract changes? After one year, was there a potential for AHCCCS to be a desirable health

Table 11.13   Bids from St. Joseph's Hospital, 1983

		Initial Categories of Enrollees			
	AFDC	*Aged and Medically Indigent or Medically Needy with Medicare*	*Disabled*	*Blind*	*Medically Indigent or Medically Needy without Medicare*
Initial bids	$66.06	$54.37	$132.00	$264.00	$114.69
Revised bids after first voluntary price reduction	62.75	54.37	132.00	264.00	114.69
		Revised Categories of Enrollees			
	AFDC	*Aged and Medically Indigent or Medically Needy with Medicare*	*Disabled or Blind with Medicare*	*Disabled or Blind without Medicare*	*Medically Indigent or Medically Needy without Medicare*
Second bids	56.81	46.76	113.52	227.04	98.64
Final payment rate	51.50	65.00	85.00	200.00	No award

care opportunity? Again, consider this question from the perspective of the managers at St. Joseph's.

3. To what extent was the "backing-in" approach used to derive the per patient costs in the 1983 bids an appropriate methodology? What methods should have been employed to produce a more accurate bid?

4. Attempt to construct a financial analysis of the revenues and expenses that Mercy Care Plan and St. Joseph's Hospital will experience.

Decision process

5. Assess the decision process in 1982. Specifically consider the participation (or lack thereof) of board members, physicians (both primary care physicians and specialists), executives of the parent organization, and other players in the decision.

Table 11.14   Bids from Other AHCCCS Plans, 1983

		Revised Categories of Enrollees			
	AFDC	Aged and Medically Indigent or Medically Needy with Medicare	Disabled or Blind with Medicare	Disabled or Blind without Medicare	Medically Indigent or Medically Needy without Medicare
CIGNA Health Plan	$58.03	$31.33	$31.40	$245.64	No award
ACCESS Patients Choice	46.97	68.32	74.68	211.08	No award
Phoenix Health Plan	65.53	61.91	69.19	197.56	No award
Maricopa Health Plan	48.98	58.48	62.72	167.33	No award
AZ Family Physicians	64.50	58.74	54.29	208.61	$92.00
Health Care Providers	59.76	58.11	58.87	235.92	84.75

6. Discuss the decision to forgo bidding for an AHCCCS contract in 1982. If the decision appears incorrect, what would have been the ideal strategy?

7. Assess the decision process in 1983. What were the appropriate roles for the board of trustees and for hospital-affiliated physicians in making a decision to bid for a capitated contract? How is that different from and similar to the process in 1982?

8. Discuss the decision to bid for an AHCCCS contract in 1983. If the decision appears incorrect, what would have been the ideal strategy?

Future considerations

9. What problems do you foresee in the future for St. Joseph's Hospital and the Mercy Care Plan?

10. How should the management of Mercy Care Plan be organized? Should various staff and resources (such as computer systems) be allocated to this new organization, or should the plan be a "paper" organization, which purchases management services from St. Joseph's Hospital? Keep in mind the scope of the program and the existing resources within St. Joseph's Hospital.

Analyzing the Financial Performance of Hospital-Based Managed Care Programs: The Case of Humana

Joseph S. Coyne

The vertically integrated system (VIS) has been the extension of different organizational types with different capital structures. Some systems have developed from a capital-intensive acute care base, whereas others have sprung from a labor-intensive long-term care base. It is essential to study such systems and their strategies, so that the factors of success and failure can be identified to benefit future system operations. As witnessed by recent financial results, many providers have faced depressed earnings and devalued assets and consequently have turned to diversification from the acute care business. This recent trend toward a more diversified health care product will become even more popular and pronounced as providers expand their degree of vertical integration to capture market share, sometimes by assuming greater risk through a capitation agreement.

This article has been reprinted (without accompanying appendixes) from the *Journal of Health Administration Education*, Vol. 8, no. 4 (Fall 1990), with permission of the Association of University Programs in Health Administration.

This manuscript has been prepared for the University of Washington W. K. Kellogg–funded project on vertically integrated systems. The author wishes to express appreciation to the corporate offices of Humana for their cooperation in providing pertinent information and to the students of the Program in Healthcare Management, University of Southern California at the Sacramento Center, for their intellectual curiosity and ambitious efforts to apply sound financial analysis techniques.

The case of Humana is about a VIS that began in the nursing home industry and developed into a health care company and insurance company. This case has many successes but also some failures. It is the successes that have kept the organization viable, and it is the failures that have posed challenges in its development as a VIS.

Humana is a good subject for analysis and highly relevant to typical corporate health care decision making since it has experienced multiple stages of diversification and development, both on a product line and company-wide basis. The company has fervently pursued expansion into health insurance since it first offered this product in January 1984. It has also made decisions to divest itself of specific products, such as the MedFirst clinics, that are no longer profitable. The lessons learned from this analysis of Humana can be significant and practical for the health care firm launching a new product line or contracting with firms that are doing so.

These elements of corporate decision making are important to review and analyze, both for the student and for the practitioner. Each will analyze the case from a different perspective, but both will find that the case includes decisions that face administrators at many different levels: from diversification decisions at the departmental level to decisions at the corporate level. Further, the Humana case allows us to examine all of the key financial statements of a publicly traded health care company that may be important for the not-for-profit administrator to review and understand for future management contracting or mergers.

After an examination of the theoretical models as they apply to the VIS, the growth and development of Humana is analyzed in terms of stages of diversification and related financial results. Finally, the lessons learned from the case for CEOs, COOs, and CFOs are examined.

Theoretical Models for Analysis of the VIS

After first examining the recent studies conducted on the financial performance of the health care-based VIS, we examine the studies of diversification efforts among commercial businesses. Finally, the concept of partnerships as it pertains to the health care VIS is examined.

Health care-based VIS Performance

In their recent analysis of financial growth and diversification, Coyne and Cobbs study the growth strategies of ten VIS's [1]. Using a five-year historical and five-year projected financial data base, the authors compare investor-owned (IO) and not-for-profit (NFP) systems in terms of cash liquidity, debt-service coverage, and cash profitability. The following represent the major findings:

— Cash liquidity is increasing among the NFP, while it is decreasing among the IO.

— Debt service coverage is decreasing among the NFP, while it is variable among the IO.

— Cash profitability is generally decreasing among both ownership types.

This study underscores the high cost of diversification. The IO systems studied were the first to diversify and consequently faced the associated increase in expenses earlier than did the NFP systems. During the period of the study, 1982–86, the IO systems incur a 9 percent decrease in net operating income, while the NFP systems realize a 9 percent increase in net operating income. This has prompted IO systems to divest. Such findings are supported by recent reports: "The investor-owned hospital management chains, which led the industry toward diversification, now are leading the movement away from it. The change has been prompted by pressures from investors to reverse plummeting earnings and stem problems associated with the companies' acute care businesses" [2]. These difficulties with diversification are attributed to poor planning, unclear and unachievable objectives, and poor implementation. As summarized by Richard Clarke, president of the Healthcare Financial Management Association:

> The early efforts were more reactions to competing hospitals or physicians than organized plans that were integrated with hospitals' missions and strategic plans. Too often, diversification efforts were not based on sound market research [3].

Diversification among corporate businesses

As we look at the track record of past diversification efforts of business and industry, we find that the reports are not optimistic. In Porter's study of 33 large U.S. companies, 53.4 percent of the diversification efforts between 1950 and 1980 end in failure [4]. These failures result from choosing the wrong business, investing excessively in the diversified business, or ignoring whether the diversified business added significantly to the core business. Such reasons for failure must be assessed by companies like Humana to determine whether they apply and if so what the corrective strategies are.

A major question facing many companies that launch a diversification effort is how much time is required for such ventures to break even financially or even make a profit. Biggadike finds that it may take an average of eight years for a new business to reach profitable operating levels [5]. Gilbert and Coyne indicate that the target should be two years to break even or better before a new venture is abandoned [6]. Whatever the acceptable period, the investment in diversified programs is risky and should be recognized as such. Companies such as Humana need to establish their own corporate cutoff point for new products.

In discussing the losses associated with new business, Biggadike summarizes this concept well:

> Results such as these suggest that launching new businesses is risky. Achieving a balanced product portfolio appears to be more difficult in practice than in theory. Articles on the product portfolio concept reinforce this perception of risk by referring to new businesses as "wildcats," "sweepstakes," or "question marks"—hardly the most reassuring terms. From this viewpoint, corporate diversification resembles Russian roulette [7].

In the area of interorganizational relationships, much has been written about the structure and strategy of complex organizations and their related financial and managerial success [8, 9, 10, 11, 12, 13, 14]. Regarding the nature of product development, one key model is that of the product life cycle. It assumes any product or service has a definite life cycle and that the risk potentially is greatest when the products or services are most unrelated [15,16].

Chandler [17] finds that the multidivisional firms develop in four stages:

Stage 1. The initial expansion and accumulation of resources— where the start-up phase is experienced

Stage 2. The internal rationalization and consolidation of growth— where the corporate form and function is defined

Stage 3. The diversification into new products and the expansion into new markets—where significant investments occur in assets that build the company

Stage 4. The development of the decentralized, multidivisional corporation—where the corporation achieves maturity

These stages of development are found in all four of the firms Chandler studied: Du Pont, General Motors, Sears, and Standard Oil. A major component of each of these firms' development through the four stages is an adaptation to a competitive market. This type of response requires various forms of integration, consolidation, and expansion. For example, horizontal consolidation is a favorite strategy for many firms, including those in the health care industry, as part of their expansion strategy. This type of growth strategy has its limits in considering the development outside of the core business. Furthermore, a diversification strategy requires a significant change in structure to accommodate and complement new products and markets. Chandler discusses the problems in communication and the difficulties with lines of authority as a company diversifies—problems that make reorganization essential. Humana accomplished this transition through creation of a Group Health Division to manage the insurance product line.

Thompson defines vertical integration as "the combination in one organization of successive stages of production. Each stage of production uses as its inputs the product of the preceding stage and produces inputs for the following stage" [18]. Thompson points out that vertical integration is a most effective means of reducing organizational contingencies in the technologies that are characterized by multiple stages of production. This is particularly pertinent to the health care firm because it attempts to attract market share to cover its high fixed costs.

Porter [19] addresses extensively the alternative forms of achieving competitive advantage through differentiation. In discussing the value chain, which is the flow of inputs and outputs in the production process, he points out that differentiation must be viewed in terms of the specific activities that a firm conducts and how they affect the buyer. Porter believes that differentiation is the true source of superior performance. Humana has pursued such a philosophy through its Centers of Excellence.

Harrigan [20] specifies four dimensions of vertical integration. These include (1) the successive stages of integration in the production process; (2) the degree of internal transfers; (3) the breadth of integrated activities; and (4) the form of ownership to control the vertical relationship. These dimensions are important to consider for understanding the flow of inputs and outputs in the health care delivery process.

Using these four dimensions, Conrad et al. [21] build a value chain for health services. The vertical value chain displays different levels and degrees of control/integration.

Value-added partnerships

Hopkins [22] analyzes the process of vertical integration from the perspective of value added and relatedness of the lines of business. He describes the value-added concept as the difference between the benefits and costs of various types of vertical integration. He points out that when the benefits are in excess of cost there is positive value-added, whereas the opposite condition is negative value-added, or value-lost. Hopkins notes that it is important to match strengths and weaknesses in considering possible acquisition targets, "to buy companies that are strong where yours is weak, weak where yours is strong. The effect of doing this is to magnify greatly the value added" [23]. This concept is particularly important to the case of Humana: the insurance product line has been complementary, in providing 10 percent of all admissions to Humana hospitals, while the MedFirst Clinics have not proven complementary and represent a value-lost.

Johnston and Lawrence [24] discuss the value-added concept from the viewpoint of partnerships. Using McKesson Corporation as an example, the authors describe how partnerships are formed between organizations that perform adjacent tasks in the production process. Investor-owned VIS such as HCA have pursued partnerships to reduce the risk of offering the insurance product. HCA joined with Equitable Insurance to form Equicor. An essential element in the success of these value-added partnerships is the creation of a service or product that would be much most costly or extremely difficult to build without the partnership. Ultimately, the actual value added to each of the partners is financially verifiable. In the case of HCA and Equitable, the amount of the value added can now be measured by the amount at which Equicor sold.

Three Research Questions for Analysis

Vertical integration has long been an area of study for organizational theorists. The directions for analysis are provided by the following three questions:

1. What impact does the degree of business relatedness have on the success of vertical integration?
2. Is it best to diversify through a make or buy mode: that is, should diversification occur through either developing the business with current company resources or purchasing an existing business?
3. What is the appropriate time frame for achieving a break-even position on a new business line?

These questions are addressed in this case analysis of the Humana investment in developing a hospital-based insurance company. After the case analysis and discussion, these questions are revisited to synthesize the lessons learned.

Risks and Rewards of the Insurance Product

The successful development of an insurance product by a provider depends heavily on the careful and constant analysis of relative risks and rewards. As Coyne [25] points out, this requires an investment in several areas, including:

1. the development of a clinical/financial data base on patients served, by age, sex, and utilization

2. the expansion of the role and responsibilities of case management staff

3. the enhancement of the utilization management system to include all phases of review

Many health care corporations launched investments into the HMO/PPO/Indemnity triple-option product, but only a few have continued to offer the triple option. AMI, for example, developed Amicare as an insurance program to direct patients to its hospitals. After almost two years of development and $100 million of incremental capital outlays, Amicare was abandoned, its failure attributed to alienation of physicians and inadequate patient draw [26]. All of the other major investor-owned companies, such as HCA and NME, have either divested or are lessening their risk by joint venturing similar efforts.

Freeman points out several reasons for this occurrence [27].

1. The insurance product requires different skills and incremental capital for its development.

2. The insurance product has typically been underpriced and undermanaged, making the investors nervous unless returns are imminent.

3. The insurance market has become competitive and crowded with HMO types of providers.

4. The HMOs are developing with investment capital from large insurance conglomerates, making it less necessary for providers to offer this product.

5. The provider-based HMO has typically not been a source of significant revenue and is often a corporate cash drain because of adverse selection and poor contracting.

Freeman notes that most HMOs will suffer from more than one of these symptoms. He portrays the future as a tough period because there will be inadequate capital for both start-up and expansion projects. Incompetent management, he believes, is a product of the explosive growth of HMOs, as CEOs are recruited from hospitals and other predominantly fee-for-service businesses. He states: "Although it can be argued that these individuals were competent in their own fields, HMOs are extraordinary complex financial and health-care delivery systems. In essence, the poor performance of multi-institutional hospital corporations in the HMO market is a reflection of this observation" [28].

Another problem highlighted by Freeman is the strategy of setting inadequate premiums. He notes that the long time-horizons associated with contracts make the pricing strategy critical, a problem further compounded by the increasing price competition among plans. Finally, the presence of adverse selection and poor contracts causes the HMO to be a cash drain, as money is poured into services for a sicker population that results in higher-than-average physician and hospital costs.

Several studies answer the question of how improvements can be realized in both the process and the outcome of HMO management. Kenkel [29] reports on the California-based HMO, FHP, which dates its origin to 1961 as Family Health Plan. Primarily a staff-model HMO, FHP employs its own salaried physicians. With a medical-loss (expenses to revenues) ratio of only 80 percent, a 3 percent net profit margin, and a 30 percent return on equity, FHP attributes much of its financial success to its investment in executive training. The HMO has also followed a conservative expansion strategy that focuses on peripheral areas. FHP has pursued a strategy of marketing and managing the Medicare market, with over half of its revenues from Medicare.

Feldstein et al. [30] show how utilization review programs can positively impact cost and utilization levels. Through examining the insurance claims of 222 groups of employees and dependents for 1984 and 1985, the authors evaluate the impact of compulsory utilization review programs initiated by large private insurance carriers. They find that utilization review reduces hospital admissions per thousand by 12.3 percent, inpatient days by 8 percent, hospital expenditures by 11.9 percent, and total medical expenditures per insured person by 8.3 percent. The estimated savings-to-cost ratios of the utilization review programs are approximately 8 to 1.

From a survey by SGM Marketing Group of Chicago [31], the staff and network model HMO are identified as most efficient when compared with the other managed-care models. The staff model reports a medical-loss ratio of 96.2 percent, while the network model, which contracts for physician services with two or more physician groups, reports a medical-loss ratio of 97.2 percent. The average medical-loss ratio for all HMOs is 99.1 percent. IPA model HMOs, which contract with physician organizations that in turn contract with individual physicians who provide medical services to the enrollee, report break-even results. The group model, which contracts with independent multispecialty groups, reports the worst results: a medical-loss ratio of 104.15 percent.

The research of SGM also considers the age of an HMO. They find that young HMOs (three years or younger) typically report expenses in excess of revenues by about 2 percent and very little net worth per enrollee. The mature HMOs (operating four years or more) report marginal losses. When compared with the younger HMOs, the mature HMOs report that assets have increased nearly sixfold and that net worth has increased by eleven times. Besides model type and age, another critical factor in the financial performance of HMOs is ownership type. Generally, the for-profit HMOs report much less profitable results than not-for-profit plans, particularly among the younger plans.

Thompson uses the insurance firm as an example and notes that vertical integration to increase the population served can be critical to "find enough poolers of risk" and to avoid becoming "dependent on other insurance organizations through reinsurance" [32]. It is important to consider the reasons for and benefits of moving closer to the customer. Can the extension to the customer be an effective means of achieving market share? What structural forms are most conducive to bringing the product closer to the customer? How can the risk of these forms of integration be minimized? These are particularly important to the VIS in the health care industry as market share becomes such an important consideration in competitive markets.

These questions are considered in the Humana case: its vertical expansion through development of its MedFirst Clinics in 1981 and its insurance product through its Group Health Division (GHD) in 1984. Humana has pursued different strategies in the management and expansion of the clinics versus the insurance subsidiary. Perhaps this is why the case of Humana is so interesting: it realized a failure with the investment in the clinics and divested six years after beginning, and it continued to pursue the health insurance product after five years of negative financial results, with anticipation of breaking even in the 1989 fiscal year—which it did.

As we consider these studies of the insurance industry, it is clear that the percentage of those insured by HMOs is expanding. Size and location do not appear to be associated with the significant losses in the managed-care area, whereas model type, age, and ownership type appear to be significant factors. The HMO/PPO product is complex and requires new and different skills with which a provider is often not well equipped when operating primarily as a supplier of acute care services. To achieve success in the HMO market, the provider must shift technologies and people to a prepaid and revenue-constrained direction. This is a major shift that many providers believe is not worth the investment, as witnessed by the recent divestiture of this product line. The Humana case can now be examined to determine how some of the corrective strategies may be pursued, particularly in terms of the seven research questions identified in the earlier section of this paper.

The Growth of Humana's Group
Health Division (GHD)

During the past five years Humana has directed significant resources into its managed-care product, GHD. This was a definite strategic choice on the part of its management, pursued with the goal of achieving brand name identity. This has required an all-out effort to convince the public that this insurance product is equal to that of long-established products. Further, Humana has hired marketing staff from non-health-related industries, such as the food business.

As indicated by Humana's new vice president of marketing, A. Neal Westermeyer, the approach is "high touch" in style, focusing on service rather than technology. He applies his experience from Ralston Purina to link Humana's hospitals, services, and insurance products in all payer groups. This has required a campaign to convince the public that its insurance product and health delivery system are integrated.

Not until the close of the most recent fiscal year has it appeared that indeed the insurance and delivery arms of Humana are integrated, as measured by financial results. . . . Humana's 1988 Annual Report [and] 1988 10-K Report . . . show that while patient days have dropped by 0.2 percent the revenues have increased by 15.5 percent. The most dramatic change is the 42.6 percent increase in GHD members. . . . The positive results of 1987 are represented in the income statement by a 24 percent increase in the net income; the balance sheet reflects a 6.6 percent increase in the total assets. Of particular importance . . . are . . . the data about GHD relative to the hospitals; . . . the 1988 operating results of GHD are identified as a loss of approximately $1 million after allocating the portion of the loss from the reserve account of 1986. Selected financial data . . . show the approximate 60 percent increase in GHD days in Humana hospitals. This [data] also provides a financial discussion and analysis, which explains how the GHD grew through increased sales and acquisitions of plans. . . .

During the past two years GHD has recorded losses that are the result of health insurance contracts in place as of 1986 when a loss reserve had been established to provide for future losses. . . . After amortization of the relevant portion of the $106 million loss reserve, the GHD's operating losses for 1987 and 1988 are $5 million and $1 million, respectively.

According to Tim Moody of Humana management, GHD broke even in the second quarter of fiscal year 1989, which is about five years after GHD began. This is well in advance of the timeframe suggested by Biggadike, referred to in the section on theoretical models, which found that break even typically occurs about eight years after launching a new diversified product. In the 1988 Letter to Shareholders, Jones and Cherry state: "The vertical integration initially encountered operational problems that resulted in large losses for the division." Such large losses from GHD are rooted in both the revenue and expense side of the income statement, that is, a need for a long-range premium strategy to raise revenue and a need for utilization review (UR) to reduce expenses. As described by Abramowitz, Humana's past insurance losses have been largely due to "pricing 20–30% below the market and doing little UR" [33].

As reflected in the 1988 Letter to the Shareholders, the managed care plans have been viewed as a source of patient referrals to the hospitals. Not until the close of the most recent fiscal year has this plan contributed referrals to the HMO; the proportion of hospital days accounted for by plan members grew from 6.6 percent in the prior year to 10.6 percent. They have accomplished this greater integration of business lines through concentrating their health insurance expansion efforts exclusively in markets with Humana hospitals. During 1988 they expanded the Group Health membership by 43 percent: from 554,500 to 790,700. . . . This was the result of a greater emphasis on Medicare supplement insurance, acquisitions, and new group insurance sales.

Financial Ratio Analysis

As depicted in Table 12.1, there are five categories of ratios, which serve as a diagnostic tool to assess financial results [34]. The liquidity category is important to bankers and creditors, who must monitor recipients of loans in terms of their ability to meet current obligations such as payroll, trade payables, and loan (debt service) payments due within a twelve-month period. Turnover and composition are related measures of both income statement and balance sheet performance; turnover addresses the revenue-generating ability of different types of assets, while composition helps explain the turnover results by identifying the proportion of assets accounted for by the different types of assets. Capitalization ratios provide a picture of the capital structure, which is important to banks and lenders. Performance measures describe the profitability of the organization for specified periods on both a pretax and aftertax basis. These ratio categories can best be interpreted in an interrelated fashion; that is, it is possible to achieve a better understanding of the reasons for the trends by connecting the results of the ratio calculations [35].

The ratios for each of the five categories are defined in Table 12.2. There are 27 ratios defined here, which may be more than most organizations incorporate in their financial reporting systems. These 27 ratios may therefore be viewed as a comprehensive list of financial measures.

The data for calculating these ratios are derived from two financial statements: the balance sheet and the income statement. In all instances,

Table 12.1   Ratio Definitions

Ratio Category	Definition
Liquidity	Ability to satisfy short-term obligations
Turnover	Generation of net operating revenues in relation to different types of assets
Composition	Proportion of assets invested by type of asset
Capitalization (capital structure)	Relationship between long-term debt and owners' equity or total assets
Performance (profitability)	Ability to generate a profit from operations

Table 12.2   Financial Ratio Definitions

Ratios	Definitions
Liquidity	
1. Current ratio	Current assets/current liabilities
2. Acid test	Cash/current liabilities
3. Current liabilities to equity[a]	Current liabilities/owners' equity
4. Days in accounts receivable	Net accounts receivable/(net operating revenues/365)
5. Days of cash liquidity	Cash/[(operating expenses + other income − depreciation expense)/365]
6. Days of average payment period	Current liabilities/[(operating expenses + other income − depreciation expense)/365]
Turnover	
7. Current assets	Net operating revenues/current assets
8. Inventory	Net operating revenues/inventory
9. Accounts receivable	Net operating revenues/net accounts receivable
10. Cash	Net operating revenues/cash
11. Fixed assets[b]	Net operating revenues/fixed assets
12. Total assets[b]	Net operating revenues/total assets
Composition	
13. Percent fixed assets[b]	Fixed assets/total assets
14. Percent current assets	Current assets/total assets
15. Percent inventory	Inventory/current assets

Continued

Table 12.2 Continued

Ratios	Definitions
16. Percent accounts receivable	Net accounts receivable/current assets
17. Percent cash	Cash/current assets
Capitalization	
18. Assets to equity	Total assets/owners' equity
19. Assets to debt[c]	Total assets/long-term debt
20. Debt to equity[c]	Long-term debt/owners' equity
21. Average age of plant	Accumulated depreciation/ depreciation expense
22. Debt service coverage[d]	(Pretax income + dep + principal + interest)/(principal + interest)
23. Times interest earned	(Pretax income + interest)/interest
Performance	
24. Percent return on assets[e]	(Pretax income − other income)/total assets
25. Percent return on equity[e]	(Pretax income − other income)/owners' equity
26. Percent nonoperating income[f]	Other income/net income
27. Net profit margin[g]	Net income/net operating revenues

[a]Owners' equity is the total owners' equity for taxable entities.
[b]Fixed and total assets are inclusive of construction-in-progress amount.
[c]Long-term debt includes long-term leases, long-term debt, and debentures but not deferred accounts or preferred stock.
[d]Principal amounts due are the current maturities on long-term debt.
[e]Pretax income less other income is also known as net operating income.
[f]Nonoperating income is also known as other income or investment income.
[g]The net profit margin is the aftertax margin as opposed to a pretax margin.

it is far preferable to use audited data, which means using annual reports (quarterly reports are unaudited). Also, for companies such as Humana, the consolidated financial statements are most commonly available. Typically, the presentation of financial data by a subsidiary will not be in the form of a complete financial statement but will be partial data included in a financial summary. . . .

The methodology for calculating these 27 ratios is most efficiently done using spreadsheet analysis, such as Lotus 1–2–3. The spreadsheets for the balance sheet and income statement are presented in Tables 12.3 and 12.4, respectively. The relevant accounts are then referred to by formula to calculate the ratios.

Table 12.3 Balance Sheet

	1988	1987	1986	1985	1984	1983	1982	1981	1980	1979	1978
Assets											
Cash & market securities	$246.69	$211.55	$170.63	$ 82.25	$260.95	$250.00	$209.50	$197.40	$116.30	$101.70	$ 55.30
Net accounts receivable	507.14	494.03	423.14	365.85	257.68	200.50	167.80	149.70	128.40	115.50	117.40
Inventories	69.79	58.70	55.60	50.91	45.25	41.50	34.40	30.00	28.50	22.80	18.40
Other current	104.79	92.27	23.87	39.50	41.43	29.60	14.80	11.40	9.80	8.20	9.40
Total current	$928.41	$856.55	$673.24	$538.51	$605.31	$521.60	$426.50	$388.50	$283.00	$248.20	$200.50
Land	$ 168.76	$ 163.40	$ 178.90	$ 181.16	$ 165.41	$ 147.10	$ 128.10	$ 95.90	$ 82.70	$ 64.30	$ 48.00
Buildings	1,678.69	1,613.34	1,528.81	1,449.56	1,228.70	1,024.10	827.30	702.40	675.70	559.40	459.70
Equipment	1,086.37	990.57	903.85	791.67	681.76	540.90	405.70	329.10	296.70	253.90	185.40
Construction in progress	41.73	52.54	88.04	91.18	160.08	161.30	92.70	75.20	37.40	73.60	62.70
Accumulated depreciation	−987.79	−852.48	−706.09	−562.30	−452.64	−357.00	−280.10	−223.80	−173.00	−129.30	−90.90
Net PPE	$1,987.76	$1,967.37	$1,993.51	$1,951.27	$1,783.31	$1,516.40	$1,173.70	$978.80	$919.50	$821.90	$664.90
Other assets & insurance investments	$ 505.79	$ 384.85	$ 249.48	$ 230.11	$ 189.23	$ 179.80	$ 145.00	$ 134.90	$ 66.10	$ 59.50	$ 47.20
Intangibles	0.00	0.00	0.00	0.00	0.00	0.00	0.00	0.00	58.00	60.50	39.10
Total assets	$3,421.96	$3,208.77	$2,916.23	$2,719.89	$2,577.85	$2,217.80	$1,745.20	$1,520.20	$1,326.60	$1,190.10	$951.70
Liabilities and Equity											
Accts. pay.	$107.67	$ 82.34	$ 80.88	$ 85.26	$ 88.32	$ 82.40	$ 67.50	$ 53.00	$ 46.10	$ 33.50	$ 28.20
Accrued expenses	397.91	364.35	351.02	172.94	150.23	136.40	105.00	78.40	63.00	51.60	43.20
Income taxes	95.47	82.43	26.10	48.97	59.96	34.90	61.40	100.20	60.30	52.90	28.70
Long-term debt—current	32.68	55.63	71.38	57.82	53.72	50.70	39.90	43.10	34.80	28.50	31.30
Total current	$633.73	$584.75	$529.38	$364.99	$352.23	$304.50	$273.80	$274.70	$204.20	$166.50	$131.40

Long-term debt	$1,210.62	$1,237.47	$1,215.63	$1,205.56	$1,286.53	$1,067.70	$ 864.40	$ 733.10	$ 722.40	$699.70	$542.20
Deferred credits and other	422.99	374.51	274.86	246.49	195.91	176.40	161.20	133.20	117.80	88.80	55.10
Minority interest	0.00	0.00	0.00	0.00	0.00	0.00	0.00	0.00	0.00	0.00	56.80
Total liabilities	$2,267.34	$2,196.73	$2,019.87	$1,817.04	$1,834.67	$1,548.60	$1,299.40	$1,141.00	$1,044.40	$955.00	$785.50
Preferred stock	$ 0.00	$ 0.00	$ 0.00	$ 0.00	$ 0.00	$ 60.60	$ 60.50	$ 63.90	$ 65.90	$ 65.50	$ 65.10
Common stock	16.32	16.28	16.24	16.22	16.14	13.30	12.60	9.30	6.00	3.00	2.50
Paid-in-capital	233.90	229.74	226.10	223.39	219.22	212.20	96.00	91.20	79.10	79.70	37.40
Retained earnings	915.45	769.44	661.68	679.32	527.16	395.90	286.10	196.80	131.20	86.90	61.20
Other adjustments	−11.05	−3.42	−7.66	−16.08	−19.34	−12.80	−9.40				
Total equity	1,154.62	1,012.04	896.36	902.85	743.18	669.20	445.80	361.20	282.20	235.10	166.20
Total liabilities and equity	$3,421.96	$3,208.77	$2,916.23	$2,719.89	$2,577.85	$2,217.80	$1,745.20	$1,502.20	$1,326.60	$1,190.10	$951.70

Table 12.4 Income Statement (in millions of dollars)

	1988	1987	1986	1985	1984	1983	1982	1981	1980	1979	1978
Net revenues[a]	3,435.40	2,973.64	2,710.59	2,283.51	2,038.01	1,827.05	1,569.01	1,389.31	1,152.36	955.35	660.47
Operating expenses	2,786.23	2,340.18	2,316.56	1,641.00	1,497.25	1,372.35	1,207.29	1,083.28	897.43	755.20	529.12
Depreciation and amortization	195.65	180.20	179.08	147.34	120.56	94.70	78.20	69.20	59.20	50.90	35.83
Interest expenses	145.94	154.16	154.77	159.50	123.72	104.38	95.35	87.14	85.40	74.80	40.30
Other [income] expenses[b]	−46.06	−30.92	−30.46	−40.68	−35.77	−33.13	−39.49	−27.26	−9.60	−6.80	−3.00
Total operating expenses	3,081.76	2,643.62	2,619.95	1,907.16	1,705.76	1,538.30	1,341.35	1,212.36	1,032.43	874.10	602.25
Income before tax	353.64	330.02	90.64	376.35	332.25	288.75	227.66	176.95	119.93	81.25	58.22
Income tax	126.60	147.20	36.20	159.88	138.91	128.10	100.70	83.70	55.30	40.40	30.40
Minority interests & extra items	0.08	0.00	0.00	0.00	0.00	0.00	0.00	0.00	0.00	0.00	−5.70
Net income before preferred dividend	227.12	182.82	54.44	216.47	193.34	160.65	126.96	93.25	64.63	40.85	22.12
Preferred dividends	0.00	0.00	0.00	0.00	0.00	6.50	6.90	7.60	7.60	7.60	4.40
Net income	227.12	182.82	54.44	216.47	193.34	154.15	120.06	85.65	57.03	33.25	17.72
Average shares outstanding	103.32	103.06	97.41	102.78	96.49	94.51	89.99	88.05	89.20	80.85	74.50
Earnings per share[c]	2.20	1.77	0.56	2.11	2.00	1.63	1.33	0.97	0.64	0.41	0.24

Source: Humana Consolidated Statements. Data is accurate as of June 1989 and subject to change from restatements.
[a]Net revenues are gross revenues less discounts and doubtful accounts.
[b]Other income is reported as a reduction of operating expense but for the ratio analysis is recognized as nonoperating income.
[c]Earnings per share is calculated by dividing the net income by average shares outstanding.

Norms, provided in Table 12.5, are benchmarks to which the interpretation in Table 12.5 refers. These benchmarks are intended to provide comparative data from similar firms except that they were not engaging in the same degree and scope of vertical integration as Humana.

It should be clear that a higher number does not always represent better performance, as in ratio #4, days in accounts receivable. Likewise, greater relative values, such as greater debt financing, do not always represent a desirable financial position [36].

Tables 12.3 and 12.4 represent eleven years of Humana's financial history. These data are consolidated for all of Humana's operations, both hospitals and GHD. There are two accounts that are unique in their presentation: revenues are presented only net of discounts (see note b of Table 12.4) and other income is presented as an offset to interest expense (see note c of Table 12.4), since Humana is an insurance company that earns interest from invested prepaid premiums.

The ratio trends for Humana are presented in Table 12.6. This provides a basis for interpreting the long-term financial history of Humana within all five categories of financial ratios.

Liquidity

Humana's liquidity appears stable and adequate. The current ratio and acid test show that Humana has a history of relatively high liquidity, while its reliance on short-term financing has been historically higher than average. Both the current ratio and the acid test ratio decreased significantly in 1986 from the average historical levels, while the current liabilities increased, indicating higher reliance on short-term financing. This period of 1986 represents the biggest earnings drop in Humana's history. The days in accounts receivable show an upward trend since 1985, with the average age of receivables approximately fifty-five days. During this same period the cash liquidity shows a downward trend, from about sixty days to thirty days of liquidity.

This series of liquidity ratios indicates a common trend: significant liquidity reduction in the period since diversification into health insurance. As cash is absorbed during the start-up phase of launching a newly diversified product, the days in receivables and current liabilities increase to adjust for the decrease in liquidity. Likewise during this same period, Humana was divesting itself from another diversification effort, the MedFirst Clinics. This contributed to the losses through write-offs in the disposition of these assets. Hence, diversification has had two impacts since 1984: one in the current losses in GHD and the other in write-offs from MedFirst.

Table 12.5 Financial Ratio Norms

Ratios	Norm	Interpretation[a]
Liquidity		
1. Current ratio	1.46	Higher number means greater liquidity & ability to pay
2. Acid test	0.38	Higher number means greater cash liquidity & ability to pay
3. Current liabilities to equity	0.44	Higher number means greater reliance on short-term financing
4. Days in accounts receivable (AR)	52.92	Lower number of days means greater ability to collect on AR
5. Days of cash liquidity	28.00	Higher number of days means greater cash liquidity & ability to pay
6. Days of average payment period	72.25	Higher number of days means greater reliance on short-term financing
Turnover		
7. Current assets (CA)	4.06	Higher number means greater revenue-generating ability per dollar of CA
8. Inventory	33.00	Higher number means greater revenue-generating ability per dollar of inventory
9. Accounts receivable (AR)	6.90	Higher number means greater revenue-generating ability per dollar of AR
10. Cash	15.58	Higher number means greater revenue-generating ability per dollar of cash
11. Fixed assets (FA)	1.38	Higher number means greater revenue-generating ability per dollar of FA
12. Total assets (TA)	0.82	Higher number means greater revenue-generating ability per dollar of TA
Composition		
13. Percent fixed assets (FA)	0.63	Higher percentage means a greater proportion of FA
14. Percent current assets (CA)	0.22	Higher percentage means a greater proportion of CA
15. Percent inventory	0.12	Higher percentage means a greater proportion of inventory
16. Percent accounts receivable (AR)	0.59	Higher percentage means a greater proportion of AR
17. Percent cash	0.26	Higher percentage means a greater proportion of cash

Capitalization

18. Assets to equity	3.50	Lower number means greater equity financing
19. Assets to debt	2.27	Lower number means greater debt financing
20. Debt to equity	1.36	Lower number means lower debt financing
21. Average age of plant	3.22	Lower number means less depreciated and newer assets
22. Debt service coverage	2.20	Higher number means greater ability to pay the principal and interest on loans
23. Times interest earned	1.77	Higher number means greater ability to pay the interest on loans

Performance

24. Percent return on assets (ROI)	0.08	Higher percentage means greater profitability from operations
25. Percent return on equity (ROE)	0.28	Higher percentage means greater profitability from operations
26. Percent nonoperating income	0.12	Higher percentage means greater profitability from investments
27. Net profit margin	0.07	Higher percentage means greater profitability overall

Source: The above norms are for investor-owned hospitals based on the data base and results of several studies by the author [34,35,36].
[a]The "higher number" means higher relative to the norm, white "greater" amount means greater than that associated with the norm.

Table 12.6 Financial Ratio Analysis

	1988	1987	1986	1985	1984	1983	1982	1981	1980	1979	1978
Liquidity											
1. Current ratio	1.46	1.46	1.27	1.48	1.72	1.71	1.56	1.41	1.39	1.49	1.53
2. Acid test	0.39	0.36	0.32	0.23	0.74	0.82	0.77	0.72	0.57	0.61	0.42
3. Our liab/eq	0.55	0.58	0.59	0.40	0.47	0.46	0.61	0.76	0.72	0.72	0.79
4. Days in AR	53.88	60.64	56.98	58.48	46.15	40.06	39.04	39.33	40.67	44.13	64.88
5. Cash liquid	30.71	30.96	25.20	17.67	58.76	61.79	58.70	61.56	43.19	44.72	35.45
6. Avg pmt per	78.89	85.57	78.19	73.99	79.31	75.26	76.72	85.67	75.84	73.22	84.23
Turnover											
7. Our asset	3.70	3.47	4.03	4.24	3.37	3.50	3.68	3.58	4.07	3.85	3.29
8. Inventory	49.22	50.66	48.75	44.85	45.04	44.03	45.61	46.31	40.43	41.90	35.90
9. Accts. rec.	6.77	6.02	6.41	6.24	7.91	9.11	9.35	9.28	8.97	8.27	5.63
10. Cash	13.93	14.06	15.89	27.76	7.81	7.31	7.49	7.04	9.91	9.39	11.94
11. Fixed asset	1.73	1.51	1.36	1.17	1.14	1.20	1.34	1.42	1.25	1.16	0.99
12. Total asset	1.00	0.93	0.93	0.84	0.79	0.82	0.90	0.92	0.87	0.80	0.69
Composition											
13. FA/TA	0.58	0.61	0.68	0.72	0.69	0.68	0.67	0.65	0.69	0.69	0.70
14. CA/TA	0.27	0.27	0.23	0.20	0.23	0.24	0.24	0.26	0.21	0.21	0.21
15. Inven/CA	0.08	0.07	0.08	0.09	0.07	0.08	0.08	0.08	0.10	0.09	0.09
16. AR/CA	0.55	0.58	0.63	0.68	0.43	0.38	0.39	0.39	0.45	0.47	0.59
17. Cash/CA	0.27	0.25	0.25	0.15	0.43	0.48	0.49	0.51	0.41	0.41	0.28

Capitalization											
18. TA/Eq	2.96	3.17	3.25	3.01	3.47	3.31	3.91	4.16	4.70	5.06	5.73
19. TA/LTD	2.83	2.59	2.40	2.26	2.00	2.08	2.02	2.05	1.84	1.70	1.76
20. LTD/Eq	1.05	1.22	1.36	1.34	1.73	1.60	1.94	2.03	2.56	2.98	3.26
21. Avg age PLT	5.05	4.73	3.94	3.82	3.75	3.77	3.58	3.23	2.92	2.54	2.54
22. Debt svce	4.08	3.43	2.19	3.41	3.55	3.47	3.26	2.89	2.49	2.28	2.31
23. Times INT	3.42	3.14	1.59	3.36	3.69	3.77	3.39	3.03	2.40	2.09	2.44
Performance											
24. Return on TA	0.09	0.09	0.02	0.12	0.12	0.12	0.11	0.10	0.08	0.06	0.06
25. Return on eq	0.27	0.30	0.07	0.37	0.40	0.38	0.42	0.41	0.39	0.32	0.33
26. Nonop inc/ni	0.20	0.17	0.56	0.19	0.19	0.21	0.31	0.29	0.15	0.17	0.14
27. Net prof mar	0.07	0.06	0.02	0.09	0.09	0.09	0.08	0.07	0.06	0.04	0.03

Turnover and composition

Since the first year of GHD (1984) and the subsequent divestiture of the MedFirst Clinics (1986), the turnover and composition ratios reflect trends similar to the liquidity trends, all three of which show a need for increased working capital. The most evident ratios here are those related to accounts receivable and cash. The accounts receivable turnover declined because of an increase in receivables, as evidenced by composition ratio #16. Cash turnover increased because of the decrease in cash balances in 1985, as evidenced by ratio #17. These ratios add to the notion that Humana paid for its diversification into health insurance and divestiture of urgent care and has since taken corrective action. As stated in the 1986 annual report: "Sound strategy, partial success, errors in execution, corrective steps taken."

Capitalization

Debt levels in Humana have historically been high, particularly prior to TEFRA and the implementation of DRGs in 1982. A related trend is seen in the areas of debt service and interest coverage, which have been higher since 1982, when debt levels decreased. The trend for the average age of plant shows increasing age, reflecting less replacement and fewer new construction projects. These capitalization trends depict a company that has targeted and practically achieved a one-to-one relationship of dollars of debt to dollars of equity. This reduced reliance on debt also depicts a company that is changing its product mix from just a hospital company to both a hospital company and a health insurance carrier. Such a move obviously has its impact on both the income statement and balance sheet.

Performance

The profitability levels of Humana on a companywide basis have been relatively high. The return on assets and equity and the net profit margin are represented by trend lines that are similar: increasing throughout the period up to 1985 and with a major decline in 1986, when the company wrote off losses on the disposal of MedFirst Clinics and provided for anticipated losses on insurance contracts. These write-offs and provisions are unusual operating charges that caused the decline in performance in 1986. The nonoperating income is generally higher than average and comes primarily from interest earnings from the insurance investments.

A financial growth analysis is shown in Table 12.7. These data show that appreciation of assets is strong at a rate of 14 percent. This is not a measure of how much the assets have appreciated in value but of

Table 12.7   Financial Growth Analysis

Compound Growth Rates	Values	Guess	Rate
Total assets	−951.70	0.30	
	0.00		
	0.00		
	0.00		
	0.00		
	0.00		
	0.00		
	0.00		
	0.00		
	0.00		
	3421.96		0.14
Stockholders equity	−166.20	0.30	
	0.00		
	0.00		
	0.00		
	0.00		
	0.00		
	0.00		
	0.00		
	0.00		
	0.00		
	1154.62		0.21
Net income	−22.10	0.30	
	0.00		
	0.00		
	0.00		
	0.00		
	0.00		
	0.00		
	0.00		
	0.00		
	0.00		
	227.12		0.26

how much the asset base has grown from acquisitions. The stockholders' equity has increased at a rate of 21 percent, which is primarily because of earnings growth . . . as opposed to increases in the number of common stock shares outstanding. To support this point, the net income growth of 26 percent has been higher than growth of both assets and equity. This shows that Humana has effectively built equity through its earnings.

The Lessons Learned

In reflecting on the lessons learned, the three research questions should be revisited. The Humana growth analysis, including data on the development of GHD and the divestiture of MedFirst, and the financial ratio analysis provide a basis for answering these questions.

1. What impact does the nature and degree of business relatedness have on the success of vertical integration?

The impact is significant. When Humana established MedFirst, it failed to understand the nature of the relationship with physicians in the community served by the urgent care clinic. If it had more carefully assessed the nature of the business relatedness between the clinics and the physicians, then it might have avoided the conflicting and competitive relationship with the local physicians. Likewise, if Humana had more carefully and strategically planned the marketing of its health insurance product, then it might have avoided the reliance on non-Humana hospitals, which increased expenses. Humana's most recent success with the GHD has come about because of the emphasis on expanding GHD exclusively in the Humana hospital markets. The lesson here is that the more compatible or related the business, the more likely the new diversified business will succeed.

2. Is there a best approach to take in developing or expanding from the core business—forward integration with the outputs or backward integration with the inputs of the core business?

From this case study, it would appear that if not implemented properly, either form of integration (forward or backward) can fail. As depicted by Conrad et al. [37] in their development of a health services value chain, physician services can be viewed as an input to the acute care hospital, while the HMO/PPO insurance product can be viewed as an output. With the MedFirst operations, Humana expanded in a backward direction to capture the inputs through the physicians in the clinics, an effort that failed for many reasons. Perhaps the integration process involving physician inputs in the health services value chain is more difficult than forward integration because of the potential or actual competition between services offered in the physician office and in the hospital or clinic. Comparatively, the integration process involving expansion into the insurance product line may involve less potential for conflict and more potential for complementing the delivery of services.

From a profitability perspective, Graham finds in a recent study [38] that urgent care centers (such as MedFirst) are among the least profitable. However, other forms of backward integration are profitable, such as ambulatory surgery and radiation therapy. The lesson here is that there does not appear to be one direction—either forward or backward—that represents a best approach to diversification; but when the core business (i.e., the hospital) integrates to the detriment of its critical inputs (i.e., physicians), then the vertical integration is most likely to fail.

> 3. What is the appropriate time frame for achieving a break-even position on a new business line?

When Humana first offered the insurance product through GHD in 1984, it began with 4,000 members, all located in one market. Not until two years later did the Humana health insurance plan members begin to contribute to the hospital business. In 1985 the enrollees of the Humana health plan represented 1 percent of both the Humana hospital days and revenues. In 1988, as indicated earlier the enrollees represented 10.6 percent of the hospital days and 3.5 percent of the hospital revenues. The time lapsed has been approximately five years, and management is hoping for a turnaround in year six.

Given this timing to achieve profitability, it would appear that a firm has to wait about as long as that indicated as average by Biggadike—eight years. If divestiture of an unprofitable product line is delayed, then the negative results could be felt in the long term through the write-offs on the disposal of undervalued assets. It is important to recognize that a delay in a decision to divest affects both the income statement (short-term results) and the balance sheet (long-term impact). The lesson here is that if profitability is not present, or at least a trend toward profitability in a reasonable period of time, then there should be serious questions raised on the financial viability of the new product or service.

This completes the revisiting of the three research questions. The experiment has proceeded far enough along to examine the application of theory to assist us in formulating some "lessons learned" for future ventures of this type. Obviously, such empirically based conclusions require future revisiting and reflection to assess the need for revision.

Conclusions and Forecast

In considering the future role of investor-owned companies in the offering of managed care products, some hold that it is too soon to say whether investment into managed care on the part of investor-owned systems will achieve targeted rates of return [39]. The factors critical to success are most often identified as the need to adjust to the prepaid financial incentives. More specifically, there is a need to develop locally strong marketing programs, a long-range premium strategy, and effective cost controls. In addressing these factors, Humana management had indicated as follows: "Our experience has been that the plan works best when there's a strong support from Humana facilities in the same city where Humana Care Plus is being sold" [40]. This is accompanied by a strategy of raising prices and tightening controls to ensure greater use of Humana facilities.

Can the GHD fulfill management's dream of achieving profitability to support the product line? Will the management's effort to market a brand name be successful in selling the insurance and health care products? Has the product life cycle been stretched to the limits of its start-up phase?

These questions all require further study to determine the success of Humana's investment. As with most efforts of this type, the need for new management talent and insight into managing the less familiar product line is essential to the future success of this VIS.

The future managed-care environment will be increasingly competitive. Multiple-option plans will be essential for the HMO's survival, as health benefits managers seek both indemnity and managed-care coverage for the employee [41]. Price competition will also increase as federal regulations are softened regarding community rating to permit the federally qualified HMO to price its products at different rates for different employer groups [42]. Furthermore, most premiums will be increased by 10 percent per year on average, instead of the historical rate of 5 percent, as state regulations enforce requirements for cash reserves [43]. Finally, as pointed out by Sorbo et al. [44], providers will increasingly share the risk as health plans increase their efforts to control costs through capitation.

The future is unfolding for managed care, with an important chapter to be written through the Humana case prior to 1990, assuming that the GHD does indeed break even during fiscal year 1989. We can explore new directions for the VIS at that time. Until then, we need to test and apply our analytic skills in understanding the reasons for success and failure as the complex machinery of the VIS is fine-tuned in the future.

References

1. Coyne, J., and D. Cobbs. *Financial Growth and Diversification of Hospitals and Multihospital Systems.* Chicago, IL: American Hospital Publishing, forthcoming.
2. Graham, J. Diversified Hospitals Review Plans after Some Bumpy Rides. *Modern Healthcare,* August 14, 1987, 30–31.
3. Graham, J. See number 2, p. 30.

4. Failures in Diversification Top Successes, Study Says. *Wall Street Journal*, May 7, 1987, 3.
5. Biggadike, R. The Risky Business of Diversification. *Harvard Business Review*. 57 (May–June): 103–11, 1979.
6. Gilbert, R., and J. Coyne. Should Hospitals Rush to Diversify? *Healthcare Financial Management* 41 (February): 91–92, 1987.
7. Biggadike, R. See number 5, p. 103.
8. Coyne, J. Hospital Performance in Multihospital Systems: A Comparative Study of System and Independent Hospitals. *Health Services Research* 17 (Winter): 11–30, 1983.
9. Neuhauser, D. The Really Effective Health Service Delivery System. *Health Care Management Review* 1 (Winter): 1976.
10. Starkweather, D. US Hospital: Corporate Concentration vs. Local Community Control. *Public Affairs Report* (April): 1–2, 1981.
11. Coyne, J., ed. Financial Strategies of MIOs in Price-Competitive Markets. *Topics in Health Care Financing* 11 (Winter): 1984.
12. Finkler, S., and X. S. Horowitz. Merger and Consolidation. *Healthcare Financial Management* 39 (January): 19–27, 1985.
13. Rumelt, R. *Strategy, Structure and Economic Performance.* Cambridge: Harvard University Press, 1974.
14. Hopkins, T. *Mergers, Acquisitions, and Divestitures.* Homewood, IL: Dow Jones-Irwin, 1983.
15. Clement, J. Vertical Integration and Diversification of Acute Care Hospitals: Conceptual Foundations. *Hospital and Health Services Administration* 33 (Spring): 99–110, 1988.
16. Galbraith, J. *Designing Complex Organizations.* Reading, MA: Houghton Mifflin, 1952.
17. Chandler, A. *Strategy and Structure.* Cambridge: MIT Press, 1962.
18. Thompson, J. *Organizations in Action.* New York: McGraw-Hill, 1962.
19. Porter, M. *Competitive Advantage: Creating and Sustaining Superior Performance.* New York: Free Press, 1985.
20. Harrigan, K. *Strategic Flexibility.* Lexington, MA: Lexington Press, 1985.
21. Conrad, D., et al. Vertical Structures and Control in Health Care Markets: A Conceptual Framework and Empirical Review. *Medical Care Review* 45 (Spring): 49–100, 1988.
22. Hopkins, T. See number 14.
23. Hopkins, T. See number 14, p. 46.
24. Johnston, R., and P. Lawrence. Beyond Vertical Integration—The Rise of the Value Adding Partnership. *Harvard Business Review* 66 (July–August): 94–101, 1988.
25. Coyne, J. Developing a Business Plan for Home Health Contracts: Managing Risk and Reward. *Home Health Management Advisor* 3 (November): 1, 7, 8, 1988.
26. Graham, J. See number 2, p. 36.
27. Freeman, R. Why HMOs Fail. *Medical Interface* (April): 10–12, 1988.
28. Freeman, R. See number 27, p. 12.

29. Kenkel, P. Calif.-based HMO Outperforms Industry By Emphasizing Training, Cautious Growth. *Modern Healthcare* 18 (May 20): 39–41, 1988.
30. Feldstein, P., et al. The Effects of Utilization Review Programs on Health Care Use and Expenditures. *New England Journal of Medicine* 318: 1310–14, 1988.
31. *Marion Managed Care Digest 1987 Update*. Kansas City, MO: Marion Laboratories, 1987.
32. Thompson, J. See number 18, p. 42.
33. Abramowitz, K. *Bernstein Research: The Future of Health Care Delivery in America*. New York: Sanford C. Bernstein, 1986, 52.
34. Coyne, J. A Comparative Financial Analysis of Multi-Institutional Organizations: Not-forProfit vs. Investor-Owned. *Hospital and Health Services Administration* 30 (November–December): 48–63, 1985.
35. Coyne, J. Measuring Hospital Performance in Multi-Institutional Organizations Using Financial Ratios. *Health Care Management Review* 10 (Fall): 35–43, 1985.
36. Coyne, J. A Financial Model for Assessing Hospital Performance: An Application to Multi-Institutional Organizations. *Hospital and Health Services Administration* 31 (March–April): 28–40, 1986.
37. Conrad, D., et al. Vertical Structures and Control in Health Care Markets: A Conceptual Framework and Empirical Review. *Medical Care Review*. 45 (Spring): 54, 1988.
38. Graham, J. See number 2, p. 40.
39. McLaughlin, N. Experts Say It's Too Soon to Predict Fate of Chain-Insurer Managed Care. *Modern Healthcare* 18 (January): 40–41, 1988.
40. McLaughlin, N. See number 39, p. 40.
41. Kenkel, P. Triple-Option Plans Thrive. *Modern Healthcare* 18 (February): 25–32, 1988.
42. Wagner, L. States Exerting More Control over HMOs. *Modern Healthcare* 18 (February): 22–25, 1988.
43. Kenkel, P. HMOs Boosting Premiums. *Modern Healthcare* 18 (February): 33, 1988.
44. Sorbo, A., et al. Surviving and Thriving with Capitation Contracts. *Healthcare Financial Management* 42 (March): 64, 74, 1988.

Part **IV**

Integrating the Strategic
Adaptation Process

The Institute for Preventive Medicine Health Plan

Gordon D. Brown, Keith E. Boles, and L. Jerome Ashford

Start Up and the Early Years

The creation of the Institute for Preventive Medicine

The Institute for Preventive Medicine was incorporated as a California nonprofit corporation on 17 June 1975, classified by the Internal Revenue Service (IRS) as a nonprofit corporation under Section 501(c)(4) of the Internal Revenue Code. Samuel Miller, M.D., a physician from Alameda County, created the corporation to take advantage of new state legislation providing funds for the development of programs in preventive medicine.

Miller was interested in initiating education and research programs in preventive medicine, given his background and specialty training in this area. To form the corporation, he enlisted the assistance of friends, Lane Johnson, a lawyer, and James Kuehne, a local investment banker, as the two corporate officers. Both were entrepreneurial and were always

This case was prepared for the National Center for Managed Health Care Administration, a cooperative venture of the Health Services Management Program, University of Missouri—Columbia, and the Bloch School of Business and Public Administration, University of Missouri—Kansas City, and funded by a grant from Marion Laboratories, Inc. (now Marion-Merrill-Dow, Inc.).

looking for new development opportunities. The corporation was organized with the three members constituting the board and the bylaws
specifying as its purpose to "pursue the provision of preventive health
care services."

Considerable interest in preventive medicine followed the 1960s.
This interest was in part due to changes in attitude about individual
responsibility for one's own health. It was the dawn of an era of better
nutrition, physical fitness, less cigarette smoking, physical examinations,
early detection, and minimal medical intervention. The second factor
causing a focus on preventive medicine was the skyrocketing costs of
medical care. The medical care system was increasingly viewed as un-
affordable and potentially less essential than historically thought for
maintaining good health. It was the era of *Medical Nemesis* (Illich 1976),
multiphasic screening, wellness, and the conference at Alma-Ata (World
Health Organization 1978).

Against this backdrop of interest in preventive medicine and primary care, and very much an outgrowth of it, was the interest in prepaid
health care systems. Their emphasis on prevention, education, early
detection, and primary care fit the social mood of the area and was
considered to be the most effective means of addressing the issue of
increasing costs in medical care. It also fit the political mood of the
country, which was shifting to a more conservative set of values, less
government regulation, and more procompetition attitudes. This political
climate gave rise to the HMO Act of 1973, the demise of comprehensive
planning, and a shift from cost-based to case-based reimbursement under
the Social Security Act. No state was more caught up in this wave
than California. It emerged as the trend-setting state in everything from
values, behavior, and politics to prepaid health plans.

The early years

Miller was pleased with the ease with which IPM was incorporated and
received its IRS ruling. He recognized the potential of preventive health
care and was strongly committed to developing and testing clinical procedures and their delivery. The corporation gave him the perfect vehicle
for pursuing state monies to support his research and demonstration
interests, and as president of the corporation, he was renewed in his
commitment to these interests. He immersed himself in his practice and
in his study of primary care.

At the time of the formation of the corporation, a member of the
board had been involved in negotiations just completed between the
union and management of the Southern Pacific Transportation Company

giving all employees an option of a comprehensive health benefits package provided on a prepaid basis. This board member was aware that the current insurer did not offer a prepaid plan and felt that through his contacts with Southern Pacific Management, IPM might be able to develop such a plan. His friends at Southern Transportation indicated that they were agreeable to such a deal but indicated that the union was the major force behind the movement and that he would have to get their support. He met with the union representatives and indicated to them that they could have representation on the board of IPM and in effect have their own health plan serving their needs. The union was quite taken with this idea of self-determination and agreed, with the proviso that they would have majority representation on the board of directors. They had little trust of management, and that included lawyers and investors.

Miller had not been a part of the negotiations taking place between the board member and the union and indeed was not even aware that they were taking place. He was dumbfounded with this direction and the extent to which developments had taken place, all without his knowledge. He felt strongly that the prepaid health plans and the general provision of health services were outside the intent of the corporate bylaws and that this venture should not be pursued. His partners, however, saw an opportunity to expand the corporation and voted to pursue the contract with Southern Pacific. Miller then left the corporation, and the partners brought in Benjamin Peay, a lawyer. Kuehne assumed the position of president of IPM and chairman of the board. To allow time for his new responsibilities, he resigned from the bank and established offices in downtown Vallejo as an investment advisor.

The Institute for Preventive Medicine then proceeded to create vertical linkages with both physicians and hospitals in the cities of Oakland, Hayward, San Jose, San Francisco, and Vallejo. These cities represented the area within which Southern Pacific operated and in which its employees lived. Through these contracts, IPM felt it could deliver a full range of services to all employees.

In October 1975, IPM applied for and was granted a state license to operate a limited prepaid health care plan under the provisions of the Knox-Mills Act. IPM entered into an agreement with the Southern Pacific Transportation Company to offer secondary coverage, on a prepaid basis, of medical and hospital services to employees and their dependents. While IPM had contracts to provide the full range of basic and supplemental health care services and operated in the manner of a prepaid health plan as required by state law, IPM's risk was secondary to that of Traveler's Insurance Company, which covered railway workers under a national union contract. The premium for this secondary coverage amounted to $10 per member per month. This supplemental risk arrangement was IPM's major line of business through late 1978.

To meet commitments made to the union of Southern Pacific, it was necessary for IPM to alter its corporate structure. It continued with the same president, and previous board members, but the board of directors had to be expanded to seven positions, with four to be filled by union members. This gave the union the majority representation as agreed to in the negotiations. IPM rented office space and employed a small staff, consisting of an accountant, secretaries, and some staff for claims processing. IPM in effect was a prepaid health insurance company, with one major employee group.

Family Doctor Medical Group joins IPM

The monopolistic position of the Kaiser Health Plan in the northern California area was causing concern with many medical groups in the region, and the lack of alternative choices was a concern of many residents. Kaiser was the overwhelmingly dominant plan in the area and had greatly benefited from the growing popularity of prepaid systems.

Family Doctor Medical Group (FDMG) was a multispecialty group practice located in Solano County, an area where Kaiser's impact was increasingly being felt. In fact, Kaiser had enrolled 60 percent of the total population of Solano County. FDMG knew its future was limited if it did not somehow respond to the threat being posed by Kaiser. The group decided it should explore the possibility of getting into the prepaid health care business.

Family Doctor Medical Group became aware of IPM and entered into an alliance to form an HMO in southern Solano County. FDMG agreed to provide financial backing for the venture and in turn was given representation of three members on IPM's board. The new board structure now consisted of the three business partners, three consumers, and the three FDMG members. It was not immediately apparent nor ever completely clear to the union representatives from Southern Pacific that they were no longer on the board and not involved in the corporation. The linkages being formed now included contracts with physicians and hospitals for the provision of health services and the appointment of physicians to the board of directors.

The venture relationship with FDMG was loosely defined in terms of control and financial responsibility. FDMG agreed to provide $750,000 to stabilize IPM financially, although no notes payable account or formal agreement was ever signed. FDMG saw IPM as a way of quickly getting into the prepaid health care business and competing with Kaiser.

IPM's objective was one of growth and expansion consistent with long-term viability.

On 18 January 1979, IPM was granted a license under California's Knox-Keene Health Care Service Plan Act of 1975 (successor to the Knox-Mills Act). In April 1979, IPM first offered a prepaid comprehensive health plan (IPM Health Plan) to employer groups in southern Solano County. FDMG contracted to provide physician services on a capitated basis, and Vallejo General Hospital entered into an agreement to provide hospital care on a fee-for-service basis. The difference in these agreements resulted from the fact that the physicians were willing to accept some of the risk to secure a share of the market from Kaiser, while the hospitals had no need to accept any of this risk due to the relatively insignificant marketshare of IPM.

IPM moves to Solano County

Organization. To support its new enterprise in the North Bay region, IPM moved its offices to Vallejo, renting office space initially in the FDMG building and later 3,000 additional square feet in a small office building. Among the benefits of an office in Vallejo were an abundance of reasonably priced office space and the availability of staff personnel who lived in the area and would rather work in Vallejo than commute to San Francisco or the East Bay area.

The staff was expanded to include a part-time director of marketing, managers of claims processing and fiscal operations, and a new director of systems and operations (see Figure 13.1). The recognition of at least some importance of the marketing function was an important step for IPM. The same is true of the addition of the director of fiscal operations, although the function was more for bookkeeping than for financial management. The staff was highly motivated to be involved in the new corporation and a new field of endeavor. They were all local people and developed a comfortable and informal atmosphere in which to work.

The Institute for Preventive Medicine employed two new sales representatives who made contacts with the many small firms in the area that had expressed interest in IPM or that had been referred by another corporation. The salespeople saw their role primarily as one of describing the health plan of IPM and taking orders during open enrollment periods or for new enrollees. The marketing function was mostly performed by word of mouth, which seemed to be effective, since the salespeople were kept busy and the new enrollees were coming into IPM at a rapid rate. Strategic planning and marketing research were terms not yet being discussed at IPM.

Figure 13.1   Institute of Preventive Medicine Organization
Diagram, 1982

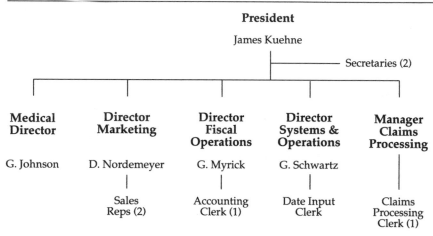

The new manager of systems and operations was a highly motivated and capable computer programmer who was faced with the immediate task of expanding the current claims processing and business systems to a claims management system. He gathered considerable information and was visited by representatives from several vendors but felt that the systems were too expensive for the corporation and were not well fitted to their needs. He recommended to the president that IPM purchase the hardware and that he develop its own system. He estimated that that could save $20,000 for the corporation. The president agreed to the purchase. The data system provided timely information on new enrollments, claims received, claims payable, premium billing, and subscriber lists.

Solano County. Solano County consists of seven subregions consisting of cities and unincorporated areas. The areas of Vallejo and Benecia make up the area classified as southern Solano County (see Figure 13.2). The demographics and employment picture of Solano County was dynamic. Total population in Vallejo and Benecia was nearly 100,000 in 1980 and growing at a rate of over 3.5 percent per year. There were 39,000 reported jobs in 1980 and 44,600 employed residents in the Vallejo and Benecia region. The rate of residential growth was rapidly exceeding job growth, so the area was expected to be a major labor source for the rest of the region (see Table 13.1).

The county was characterized by many small firms representing a range of jobs in agriculture, mining, manufacturing, wholesale, service,

Figure 13.2   Solano County Subregional Study Areas

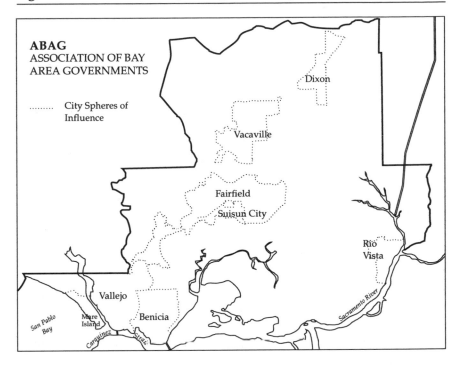

and retail industries. Most companies had fewer than 100 employees; many had only 10 to 15 employees. The largest private employers in the county were the Kaiser Health Plan, with 1,800 employees, and Anheuser Busch, with 500. The largest employer in the county was Mare Island Naval Shipyard, with 14,000 employees. Other public employers included the County of Solano and various school districts.

IPM secures a market

The Institute for Preventive Medicine successfully pursued contracts with small companies and with individuals in southern Solano County during its early years. These small corporations were not actively solicited by Kaiser Health Plan and saw IPM as an alternative to Kaiser. Because enrollments came from individuals and small firms there was a rather slow rate of growth, with enrollment totaling only 2,500 in 1979.

   Another factor limiting the growth potential of IPM was its limited delivery system. It was limited to southern Solano County and thus could not service large corporations with employees living outside the region.

Table 13.1   Total Population, Residents Employed, and Total Jobs in
Solano County, by Subregional Area, 1980 and 2000

Subregional Area	Total Population		Employed Residents		Total Jobs	
	1980	*2000*	*1980*	*2000*	*1980*	*2000*
Benicia	15,696	28,300	7,542	15,100	4,656	11,200
Dixon	7,775	13,900	3,057	6,000	3,353	5,100
Fairfield	59,483	104,500	26,993	55,100	32,076	50,600
Rio Vista	3,448	7,600	1,573	3,900	1,367	1,900
Suisun City	12,463	30,900	5,150	14,300	2,674	4,100
Vacaville	44,079	87,500	18,192	38,900	11,206	26,400
Vallejo	82,790	117,400	36,076	61,600	34,875	48,700
Remainer	9,469	14,400	4,051	7,100	476	600
Total Solano County	235,203	404,500	102,634	202,000	90,683	148,600

However, IPM was well positioned to pursue its strategy of enrolling individuals and small corporations. It drew on the personal and small town relationships between IPM and the community, particularly the relationships between local businesspeople and the physicians of FDMG.

In September 1979, IPM decided to extend its delivery system and affiliated with the Fairfield Medical Group and Intercommunity Hospital in northern Solano County. This strategy was intended to allow IPM to market the plan to larger employers with employees living outside southern Solano County, as well as to new populations of residents and corporations outside southern Solano County.

From 1979 to 1982, IPM pursued a very aggressive marketing effort. It employed two new professional salespeople who had over 20 years of combined experience in sales, including insurance, encyclopedias, and automobiles. They were given the green light to bring in the business and enjoyed considerable stature within the organization. Their high-pressure tactics, making promises they did not always understand, or that could not be met, was a clear departure from the marketing approach previously pursued by IPM. IPM regarded itself as entering the big time and needing to employ large company strategies.

As a result of the intensive marketing effort, plan enrollment increased at a modest but steady rate, from 2,500 in 1979 to 4,500 in 1982. An increase of almost 100 percent was viewed as a most impressive growth rate. However, it was not sufficient to make IPM into a profitable organization. Prepaid health plans were widely accepted in the county, given the large enrollment experience of Kaiser, but penetration into small businesses was a difficult and slow process.

The Institute for Preventive Medicine became concerned that the growth rate was not sufficient to enable it, within the necessary time period, to reach 20,000 members, the level it believed was necessary to sustain itself. It was decided that increased marketing efforts would be needed to expand its marketshare.

Seizing the Initiative

The issue of federal qualification

During the process of marketing the IPM plan, there was considerable interest expressed by employers in having the plan meet federal qualifications. There were many reasons employers valued this criterion, including external validation of the quality and availability of services. There was a belief that federal qualification provided an assurance of the financial viability of the plan. Sales representatives also felt that the lack of federal qualification was frequently given as an excuse for employers to terminate further negotiations with plans that were trying to gain entry into the corporation.

In addition to the marketing advantages of federal qualification, IPM was interested in getting access to grants and loans available to federally qualified plans. It was felt that such funds could be used to stabilize the plan until it became larger and stronger.

In 1980, IPM made its first application for federal qualification and was denied. It applied twice more between 1980 and 1982 and each time was denied. The Office of Health Maintenance Organizations (OHMO), through its consultant, worked with IPM to prepare an application and to address certain areas of noncompliance. The office informally advised the board that its financial position, organizational structure, and management capacity was such that it was doubtful if it would ever become qualified.

IPM gets new leadership

In August 1982, the board hired Jerome Ashford to assume the position of president of IPM. Ashford had been a consultant to IPM from the OHMO and impressed the board with his experience and insight into the operation of prepaid health systems.

Ashford had received his baccalaureate degree in business administration from Boston University and a master's degree in public administration from the University of Southern California. He had worked as a marketing representative for Exxon Corporation and had served as executive director of Mahoney Community Health Center in Boston and as director for community health programs and administrator of the Mission Hill Center of the Harvard Community Health Plan in Boston.

In 1973, Ashford had become the first CEO of the National Association of Community Health Centers in Washington, D.C., where he was instrumental in increasing the organizational membership from 30 to 275. While with the National Association of Community Health Centers, he developed and administered an on-job/on-campus master's degree program for administrators of community health centers with the University of Michigan and the University of Southern California.

In 1979, Ashford became senior research fellow and expert consultant in the OHMO, U.S. Department of Health and Human Services. In this position he organized and managed the National HMO Fellows Program and conducted management assessments of unstable HMOs. From 1981 to 1982, he was the director of corporate planning and development for Jurgovan and Blair, a consulting firm in Rockville, Maryland. It was in this capacity that he became a consultant to IPM. When he assumed the position of president of IPM, he became the first African American chief executive of a general prepaid health plan.

IPM restructures

On assuming the presidency of IPM in August 1982, Ashford undertook several changes within the organization. He had a mandate to get IPM federally qualified and to increase the plan enrollment. He knew that the plan must become federally qualified to increase its current market appeal and to secure federal grants and loans. To become qualified, the plan would have to be financially stabilized in the short run and demonstrate a sound planning strategy.

His first action was to bring in a new management team and to restructure the organization. Donald Bailey was recruited as executive vice president. He had been a very successful director of marketing at a plan in New York. Janet Jones, the previous director of marketing, was employed full-time and given more responsibilities. The marketing staff was expanded, creating both a member marketing function as well as group sales. Other members of the staff were also promoted and given additional responsibilities. This reorganization was designed to increase the importance and relevance of the marketing function and to improve the operating efficiency of the organization. The internal reorganization also increased accountability.

The reorganized staff took immediate action to complete the application for federal qualification. Part of the application requested a loan to help stabilize the plan financially. There was some concern that including the loan request as part of the application would make the approval of the application less likely. With a loan request included as part of the application, approval of the application meant approval of the loan. It was decided to leave the loan request as part of the application. While the application for qualification was in process with the OHMO, the government closed down the federal loan program. This potential source of funding to achieve stabilization was eliminated.

The demise of the federal loan program meant that alternative sources of financing had to be found. The management had already been in the process of discussing with the corporate lawyers the possibility of establishing a limited partnership for the purpose of providing capital for the IPM Plan. The details of the relationship were already worked out and several potential investors identified.

In October 1982, Empire Development Associates (EDA) was formed as a limited partnership, involving 28 physicians from FDMG and Fairfield Medical Group and two local investors. The partnership created shares worth $1,000 each and specified that any partner could not hold fewer than five shares. Investors were limited to the two medical groups, although there were additional groups with contracts with IPM. The rationale was that the partnership should be tightly held for purposes of control.

The IPM corporation was restructured to include a board made up of the 28 physicians from the two medical groups, the three original founders, and three consumers. Kuehne remained as chairman of the board, with Ashford as the president. Board committees included long-range planning, compensation, the executive committee, and the committee on medical affairs. Most committees met when items were brought to them by the executive committee and met infrequently. The executive committee was made up of Kuehne, Johnson, and Peay, along with Ashford and Drs. Graham and Body from FDMG.

Empire Development Associates sold 791 units with individual investors holding between $5,000 and $40,000 worth of shares. In addition to the cash funds, EDA guaranteed a $400,000 line of credit for IPM at the Wells Fargo Bank in Vallejo. These funds were used to satisfy the tangible net equity requirements of the State of California, to meet requirements for federal qualification, and to provide cash for operations and expansion.[1] In April 1983, IPM was granted federal qualification.

Rapid expansion

East Bay area. With the infusion of new capital, IPM initiated efforts to expand the market and level of enrollment. A major effort was made to extend coverage into the Eastern Bay area of Alameda and Contra Costa Counties. These counties would give IPM access to a sizable and rapidly growing population area that it did not currently possess. The population of the two counties in 1980 was over 1.7 million people and growing at a steady rate (see Table 13.2).

Alameda County includes the metropolitan area of Oakland, as well as several smaller cities and suburban areas. It has a population base of 1.1 million people, 350,000 of whom live in Oakland. There are four areas with populations of more than 100,000, and the total population is estimated to increase 70 percent by the year 2000. There has been a shift in industry mix from heavy industry to office and service-related industry, with long-term potential for high-technology industry. The industrial base is diversified and geographically spread, with the employment opportunities growing more rapidly than the total number of employees.

Contra Costa County had a total population of 656,000 in 1980 and was projected to have the highest percentage of employment increase in the Bay area in the coming decade. The area had already experienced a rapid increase in jobs by 1982, mostly due to corporate consolidations and job transfers. Most of the growth in industry had been in the central part of the county, while the growth in residential areas was in the eastern and western parts of the county. It was estimated that over 45 percent of the new employees in the county would live in other regions, primarily

Table 13.2   Historical Population Growth in the San Francisco Bay Region

County	1940	1950	1960	1970	1980	Change 1940–80
Alameda	513,011	740,315	908,209	1,073,184	1,105,379	115%
Contra Costa	100,450	298,984	409,030	558,389	656,380	553
Marin	52,907	85,619	146,820	206,038	222,568	321
Napa	28,503	46,603	65,890	79,140	99,199	248
San Francisco	634,536	775,357	740,316	715,674	678,974	7
San Mateo	111,782	235,659	444,387	556,234	587,329	425
Santa Clara	174,949	290,547	642,315	1,064,714	1,295,071	640
Solano	49,118	104,833	134,597	169,941	235,203	379
Sonoma	69,052	103,405	147,375	204,885	299,681	334
Region	1,734,308	2,681,322	3,638,939	4,628,199	5,179,784	199%

Source: Census, April 1 of each year.

in Alameda County. This would put a strain on the already burdened transportation system.

In addition to the access to a large population base, IPM would also increase its marketing potential because it would become a regional plan. IPM would become more attractive to larger corporations and to corporations with more than one plant that had employees who resided anywhere in the East Bay area. This was considered to be a major strategic advantage for IPM in its pursuit to increase marketshare and size.

Considerable time and effort of the top management team was spent developing contracts with hospitals and medical groups in Alameda and Contra Costa Counties. Fourteen hospitals and six medical groups were brought into the IPM network between March and October 1983 (see Table 13.3, Figure 13.3). These additions increased the geographic coverage and service capacity of the IPM system fivefold. These contracts were developed rapidly and with very little visibility or acknowledgment in the health community or with competitive plans.

The Institute for Preventive Medicine contacted employers about extending coverage into the East Bay region and received considerable interest and acceptance and good initial enrollment. Much of the enrollment came from industries with whom IPM already had contracts. Other firms were interested because the East Bay area was underserved by health plans and many firms were moving into and expanding in that area. Many of them had employees living in other counties and were attracted to the concept of a regional health plan.

The Institute for Preventive Medicine applied for state approval for a service area expansion into Alameda and Contra Costa Counties, based on the impressive network of facilities and services it had established. IPM marketed services to firms in the area to be initiated 1 October 1983. Fortunately, IPM received state approval for a service area expansion on 1 October and aggressively moved to initiate operations in these counties.

While IPM was extending its coverage into Alameda and Contra Costa Counties, several plans were performing feasibility studies of the area, pursuing decisions within their corporate hierarchies to move into these counties, and cautiously moving to explore service contracts. Competing health plans were surprised by the unveiling of the delivery network and aggressive marketing tactics of IPM. Some word had leaked out from providers that IPM was gearing up to go into these counties, but few thought IPM could undertake it, and those who tried to verify it with the state were informed that there was no record of approval on file for IPM to operate in these areas (since the approval was not given until 1 October). IPM's small size permitted it to move swiftly in pursuing its strategy of increasing market size. The management team knew its small size was a strength in pursuing its

Table 13.3   Institute of Preventive Medicine Health Plan Medical Group Locations and Affiliated Hospitals

Counties	Medical Groups	Hospitals
Alameda	Oak Hill Medical Group, Oakland Oak Hill Medical Group, San Leandro Fremont Medical Group, Fremont Hayward Medical Group, Hayward Hayward Family Health Clinic, Hayward Pleasanton Family Health Clinic	Peralta Hospital, Oakland Samuel Merritt Hospital, Oakland Vesper Memorial Hospital, San Leandro Hayward Vesper Hospital, Hayward Valley Memorial Hospital, Livermore Washington Hospital, Fremont Providence Hospital, Oakland
Contra Costa	Family Doctor Medical Group, Martinez Oak Hill Medical Group, Lafayette Oak Hill Medical Group, Concord East County Medical Group, Pittsburg	John Muir Hospital, Walnut Creek Mount Diablo Hospital, Concord Los Medanos Hospital, Pittsburg
Solano	Family Doctor Medical Group, Vallejo Fairfield Medical Group, Fairfield Family Doctor Medical Group, Benicia Fairfield Medical Group, Vacaville	Vallejo General Hospital, Vallejo Intercommunity Hospital, Fairfield
Specialty Hospitals		Children's Hospital of San Francisco Children's Hospital of Oakland St. Mary's Hospital, San Francisco Alta Bates Hospital of Berkeley Mt. Zion Hospital, San Francisco

Figure 13.3 Institute of Preventive Medicine Health Plan Facilities

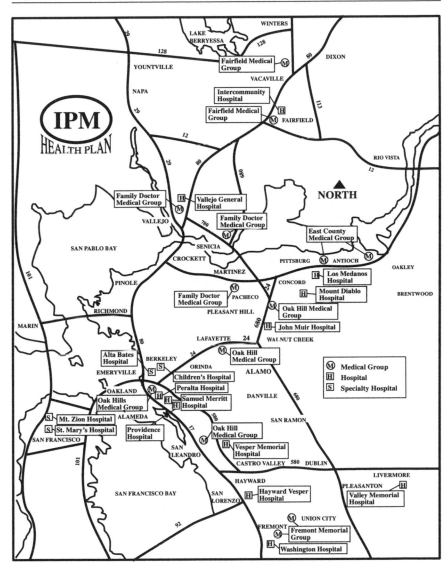

aggressive strategy and took full advantage of it. It felt it could deal with whatever followed.

The Kaiser Health Plan was already well-established in the region, and seven additional plans were already there or in the process of exploring coming in. They included Lifegard, HEALS, Contra Costa

Health Plan, Health Plan of America, Rockridge Health Plan, Foundation Health Plan, and TAKECARE. This surprise move by little IPM was described by one executive as "guerrilla warfare," and it opened the area to aggressive competition. TAKECARE and Foundation Health Plan had recently converted from nonprofit to for-profit status, and Rockridge was negotiating with Health Plan of America for a sale. In addition to these plans, Maxicare and Bay Pacific were also studying the East Bay region to test the market (see Table 13.4).

Federal Employees Health Benefit Programs. At the same time that IPM was expanding into the East Bay Area, initiatives were being taken to extend coverage to employees covered by the Federal Employees Health Benefit Program (FEHBP) in Solano County. This expansion had been included in the business plan submitted to the federal government as part of the application for qualification, but the move was made a year before it was planned. Approval was received on 1 January 1984, and enrollment started in early 1984.

Approval for the FEHBP opened up the largest employee group in Solano County. It included over 30,000 persons who were working in federal facilities and living in Solano County. Employers included Travis Air Force Base, Mare Island Naval Shipyard, post offices, and other federal installations. The FEHBP does not require that the plan be federally qualified, nor does federal qualification satisfy its participation requirements; the FEHBP has its own strict requirements for the delivery system. IPM was the only plan in Solano County approved to offer benefits under the FEHBP.

The FEHBP accounted for the major portion of the growth in enrollees between 1984 and 1986, because they were familiar with IPM and its services and many of them previously used IPM physicians as their personal physicians. In addition, many employees who had had only Kaiser as an option for a prepaid health plan switched when a second option became available. From 1 January 1984, when the FEHBP began enrolling members, to June 1986, the number of IPM enrollees increased from 10,314 to 18,528. It had almost achieved its 20,000-member objective.

IPM comes of age

The expanded size and complexity of operations of IPM made it necessary to increase the organizational and managerial capacity of the corporation. Ashford increased both his staff size and quality during the latter part of 1983 and early 1984, developing several new positions, replacing others, and upgrading many of the management systems. Sarah Sanders, the new full-time marketing director, came in from another

Table 13.4 Health Plans Serving the Bay Area

Plan and Date Originating	Control	Owner Affiliation	Enrollment Size*	Type	Federal Qualification	Clinics	Hospitals*
Kaiser Health Plan, Jan. 1945	Nonprofit	Kaiser Foundation	800,000	HMO	Yes	—	—
HEALS, July 1981	Nonprofit	Independent	30,000	IPA	Yes	10	7
TAKECARE, June 1978	Profit	Blue Cross	70,000	Net	Yes	35	28
Health Plan of America, Nov. 1980	Nonprofit	Catholic Hosp. Assn., Calif.	20,000	IPA	Yes	11	9
Contra Costa Co. Health Plan, Jan. 1980	Public	County	4,000	Staff	Yes	5	3
Foundation Health Plan, Dec. 1977	Profit	Americare	10,000	IPA	Yes	10	8
LIFEGUARD, Feb. 1979	Nonprofit	Independent	80,000	IPA/PPO	Yes	25	18
Rockridge, Jan. 1979	Nonprofit	Independent	15,000	HMO	Yes	5	3

*Including Northern California Region.

plan in Los Angeles. The marketing staff was expanded, creating both a member marketing function as well as a group sales function (see Figure 13.4). The latter office was also expanded in size. A new manager of health systems was recruited from another plan in San Francisco, with the charge to develop a quality assurance and utilization review system. Several new reporting relationships were established and new staff brought in. Some of the new people were recruited to fill vacancies created by the resignations of several staff, who took other jobs in the community or with other managed care systems in the Bay Area.

The major management system developments were in the areas of quality assurance, utilization review, and management information. With the greatly expanded provider system, it was necessary to develop a more formalized process of utilization review and quality assurance, including the creation of a quality assurance committee of the board and the development of a policies and procedures document (see Appendix A).

The management information system was expanded to provide additional reports and to process additional transactions. Additional processing capacity was purchased and additional programs were designed, written, and loaded. The system was found to be fully capable of handling the additional data needs, which pleased its designer, Greg Schwartz. The information reports and their schedules are presented in Table 13.5. In addition to the routine reports, the system was capable of providing special analysis reports and word processing. Examples include special reports by age and gender of subscriber, the percentage of subscribers covered by Medicare, and claim vouchers by service.

Financial characteristics and developments

Between July 1981 and July 1984, the number of enrollees in IPM's prepaid health plans increased from 4,478 to 11,017 (see Table 13.6, Figure 13.5). During this same time period, the retained earnings of IPM were diminished from a positive $4,601 to a negative $1,040,597, or an average loss of $346,866 per year. To remain in operation over this time period, loans were made to IPM by EDA in the amount of $1,384,497. These loans had favorable interest rates (2 percent over prime) and were not anticipated to be repaid until IPM was profitable. These loans were justifiably classified as long term, while most of the funds were being used to support short-term operations.

The first major infusion of funds from EDA during 1983 amounted to $467,250. These funds were used to support the excess of expenses over revenues of $342,839, increase the cash balance from an uncomfortable $6,598 in 1982 to a more secure $94,518 and to reduce claims payable,

Figure 13.4 Institute of Preventive Medicine Organization Diagram, 1984

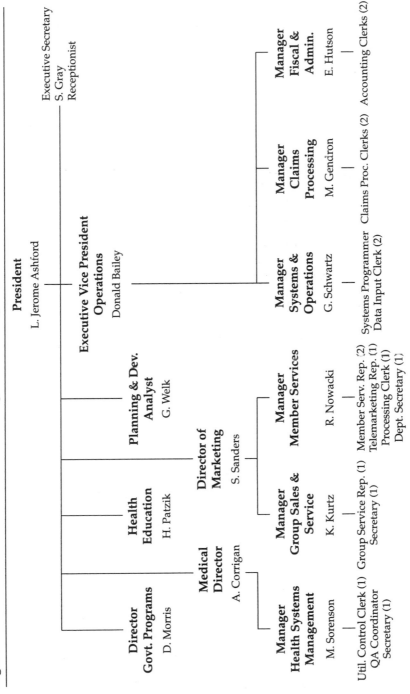

President
L. Jerome Ashford

Executive Secretary
S. Gray
Receptionist

Executive Vice President Operations
Donald Bailey

Planning & Dev. Analyst
G. Welk

Director Govt. Programs
D. Morris

Health Education
H. Patzik

Medical Director
A. Corrigan

Director of Marketing
S. Sanders

Manager Health Systems Management
M. Sorenson

Util. Control Clerk (1)
QA Coordinator
Secretary (1)

Manager Group Sales & Service
K. Kurtz

Group Service Rep. (1)
Secretary (1)

Manager Member Services
R. Nowacki

Member Serv. Rep. (2)
Telemarketing Rep. (1)
Processing Clerk (1)
Dept. Secretary (1)

Manager Systems & Operations
G. Schwartz

Systems Programmer
Data Input Clerk (2)

Manager Claims Processing
M. Gendron

Claims Proc. Clerks (2)

Manager Fiscal & Admin.
E. Hutson

Accounting Clerks (2)

Table 13.5   Management Information System Report Schedule

Report	Frequency
Marketing/member services reports	
Master membership list	Daily
Member addition list	Weekly
Member suspense list	Weekly
Member change list	Weekly
Master clinic membership list	Monthly
Pharmacy membership list	Monthly
Optics membership list	Monthly
Employer group report	Weekly
Rate notification report	Monthly
Premium billing report	Variable
Utilization control/claims control reports	
Hospital reserve report	Monthly*
Hospital reserve analysis	Monthly*
Hospital utilization summary report	Monthly*
Claims received reports	Monthly
Incurred but unreported claims report	Monthly*
Monthly claims payable (by group, etc.)	Monthly*
Claims paid	Monthly
Capitation report (by medical group)	Monthly*
Budget variance analysis	Monthly*

*Descriptions and copies of these reports are found in Appendix A.

which were being paid off in 113 days during 1982, to a more acceptable level of 65 days at the end of 1983.

Due to an 11.7 percent increase in enrollments, total revenues increased 42 percent, while increasing almost 19 percent per enrollee (due to increased premium rates). Unfortunately, medical care costs and other operating expenses increased 26.5 percent per enrollee, resulting in a loss of $5.33 per enrollee.

During 1984, the number of enrollees increased 94 percent, a substantial and admirable increase. EDA provided an additional $670,473 to support an excess of expenses over revenues of $589,179. Revenues increased almost 77 percent, while decreasing slightly per enrollee (see Figure 13.6). This decrease was due to the timing of enrollments and was not the result of a decrease in premiums. This decrease was associated with a 76 percent increase in total expenses, thereby presenting a slight improvement in the overall financial picture. The loss of $4.76

Table 13.6   Institute of Preventive Medicine Enrollment Chronology

Date	Enrollments	Significant Events
1 January 1979	2,500	
30 June 1982	5,000	
August 1982		Jerome Ashford hired
October 1982		EDA formed
1 January 1983	5,538	
1 April 1983		Federal qualification received
30 June 1983	5,587	
1 October 1983		Service area expansion
		Delivery system expansion
1 January 1984	10,314	Admission to FEHBP
30 June 1984	11,017	
1 January 1985	16,030	
30 June 1985	18,528	
1 July 1985		Change in fiscal year from June 30 to December 31
1 January 1986	18,500	
1 October 1986		Conversion to taxable corporation
1 January 1987	23,272	
30 April 1987	24,229	
1 January 1988	25,037	
30 April 1988	26,182	

per enrollee was a reduction of almost 11 percent from the loss for fiscal year 1983. A large portion of the increase in operating expense was due to a 219 percent increase in the advertising and marketing expenses and a 137 percent increase in professional services. Marketing and advertising increased almost 66 percent per enrollee. The resulting increase in enrollments was proportional, although the impact of the increased marketing expenses should have long-term implications.

Consolidation and Maturity

Health system enhancement and increased competition

The period January 1984–June 1987 was one dedicated to increasing marketshare in the expanded service area and strengthening the financial and organizational position of IPM. This goal was complicated by the fact that it was an era of rapidly increasing competition in the Bay area. Since IPM entered the Contra Costa and Alameda markets, four new plans had started operations there: CIGNA, Metlife, Bay Pacific, and Maxicare.

Figure 13.5   Institute for Preventive Medicine Total Enrollees

Enrollees (in thousands)

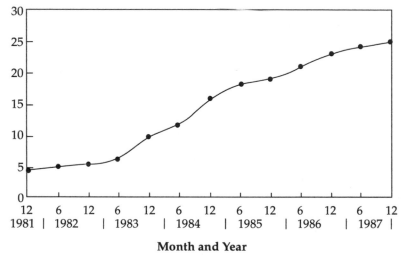

Month and Year

Maxicare had become a major force in the region with its purchase of Health Plan of America, which had previously purchased Rockridge Health Plan. That brought to ten the number of regional and national plans operating in the East Bay area. Some, like Contra Costa Health Plan, were small and confined their operations to specialized services, such as Medicaid. Others, like Maxicare, were multistate organizations pushing toward national plans (see Table 13.4).

As a result of the increasing competition, there was a need to greatly enhance the existing service delivery system. The existing system was adequate from a regulatory perspective but had gaps in terms of service coverage that proved to be costly from a marketing perspective. To be more competitive, each plan developed and expanded through vertical integration. The IPM system was enhanced to include primary care services in 21 new locations, adding three new medical groups and specialty services in many existing groups. There was considerable investment of time and resources in the development of management systems and marketing capacity.

In addition to the cost of developing the service delivery system, the cost of operations increased as a result of increasing competition. Operating costs such as advertising increased by 100 percent due to competitive pressures. In addition, rapid escalation in the sophistication of the advertising campaigns increased the stakes in the advertising

Figure 13.6   Institute for Preventive Medicine Revenue and Expense per Member per Month

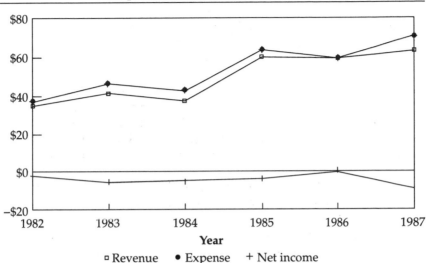

game. The advertising expenses for IPM had averaged about $60,000 per year going into this era, a figure that was regarded as high by management, given the size of the operation. During one six-month period at that time, Maxicare spent $1.5 million on advertising. Other plans responded by rapidly increasing their advertising budgets. IPM had indeed entered the big time.

Another competitive strategy of the same plans in the region was to increase the level of capitation provided to the physicians. This strategy was effective in signing up new medical groups as well as increasing the physician acceptance and promotion of these plans.

A slight change in capitation levels was found to cause rapid shifts in physician loyalty. Loyalty was also affected by other services to the groups, most notably the time required for them to receive their capitation fees. The increase in capitation significantly added to the cost of operations. As a result of the operating losses, higher costs of doing business, and the increased risks from the increased size of the enterprise, IPM found it necessary to increase its line of credit from $400,000 to $1.7 million. This increase was also guaranteed by EDA.

The period from the middle of 1984 to the end of 1985 was one of general financial improvement as the liquidity position of IPM became less risky as indicated by the number of days of cash on hand. Cash on hand indicates the number of days worth of expenses that IPM could absorb without an additional infusion of cash receipts. In 1982 IPM had slightly over 1 day's worth of operating expenses in its cash account—an extremely risky position. This figure had increased to almost 15 days by the end of 1984 and to over 26 days by the end of 1985.

The improved liquidity position was the result of improved operating and new income. By June 1985, total assets were $2,874,073, 400 percent greater than in 1982. The cash position had improved, and an operating profit was experienced for the first time in IPM's history. However, with interest expenses of $141,867, there remained an excess of expenses over revenues. Management felt that it had turned the corner with regard to financial operations and was optimistic about the future.

Management's optimism seemed to be well founded, for in 1986, IPM produced the first positive bottom line in its history. Although relatively small, the $50,613 profit was consistent with the projected trend of the firm and was seen as an indication of profitability. Management felt that it had control over the medical cost increases, with increased economies being realized from spreading fixed costs over greater numbers of enrollees. This situation reduced the cost per enrollee, a measure that management increasingly felt was a good indicator of economic health and viability.

However, the profitability position of IPM was not gained without some cost, which would eventually have to be borne. During 1986, enrollments increased at a comfortable 26 percent. The increase in total revenues was slightly less than the increase in enrollments, resulting in a slight decrease in revenue per enrollee. The major improvement in financial performance, however, came about from the constraints placed on operating costs. The increase in operating costs was less than the increase in enrollments, resulting in a 7 percent reduction in expense per enrollee. The decrease in operating expenses came about due to limited increases in physician and hospital capitation and fee-for-service payments and a reduction in marketing and advertising expenses per enrollee. The marketing and advertising expenses during the last six months of 1985 were $216,000, while $310,000 was the total marketing and advertising expense for all of 1986.

Closer examination of the financial statements for 1986 (see Appendix B) indicate that a major financial change took place, resulting in a net loss of $466,671. This loss was an immediate recognition of funds previously expended but not yet accounted for on the income statement. However, these expenses had been recognized on the balance sheet in the form of prepaid expenses.

Services development and quality

The management staff agreed that the strengths of IPM included the range of benefit packages that it offered, the range of services covered, and the low deductibles and copayments. The package was developed to compete with the Kaiser Plan and was acknowledged by enrollees as having very good benefits and options, with most services paid in full. IPM markets three standard benefit packages to commercial accounts— the Ultra Plan, the Share Plan, and the Basic Plan. Each plan offers the same coverage but differs in its premium and copayment schedules. Optional coverage for pharmacy and vision care services are also available in conjunction with the Ultra Plan and Share Plan. In addition to these plans, IPM custom designed the plans for federal and California state employees (see Appendix C for a comparison of the benefit packages).

As of 2 January 1985, IPM did not participate in either the California Medi-Cal program or the federal Medicare program. It did participate in the Medicare program before the end of 1985 and explored the feasibility of participating in the Medi-Cal program.

Competitive response

Competitive health plans in the Bay area provided a range of benefits and options at a range of prices. Employers found that they could choose about any range of services at any price; it had become a buyers market. IPM was more than competitive on both benefit package and price and extensively marketed this fact and this image. All the promotional materials describing any of the plans always included a side-by-side comparison of the competitive plan, so that each potential enrollee could get a clear visual basis for making plan comparisons (see Appendix C). For those who did not take the time to do such a side-by-side comparison, which was most, the brochures still conveyed the message that IPM would compare favorably against all others. This marketing position was consistently held by IPM.

Competitive plans, other than Kaiser, did not have health benefit coverage comparable to IPM. They also tended to have higher copayments and deductibles. IPM had considered responding to the market by increasing coinsurance and deductibles as well as altering the option package but discovered that the management information system was not sufficiently flexible to accommodate these changes. This inflexibility was also becoming a problem in that the larger corporations were increasingly demanding tailor-made benefit packages, which IPM's data system could not accommodate. A consultant was retained to address the management information system problem and recommended a new data support system and new hardware and software packages. IPM concluded that sufficient financial resources did not currently exist to permit this expenditure.

By the third quarter of 1987, it became apparent that adjustments needed to be made in the benefit package, particularly with the deductibles and copayments, to increase the net income of the plan. A careful market assessment was carried out by the marketing department to determine the position of the competition with regard to benefits. IPM decided that at the next contract period, changes in the benefit package would have to be made but kept it within the range of the competition. The reaction to these changes was more negative than anticipated, particularly given that they were still within the competitive range. IPM decided to stay with the adjusted rates.

Conversion and Sale of IPM

Conversion

Conversion attempts. In 1985 it became increasingly apparent to management that long-term changes needed to be made to IPM, to gain greater access to capital. This need was primarily due to the nature of the increasing competition in the region. Competitors were larger, better financed, and had more sophisticated management systems. To compete in the existing service area and to continue to expand, it became apparent that IPM would have to find a partner corporation to increase its size and power. IPM initiated the search for an appropriate partner or a buyer and considered the possibility of pursuing a strategy of becoming a publicly traded entity, with or without a corporate partner. Without increased access to capital, it could not continue to compete with the large plans in the region.

The Institute of Preventive Medicine initiated the process through a series of informal discussions with corporations that they felt might be interested in a partnership. Included in the negotiations was the provision that if IPM converted to a for-profit corporation, the transfer of the value of the assets to another 501(c) organization would be the responsibility of the partner corporation. There was the recognition that the conversion of IPM to for-profit status was most likely, in that it would increase the list of potential buyers, and it was becoming clear that HMOs could increase their access to capital if they were for-profit. A valuation study was completed by Ernst and Whinney to identify up front that part of the transaction.

As the word spread that IPM might be for sale, several firms inquired about the potential terms of sale. Two firms, HealthWest and Sierra Health Services, were pursued by IPM as potential partners. Negotiations were initiated with HealthWest, a nonprofit firm, but broke down due to demands placed on the firm by members of the IPM board. During this process, the chair of the board of IPM, through the executive committee, was the chief negotiator.

Negotiations were then entered into with Sierra Health Services, a for-profit firm, but encountered difficulty due to the takeover of a nonprofit corporation by a for-profit corporation. The issue was not one of the valuation of the assets or the contribution to a 501(c) corporation but of the impact, including the cost of operations of the IPM Health Plan and the resulting increase in cost of services. The IPM lawyers developed a plan for a management agreement with Sierra Health Services that provided the assurance of continuity to IPM enrollees. The State of California denied approval of the management agreement on the basis that it would increase the cost of services to the enrollees of IPM.

While the management agreement was being negotiated with the state, a group of FDMG physicians filed a lawsuit contending that there was an oral agreement with FDMG that if IPM were ever to convert to a for-profit status, FDMG would be given a one-third equity interest in the new corporation. Sierra, as a new firm listed on the stock exchange, decided it did not want to be a part of any lawsuit and in June 1986 withdrew from the negotiations.

The conversion consummated. In June 1986, Empire Health Services (EHS), a for-profit holding company, was formed as a successor to EDA. This corporation was funded by EDA partners and the senior management of IPM, a total of 28 shareholders. The corporation sold 1,319,747 shares of stock at ten cents per share, generating capital of $131,975. Empire Health Services provided $369,906 in the form of subordinated notes. These funds were used to assist in expenses associated with the conversion process and to reduce the average payment period. However, these expenditures amounted to more than the additional funds provided, placing IPM once again in the tenuous position of having only two days' operating expenses in the form of cash.

The Institute for Preventive Medicine applied to the state for conversion and entered into negotiations on valuation, price, etc., and in October 1986 converted to a for-profit corporation, with 100 shares of common stock. EHS purchased IPM by buying the 100 shares of IPM stock and assumed the liability for the $1,021,000 charitable contribution. EHS then resumed the search for a partner.

The sale

Sale attempts. The second attempt at the sale of IPM started in October 1986 with the development of a detailed prospectus on the corporation, including a description and assessment of its current and potential delivery system, its current and potential market, the strengths of the corporation in terms of its business operations and plan, the quality of management, the strategic plan, and the consistency and unity of the direction and mission. The offer for the sale of IPM was widely announced, and a prospectus was sent to all who inquired. Those who formally expressed interest were screened with regard to predetermined criteria on size, location, capacity, and image as well as consistency of purpose. Preliminary discussions were held with several corporations that met the desired criteria. From this series of discussions, two—Pacific Mutual Insurance Company and Principal Health Care—were selected for more detailed discussions.

Ashford entered intensive negotiations with Pacific Mutual Insurance early in 1987. Pacific Mutual was new in the HMO business and was developing a start-up HMO in Bakersfield. It was interested in acquisitions to rapidly increase its market and system. At the end of six months of study and negotiation, all terms of the deal were agreed to. The two organizations seemed to be very compatible in terms of their aggressive behavior and corporate philosophies. They proceeded to initiate some cooperative activities, jointly purchased a sophisticated computer system and software package, and were recruiting some new staff and developing common policy and procedures manuals. The merged relationship was announced in the papers, and the news was widely circulated in the industry.

By June 1987, the industry had entered a period of rapid and major transformation, with several plans closing or being sold, and the stock price of those being publicly traded dramatically dropped. The day the contract was to be officially signed, at the meeting that had been called for that purpose, the chair of the board of Pacific entered the meeting and announced that it had reassessed the corporate position and decided not to enter the HMO business. The deal was off. Financial negotiations ensued to balance the activities and computer acquisitions of the previous few months.

The sale completed. In October 1987, after IPM management and staff recovered from shock and disappointment, a solicitation was again made for the sale of IPM. IPM moved more quickly to the process of selecting a short list of potential buyers, given the familiarity with some of the firms and its increased experience in conversions and sales of health plans.

On the negative side, the performance of HMOs rapidly continued to deteriorate nationally, and the market for health plans went with it. The market value of IPM in 1985 had been $15 million. By 1986 the value was about $6 million. This drop was even more significant in that the membership in IPM in 1985 was only two-thirds of what it was in 1986.

The superior proposal was from Children's Hospital in San Francisco, and IPM entered into intensive negotiations with it. In June 1988, IPM was sold to Children's Hospital. This sale was the conclusion of more than three years of intensive effort by management and staff to reposition the organization for the future. It was an effort incorporating a vision of the future and built on the successes and failures of the past as the corporation charted its course in an increasingly complex and dynamic health care system environment.

Note

1. The Knox-Keene Act requires that IPM maintain a minimum tangible net equity of $15,000. On 30 June 1982 and 30 June 1983, IPM had tangible net equity deficits of $33,079 and $17,714, respectively. On 30 July 1982 and 9 June 1983, the institute obtained subordinated loans amounting to $57,500 and $46,884, respectively, to satisfy these deficits. The tangible net equity position for IPM is calculated by taking total assets less total liabilities plus the subordinated notes payable to EDA. Prior written approval of the commissioner of the Department of Corporations of the State of California is required before these notes can be repaid.

References

Illich, I. 1976. *Medical Nemesis—The Expropriation of Health*. New York: Random House, Inc.

World Health Organization. 1978. *Alma-Ata 1978: Primary Health Care*. Report of the International Conference on Primary Health Care, Alma-Ata, U.S.S.R. Geneva, Switzerland: The Organization.

Appendix A

Utilization Management and Quality Assurance Policies

Utilization Management Program

IPM Health Plan is a Health Maintenance Organization (HMO), which is defined as an "organization of health care providing a comprehensive range of health benefits to its voluntarily enrolled members in exchange for a fixed prepaid fee." IPM is at risk for the cost of services defined under its benefit package; services are paid for in advance of when they are actually used and any cost beyond what is covered by the premium is borne by IPM Health Plan and participating providers.

IPM Health Plan manages its financial risk by delivering health services through an organized health care delivery system. This means IPM and the Plan Providers unite into a single system, creating a setting in which they share the financial risk of cost overruns beyond the budget for health care services provided to members. To prevent cost overruns in the delivery of health care services, the Utilization Control System was established.

The Utilization Management Program (UMP) is designed to monitor utilization and cost of delivering health care to assure the appropriate level of care is provided to the member in the most cost-effective manner. To achieve this goal, the UMP employs prospective, concurrent, and retrospective review of the utilization and cost of health care services provided to members.

Prospective review

The heart of the IPM health care delivery system is the primary care physician from one of the medical groups. This physician is responsible for providing or arranging for all of the health care services required by the member.

Referral authorizations. If the member requires service which the primary care physician is unable to provide, the member is referred to a provider who can meet his/her needs. In many instances, the referral provider will belong to the same medical group as the primary care physician—this is an internal referral to a Plan provider. Members may also be referred to a Plan provider in another IPM medical group—this is a cross referral. On occasion, the member will require the services of a provider who is not a member of an IPM medical group—this is an external referral to a non-Plan provider.

All referrals, internal, external, and cross, require written authorization from the medical group's Medical Director prior to services being rendered. The following services are included in this type of referral authorization:

- Specialty Care (physician)
- Home Health Care

- Durable Medical Equipment
- Prosthetics/Orthotics
- Skilled Nursing Care

Prior authorization of referral provider services gives the Medical Director an opportunity to assure that the requested services fulfill the members' needs and are cost effective.

Referrals of an urgent nature may be authorized verbally by the Medical Director. A written authorization must be completed by the first working day following the verbal authorization.

To obtain approval for a referral, the requesting provider must complete a "Referral Authorization Form Worksheet" and forward it with the member's medical record to the group's Medical Director.

The Medical Director will then approve or deny the request for referral and forward the form and the medical record to the medical group IPM Coordinator. If the referral request is denied, the IPM Coordinator returns the worksheet and the member's medical record to the provider who requested the referral.

If the request for referral is approved, the IPM Coordinator verbally notifies the requesting provider and the referral provider. The Coordinator completes the "Referral Authorization Form", a four-part NCR form, and distributes it.

Hospital authorizations. All hospital admissions must also be authorized in writing by the medical group's Medical Director. As indicated previously, this authorization helps to assure that the appropriate level of care is being provided to members in a cost-effective manner. Elective admissions, which include out-patient surgery services, require authorization prior to the member being admitted. Authorization for emergency admissions, which include obstetrical admissions, are obtained concurrently. Written concurrent authorization must be obtained the first working day following the admission.

Authorization for a hospital admission is obtained in the same manner as a referral authorization except the primary care or admitting physician must complete a "Hospital Admission Authorization Form," and forward it, with the member's medical record, to the medical group's Medical Director for action.

When a hospital admission is approved by the Medical Director, the IPM Coordinator notifies the requesting provider of the admission approval, completes and distributes the "Admission Authorization form." Copies must be sent to the HMO's Health Services Department and the Hospital Admission Department on a prospective basis.

In-area emergency services. When members are allowed to decide unilaterally when to seek emergency room services, these services are frequently utilized inappropriately. As a result, members are instructed to obtain prior authorization for emergency room services.

If members have a condition of an urgent nature and their physician's office is closed, they are instructed to call their physician prior to going to the emergency room. This gives the physician an opportunity to assess the member's condition and recommend appropriate action.

Emergency room services rendered to members in a Plan hospital must either be provided or authorized by a Plan physician. Therefore, if a member is referred to the emergency room by a Plan physician, the physician must either treat the member in the emergency room or notify the emergency room physician that the member has been referred to him/her for treatment.

If a member does not obtain prior authorization for emergency room services, the hospital emergency room staff has been instructed to call the primary care physician to determine who should treat the member. If the member's physician is not available, the hospital will contact the on-call Plan physician from the nearest medical group, who may either authorize or render treatment. However, there may be a case/encounter that does not clearly fall into these guidelines. These situations are reviewed retrospectively. Emphasis will always be placed on quality patient care.

If a life-threatening condition exists, prior authorization for emergency room services is not required. Members are instructed to go immediately to the nearest hospital in a life-threatening situation. In addition, Plan hospitals are instructed to initiate treatment immediately in life-threatening situations and notify the member's physician or the physician on call as soon as possible.

Concurrent review

Hospital, Outpatient Surgery, Home Health, DME Rental and Skilled Nursing Facilities are services which are reviewed concurrently.

Health Services Representatives of IPM monitor each category to assure that the level of care and length of stay/service is appropriate.

In addition, based on the information the Health Services Representative collects when monitoring utilization, he/she estimates the cost of each service. These estimates are used to determine IPM's liability for services known to have been provided to IPM members. Utilization data and the estimated cost of services are reported to the medical groups' Medical Directors weekly and monthly.

Retrospective review

Retrospective review involves collection and analysis of utilization data. The medical groups' Medical Directors and medical group committees review encounter data for trend analysis, problem identification and resolution. Quantity and quality of services are analyzed in this process. This gives the Medical providers an opportunity to evaluate and compare utilization and cost of services.

Retrospective review of utilization and cost data is imperative to guarantee a fiscally viable health plan. IPM has a comprehensive Management Information System for collection and analysis of utilization and cost data. In addition, the medical groups collect and report data on their utilization. Review of this data allows analysis and comparison of practice patterns of providers and is an important mechanism to assure appropriate care is provided to members in a cost-effective manner.

The data, which is collected by IPM and the medical groups, is reported to the medical group's Medical Directors and Administrators and the executive staff of IPM for their analysis and recommendations.

The Quality Assurance Program

Narrative

The IPM Health Plan is committed to the concept of providing high-quality care at reasonable cost. To assure that this commitment is met, the plan has developed a Quality Assurance Program that stresses the process and outcomes of its health care delivery system. The program incorporates ongoing review and evaluation by physicians and other health professionals and has written procedures for conducting studies, reporting results and implementing changes.

The goals of the Quality Assurance Program are to assure that quality health care is delivered to the members of IPM Health Plan; and to assure that quality care is delivered in a manner consistent with the human dignity and rights of Plan members.

While the complete essence of "quality" is difficult to define, certain attributes of quality care can be identified and monitored: accessibility, availability, adequacy, appropriateness, effectiveness, and timeliness.

The Quality Assurance Program comprises the following components:

— Standards of care which apply to the health services delivery system structure, process and outcome of care.

— A system of monitoring care prospectively, concurrently, and retrospectively.

— A system of integrated review and evaluation which identifies variations from accepted medical practice and which strives toward improvement of health care.

— A program of corrective action for the resolution of identified problems and a method for monitoring improvements and compliance with problem resolution recommendations and/or actions.

— A policy of confidentiality to ensure the cooperation of providers and the privacy of members.

The Quality Assurance Committee of IPM Health Plan is responsible for the Quality Assurance Program. It evaluates the effect of outcomes of the program on the operation of the health care delivery system.

The Quality Assurance Program is executed by the Quality Assurance Committee and the IPM Health Services Department, which derives its authority from the IPM Health Plan Board of Directors. The Quality Assurance Committee reports directly to the IPM Health Plan Board of Directors, submitting all study conclusions and recommendations to that body.

The Quality Assurance Committee (OAC). The IPM Quality Assurance Committee meets quarterly. This committee seeks to assure that the health care services available are appropriate to the members' needs and are of appropriate quality. This includes assuring that the right care at the time is provided in a cost effective manner. In addition, the Committee is working toward improving the quality of health care delivered to IPM Health Plan members.

Committee functions

— Review and analyze performance of the components of IPM's health services delivery system.

— Review proposed benefit options as they impact upon health services delivery.

— Review credentials of proposed IPM health care providers.

— Review management information reports which provide information about referrals, physician encounters, hospital admissions and length of stays, and ER utilization.

The Quality Assurance Program monitors the delivery of care in three ways:

— Prospective Review
— Concurrent Review
— Retrospective Review

Prospective and concurrent quality assurance review involves the utilization management process. Prospective review occurs with referral and pre-admission hospitalization authorizations. These authorizations require that the Medical Directors, or designated physicians, of the Medical Groups review and authorize the requests prior to the services being delivered. This process requires a quality judgment by the Medical Director, or the designated physician, on the appropriateness of the requested referral or hospitalization based on standards set forth by the Quality Assurance committee. Monitoring of hospital stay is a concurrent review undertaken by the Health Services Representative and the medical group's Medical Doctor. Hospital stays are reviewed against established length of stay targets for similar diagnosis based on standards of quality accepted by the Quality Assurance Committee. In addition, active case management is instituted to assess the appropriateness of the level of care. Working with the physician involved in each case, the HMO is able to transfer the member to the appropriate setting in a timely fashion.

Process and outcome studies, as recommended by the Quality Assurance Committee, are retrospective assessments which strive to improve health care delivery. Process studies evaluate specific care delivered to the patient by the physician and other health care providers. Outcome studies evaluate the end result of care delivered to the patient in terms of the health status of the patient. These studies are on-going at the Medical Group level. In addition, the IPM Quality Assurance Coordinator carries out similar studies on-site on a continuing basis with reports submitted to the Quality Assurance Committee for review and recommendation.

The following topics provide an overview of the Quality Assurance process of IPM Health Plan. These studies are carried out by the HMO's Health Services Department under the direction of the Plan's Quality Assurance Committee.

Medical provider information sheets. This data collection tool is IPM Health Plan's initial assessment of medical providers. It provides the potential medical group with an opportunity to review the basic elements that are required by IPM Health Plan in order to assure a quality delivery network. This information is collected prior to contract negotiations and reviewed by the Executive Staff and Department of Planning and Development. Criteria elements must be met before further discussion and development of the group.

Precontractual on-site evaluation—medical group. This review is conducted on a pre-contractual basis to apply the standards necessary for medical providers of IPM's delivery network. This review provides a baseline analysis for on-going dialogue between IPM and the medical group. IPM's Quality Assurance Coordinator applies this evaluative tool to the provider site with review and recommendations presented to IPM's Executive Staff and Quality Assurance Committee. This is an excellent opportunity to establish communication avenues with the provider community.

Precontractual on-site evaluation—IPA. This review is a modified version of the medical group evaluation to meet the IPM's requirements of an IPA setting.

Pre-contractual on-site skilled nursing facility evaluation. This review is conducted on a pre-contractual basis to apply the standards necessary to the skilled nursing facilities of IPM's delivery network. This review provides a baseline analysis for on-going dialogue between IPM Health Plan and skilled nursing facilities. In addition to the initial review of this type of provider setting, dialogue will be useful in the development of levels of care that may be appropriate for IPM Health Plan's member population. Enhancement of appropriate settings of care provide an environment that is quality oriented to provide member satisfaction.

On-site evaluations. This review is conducted on a regular basis to assist the medical groups in the assessment of Quality Assurance functions. This element of our Quality Assurance Program is critical in the development of our medical providers' on site Quality Assurance functions. Increased communication by the IPM Quality Assurance Coordinator enhances standardization of our delivery network. Similar areas needing development are identified and appropriate action plans can be established. Revisits will measure the results of corrective or developmental actions. The following elements are included in this program:

1. Utilization Management and Quality Assurance Program Assessment
2. Medical Records Charting Standards Audit
3. Medical Care Evaluation

HMO member inquiry/complaint program. The importance of analyzing members' concerns is addressed by this program. Focus is on issues such as: access, availability, quality of care and benefits. Presenting the medical providers with this detail enhances the ability to pinpoint problem areas in the delivery of care and, thus, take necessary action. This avenue of communication is conducted by IPM's Member Services Representatives. Confidential member files are maintained by IPM.

Member satisfaction survey. This survey tool is utilized to sample membership attitudes with reference to the medical providers network. This quality assurance tool includes members' comments related to accessibility, availability, quality of service, and other issues on which members wish to comment. Results of the survey are shared with the medical groups and are utilized by their internal Quality Assurance Committees.

Member disenrollment survey. As stated above, this is another survey tool utilized by the Health Plan to assess membership attitudes and concerns. These results are also shared by the Medical Group's internal Quality Assurance Committee.

Optometric quality assurance program. This is a comprehensive program geared toward the optometric provider community. Components include precontractual assessments and on-site evaluations.

Home health care agency—evaluations. This on-site evaluation is an assessment tool utilized for our home health agencies. This type of tool enhances dialogue between IPM and contracting providers that will be useful in the development of programs that will best serve IPM's members.

Appendix B IPM Financial Information

IPM Balance Sheet Information

	1982	1983	1984	1985	1985 Six Months	1986	1987
	June 30	June 30	June 30	June 30	December 31	December 31	December 31
Cash	$ 6,598	$ 94,518	$ 206,614	$ 554,099	$ 521,038	$ 81,319	$ 153,356
Receivables all for bad debts							
Net receivables	$ 413,283	$ 308,576				$ 2,531,325	$ 2,091,777
Premiums			$ 655,576	$1,429,284	$1,691,191		
Copayments & reinsurance			$ 22,525	$ 3,401	$ 270,654	$ 57,427	$ 16,420
Reinsurance reserve				$ 92,218			
Risk-sharing agreements			$ 29,406		$ 72,555	$ 174,844	$ 380,937
Parent						$ 26,024	$ 436,784
Other			$ 13,698	$ 28,115	$ 2,477	$ 130,360	
Empire Development Associates			$ 99,568	$ 133,083	$ 363,083		
Current portion—notes receivable	$ 40,000	$ 40,000	$ 31,429	$ 62,857	$ 47,143		
Total receivables	$ 453,283	$ 348,576	$ 852,202	$1,748,958	$2,447,103	$ 2,919,980	$ 2,925,918
Prepaid expenses	$ 13,274	$ 32,008	$ 224,414	$ 299,808	$ 706,096	$ 133,151	$ 39,025
Total current assets	$ 473,155	$ 475,102	$1,283,230	$2,602,865	$3,674,237	$3,134,450	$ 3,118,299
Notes receivable			$ 118,571	$ 55,714	$ 40,000		
Furniture and equipment accumulated depreciation							
Net furniture & equipment	$ 17,509	$ 29,019	$ 137,219	$ 144,203	$ 155,558	$ 220,556	$ 189,586

Deferred charges—note an accumulated amortization							
Net deferred charges	$ 83,005	$ 109,046	$ 86,090	$ 71,291	$ 51,656	$ 28,700	$ 5,774
Total assets	$ 573,669	$ 613,167	$1,625,110	$2,874,073	$3,921,451	$ 3,383,706	$ 3,313,629
Current liabilities:							
Deferred revenue	$ 185,063	$ 254,234	$ 549,778	$1,027,714	$1,183,908	$ 1,492,458	$ 1,773,254
Claims payable	$ 361,305	$ 247,272	$ 412,516	$ 912,287	$1,866,830	$ 1,262,850	$ 2,363,008
Capitation & risk-sharing payable			$ 240,191	$ 426,878	$ 481,171	$ 383,138	$ 1,417,527
Current portion—medical liabilities							$ 115,482
Accounts payable and accruals	$ 60,380	$ 14,770	$ 26,003	$ 30,886	$ 80,997	$ 46,849	$ 140,545
Current portion—capital lease			$ 21,293	$ 30,114	$ 32,483	$ 62,512	$ 47,324
Current portion—note/payable			$ 31,429				
Current portion—subordinated N/P				$ 62,857	$ 47,143		
Interest payable		$ 5,559					
Total current liabilities	$ 606,748	$ 521,835	$1,281,210	$2,490,736	$3,692,532	$ 3,247,807	$ 5,857,140
Long-term liabilities:							
Medical liabilities			$ 92,703	$ 79,836	$ 62,432	$ 106,117	$ 170,350
Capital lease obligations							$ 58,645

Continued

Appendix B Continued

IPM Balance Sheet Information

	1982 June 30	1983 June 30	1984 June 30	1985 June 30	1985 Six Months December 31	1986 December 31	1987 December 31
Note payable			$ 78,571	$ 15,714			
Subordinated notes payable:							
To parent		$ 542,750					
Other	$ 75,500		$1,213,223	$1,350,817	$1,632,815	$ 2,002,721	$ 3,085,216
Total long-term liabilities	$ 75,500	$ 542,750	$1,384,497	$1,446,367	$1,695,247	$ 2,108,898	$ 3,314,211
Total liabilities	$ 682,248	$1,064,585	$2,665,707	$3,937,103	$5,387,779	$ 5,356,705	$ 9,171,351
Shareholders equity:							
Common stock, no par, authorized, issued, and outstanding 100 shares						$ 1,511,000	$ 1,511,000
Retained earnings (deficit)						($ 3,483,999)	($ 7,368,722)
Total equity						($ 1,972,999)	($ 5,857,722)
Fund balance (prior to conversion)	($ 108,579)	($ 451,418)	($1,040,597)	($1,063,030)	($1,466,328)		
Total liabilities + equity	$ 573,669	$ 613,167	$1,625,110	$2,874,073	$3,921,451	$ 3,383,706	$ 3,313,629

IPM Revenue and Expense Statement

Statement of Operations	1982	1983	1984	1985	1985	1986	1987
Revenues:							
Premium income	$1,847,622	$2,617,448	$4,618,708	$9,710,566	$6,471,826	$16,446,351	$18,731,364
Reinsurance recoveries					$ 321,471		
Other	$ 1,873	$ 9,605	$ 24,729	$ 40,918	$ 31,040	$ 54,417	$ 289,682
Total revenues	$1,849,495	$2,627,053	$4,643,437	$9,751,484	$6,824,337	$16,500,768	$19,021,046
Expenses:							
Physician & pharmacy capitation	$1,580,153	$2,276,896	$4,179,846	$8,195,749	$6,139,777	$13,687,503	$ 9,582,616
Hospital							$ 8,103,445
Other medical care costs	$ 6,624	$ 12,132					$ 556,332
Reinsurance premiums					$ 94,380	$ 217,972	$ 244,310
Salaries & benefits	$ 208,065	$ 393,409	$ 467,318	$ 625,550	$ 428,377	$ 1,174,071	$ 1,250,751
Marketing & advertising	$ 30,771	$ 32,943	$ 105,210	$ 309,497	$ 216,648	$ 309,767	$ 627,305
General & administrative	$ 61,961	$ 139,829	$ 161,575	$ 222,706	$ 142,048	$ 634,884	$ 495,314
Professional services	$ 16,991	$ 39,306	$ 93,270	$ 120,130	$ 41,037	$ 101,883	$ 350,751
Rent & occupation	$ 45,482	$ 26,949	$ 66,468	$ 91,743	$ 51,036	$ 61,364	$ 109,800
Depreciation & amortization	$ 3,148	$ 12,558	$ 52,023	$ 66,675	$ 37,692	$ 89,666	$ 98,119
Health & education program					$ 6,358		
Refund of excess hospital reserve	$ 8,805						
	$1,962,000	$2,934,022	$5,125,710	$9,632,050	$7,157,353	$16,277,110	$21,418,743
Interest expense	$ 675	$ 35,870	$ 106,906	$ 141,867	$ 70,282	$ 173,045	$ 297,730
Total expenses	$1,962,675	$2,969,892	$5,232,616	$9,773,917	$7,227,635	$16,450,155	$21,716,473
Net income (loss)	($ 113,180)	($ 342,839)	($ 589,179)	($ 22,433)	($ 403,298)	$ 50,613	($ 2,695,427)

Appendix C IPM Health Plan Benefits and Promotional Material

IMP Health Plan Benefit and Copayment
1 January 1985

The IMP Health Plan offers three basic benefit packages which provide comprehensive coverage. Optional coverage for pharmacy and complete vision care service are available. Our basic benefit packages consist of:

Benefits	Ultra Plan	Share Plan	Basic Plan
Lifetime maximum	Unlimited	Unlimited	Unlimited
Hospital services			
Length of stay	Covered in full 365 days per year	$100,000 copayment per medical or nonsurgical admission	$500.00 copayment per admission
Room and board		$300.00 copayment per surgical or maternity admission	
Semiprivate room	Covered in full	Covered in full	Covered in full
Private room	Covered in full when authorized by Plan physician	Covered in full	Covered in full
Miscellaneous	Covered in full	Covered in full	Covered in full
Physician services			
In hospital	Covered in full	Covered in full	Covered in full
Office visits	Covered in full	Covered in full	Covered in full

Home visits	$15.00 Copayment— 9:00AM to 5:00PM $20.00 Copayment— 5:00PM to 9:00PM	$15.00 Copayment— 9:00AM to 5:00PM $20.00 Copayment— 5:00PM to 9:00PM	$15.00 Copayment— 9:00AM to 5:00PM $20.00 Copayment— 5:00PM to 9:00PM
Surgery	Covered in full	$300.00 copayment per admission	$500.00 copayment per admission
Anesthesiologist	Covered in full	Covered in full	Covered in full
Outpatient tubal ligation	Covered in full	$50.00 copayment if performed at hospital No charge when performed at medical group	$50.00 copayment when performed at medical group No charge when performed at medical group
Outpatient x-ray and diagnostic lab	Covered in full	Covered in full	Covered in full
Allergy testing and treatment	Covered in full	Covered in full	Covered in full
Hearing exams	Covered in full for members through age 16	Covered in full for members through age 16	Covered in full for members through age 16
Routine physicals	Covered in full	Covered in full	Covered in full
Routine well-baby care	Covered in full	Covered in full	Covered in full
Immunizations	Covered in full	Covered in full	Covered in full
Vision exams	Covered in full	Covered in full	Covered in full

Continued

Appendix C Continued

Benefits	Ultra Plan	Share Plan	Basic Plan
Extended care services			
Extended care facility	Care in a skilled nursing facility covered in full for a maximum of 100 days per calendar year	Care in a skilled nursing facility covered in full for a maximum of 100 days per calendar year	Care in a skilled nursing facility covered in full for a maximum of 100 days per calendar year
Home health care	Covered in full when authorized by a Plan physician	Covered in full when authorized by a Plan physician	Covered in full when authorized by a Plan physician
Private-duty nursing	Covered in full when authorized by a Plan physician	Covered in full when authorized by a Plan physician	Covered in full when authorized by a Plan physician
Ambulance	Covered in full when authorized by a Plan physician	Covered in full when authorized by a Plan physician	Covered in full when authorized by a Plan physician
Maternity			
Physician charges	Covered in full	Covered in full	Covered in full
Hospital charges	Covered in full	$300.00 copayment per admission	Covered in full
Nursery charges for baby at birth	Covered in full	Covered in full	Covered in full
Mental health			
Outpatient	Covered in full up to 20 visits per calendar year	Covered in full up to 20 visits per calendar year	Covered in full up to 20 visits per calendar year

In hospital	Covered in full for up to 30 days per calendar year	$100.00 copayment per admission	$500.00 copayment per admission
Alcoholism & drug addiction			
In hospital	Covered in full for up to 30 days per calendar year. $10.00 per day copayment for rehabilitation. No charge for detox only.	$100.00 copayment per admission. $10.00 per day copayment for rehabilitation. No $10.00 per day copayment for detox only.	$500.00 copayment per admission. $10.00 per day copayment for detox.
Worldwide emergency care	Worldwide coverage is provided for all emergency care provided as a result of life-threatening illness, accident, or injury. A $15.00 emergency room copayment is required.	Worldwide coverage is provided for all emergency care provided as a result of life-threatening illness, accident, or injury. A $15.00 emergency room copayment is required.	Worldwide coverage is provided for all emergency care provided as a result of life-threatening illness, accident, or injury. A $15.00 emergency room copayment is required.

Index

Accrual-based system, 152
Acute care, 75–76, 87, 95; and long-term care, 7
Adverse selection, 198, 205
Aid for Families with Dependent Children (AFDC), 190, 192, 195, 208
Alameda County, 258, 259, 267
Allaire, Paul, 3
Alma-Ata, 248
Ambulatory care, 60, 183–84
Amicare, 223
Anderson & Anderson, 70–71
Arizona Family Physicians, 199
Arizona Health Care Cost Containment System, 188–95; bidding, 189, 193–95, 198–200, 203–6, 209, 214–15; contractor service areas, 191; copayments, 192; deferred liability, 192–93; eligibility estimates, 197; gatekeeper system, 191; members for, 190; and reinsurance, 192; services of, 190–91; utilization control, 192, 196
Arizona Health Plan, 187, 200
Arizona Maternal Transport Program, 183
Arizona Newborn Intensive Care and Transport Program, 183

Arizona Physicians IPA, 199, 201, 206, 207
Ashford, L. Jerome, 255–56, 257, 262, 274

Bailey, Donald, 256
Barrow Neurological Institute (BNI), 182
Bay Pacific, 262, 267
Beeler Hospital, 21, 32–33, 35, 36
Bennett, Astrid, 67
Biggadike, R., 220, 226, 241
Blue Cross–Blue Shield, Arizona, 187
Boston University, 255
Budget: administration, 147–48; barriers to effective management, 147–48; of medical staff, 144, 145–46; operations, 146–47; transfer, 144
Buena Vista Clinic, 81, 82–84, 91; acquisition proposal, 86–87; and Memorial Medical Center, 86; mix of physicians of, 83; patient mix of, 87
Buyer response, 61–64

Capitation: contract, 209; rate calculation, 210–13; regionalization phases, 146
Case management programs, 166

List of Contributors

L. Jerome Ashford is Vice President and Health Plan Manager of the South California region of Kaiser Foundation Health Plan.

Keith E. Boles, Ph.D., is Associate Professor of Health Services Finance at the University of Missouri, Columbia.

Gordon D. Brown, Ph.D., is Professor and Director of Health Services Management at the University of Missouri, Columbia.

Joseph S. Coyne, Ph.D., is currently employed at the Health Care Data Bank in Santa Rosa, California.

Jenifer Ehreth, Ph.D., is Assistant Professor for the Department of Health Services, School of Public Health and Community Medicine at the University of Washington. Having earned her doctorate in business administration with a minor concentration in economics and health services, Dr. Ehreth teaches classes in health services finance and managerial ethics.

Mary Ann Goeppele is Administrator for Special Projects who joined the administrative staff of Northwest Hospital in Seattle, Washington, in 1984. Goeppele currently serves as governmental affairs officer and provides a vital link to the community through participation in numerous civic and charitable organizations. She holds a bachelor's degree in communication and a master's degree in hospital administration, both from the University of Washington.

James D. Hart, FACHE, is President/CEO for Health Resources Northwest in Seattle, Washington. Prior to 1986, Hart was President/CEO for Northwest Hospital, a subsidiary of Health Resources Northwest. His professional experience includes 30 years of administrative experience in California, Oregon, Utah, and Washington. Hart holds bachelor's and master's degrees from Brigham Young University and a second master's in hospital administration from the University of Minnesota.

Carol K. Jacobson, Ph.D., is Assistant Professor in the Department of Management at Arizona State University, Tempe.

Arnold D. Kaluzny, Ph.D., is Professor in the Department of Health Policy and Administration, School of Public Health, and is a Senior Associate at the Cecil G. Sheps Center for Health Services Research at the University of North Carolina, Chapel Hill. Dr. Kaluzny received his master's degree in hospital administration and doctoral degree in medical care organization/social psychology from the University of Michigan. He has worked extensively in the design and management of organizational systems and is particularly interested in how these systems facilitate and/or impede technological and managerial innovations.

Bradford Kirkman-Liff, Dr.P.H., is Professor in the Graduate Program in Health Services Administration, School of Health Administration and Policy, College of Business, at Arizona State University, Tempe. He teaches courses addressing the management of HMOs and multispecialty group practices, health care information systems and total quality management, and comparative health care systems in industrialized countries. He has directed four large surveys on access to health care in Arizona and has extensively studied Arizona's program for mandatory use of managed care plans by Medicaid recipients from the perspective of patients and hospital managers.

R. Scott MacStravic, Ph.D., is Vice President for Marketing and Planning with Provenant Health Partners, a Denver, Colorado multihospital system. He is a member of the clinical faculty in the Executive Program in Health Management at the University of Colorado, Denver, where he teaches tactical marketing. He has authored eight books and 100 articles on health care planning and marketing and has consulted with health care providers and governments across the country.

Robert C. Myrtle, D.P.A., is Professor in the School of Public Administration and the Leonard Davis School of Gerontology at the University of Southern California. He is also Director of the Programs in Health Services Administration. His current research interests involve the strategic behavior of managers and organizations with a focus on intuitive and thinking processes of successful managers and leaders. Dr. Myrtle has authored more than 70 books, articles, monographs, and research reports addressing management and public policy concerns. He has been appointed to several public commissions and has served as a consultant to many public and private sector organizations, both domestic and abroad.

Nancy J. Packard, Ph.D., R.N., M.P.H., is Assistant Professor in the School of Nursing at the University of Washington. Her areas of research are health service access and utilization patterns among chronically ill adults and vertically integrated care systems and chronically ill populations.

David B. Starkweather, Dr.P.H., is Professor of Health Services Management in the School of Public Health and the HAAS School of Business Administration, the University of California, Berkeley.

About the Editors

Douglas A. Conrad, Ph.D., is Professor in the Departments of Health Services and Dental Public Health Sciences and Adjunct Professor in the Department of Finance and Business Economics at the University of Washington. Among his research interests are the influence of managed care on hospital efficiency, the effect of malpractice law on dentist behavior, and the resource costs of treatment for low back pain in the United States. Dr. Conrad has been editor of *Frontiers of Health Services Management* since 1989, serves on the editorial board of the *Journal of Health Politics, Policy and Law*, and is a past chair of the Accrediting Commission on Education in Health Services Administration.

Geoffrey A. Hoare, Ph.D., received training in systems thinking, planning, and social systems design at the Wharton School and has taught at the University of Pennsylvania, Temple University, Tulane University, and most recently, the University of Washington's School of Public Health and Community Medicine. His consulting research has focused on organizational learning, adaptation, and redesign. This work—as facilitator, analyst, or writer—has included decision making in complex health care organizations, developing integrative managed care systems, improving public health practice, developing survival strategies for rural hospitals, and implementing health care reform. Dr. Hoare has produced a variety of educational materials, reports, and journal articles; he has trained graduate students, mid-career professionals, and top management in systems thinking, strategic management, public health practice, organizational assessment, management change, total quality management.